G00254240

IN
THE PUBLIC
INTEREST

IN
THE PUBLIC
INTEREST

A DEVASTATING ACCOUNT
OF THE THATCHER GOVERNMENT'S
INVOLVEMENT IN THE COVERT ARMS TRADE –
BY THE MAN WHO TURNED ASTRA FIREWORKS
INTO A £100M ARMS MANUFACTURER

Gerald James

LITTLE, BROWN AND COMPANY

A *Little, Brown* Book

First published in Great Britain in 1995
by Little, Brown and Company

Copyright © Gerald James 1995

The moral right of the author has been asserted.

All rights reserved.
No part of this publication may be reproduced,
stored in a retrieval system, or transmitted, in any
form or by any means, without the prior
permission in writing of the publisher, nor be
otherwise circulated in any form of binding or
cover other than that in which it is published and
without a similar condition including this
condition being imposed on the subsequent purchaser.

A CIP catalogue record for this book
is available from the British Library.

ISBN 0 316 87719 0

Typeset in Bauer Bodoni by M Rules
Printed and bound in Great Britain by
Clays Ltd, St Ives plc

Little, Brown and Company (UK)
Brettenham House
Lancaster Place
London WC2E 7EN

To my family – Gisela, Christian, Andrew and Alexander – who have given me support when it was most needed.

CONTENTS

INTRODUCTION

Most people who are not authors write books to crown a successful life and to leave some lasting account or memorial. Others may
write because they feel it is the latest trend or fashion and it is
somehow smart to do so. There are, however, other categories of
author who have come to the conclusion that only through a book
is it possible to chronicle events which are out of the ordinary
and which touch sensitive areas of politics, industry and the City
and which are of a complex nature.

My book seeks to unravel some of those strange and scan-
dalous events of the 1980s involving high politics and the arms
trade. It is part of one of the strangest episodes in the history of
this country, the full truth of which may never be revealed or
told. Mine is a true story of murder, intrigue and big money, where
the losers are always the hard working and straightforward (who
make all possible) and the winners, the small band of elite manip-
ulators who run everyone's lives through the political and business
structure of our society.

It is the story of unaccountable security services and intelligence
services and how these services relate to politics and business and
to those who have the inside track. It is a story of corruption best
summarised by the anonymous civil servant who said, 'Rules are
for the obedience of fools and the guidance of wise men.' The wise
men in this case being those who are not even accountable to
Parliament and who, unseen and unelected, control all our institutions. Their protection is the obsession with secrecy of British
Society, and a National Interest which has different meanings for
different men and which is truly the last refuge of scoundrels.

I think Ari Ben-Menashe has captured the reality in his book *Profits of War*:

> *It is a tale of the 1980s – of big money, insatiable greed, and unfathomable corruption. It is a tale of government by cabal – how a handful of people in a few intelligence agencies determined the policies of their governments, secretly ran enormous operations without public accountability, abused power and public trust, lied, manipulated the media, and deceived the public. Last but not least it is a tale of war – armies, weapons, hundreds of thousands of deaths – war run not by generals on the battlefield but by comfortable men in air-conditioned offices who are indifferent to human suffering.*

Those of us born in the 1930s have seen times of momentous change. My lifetime has witnessed what I can only call a permanent decline of British influence and power. At school it appeared that most of the world map was red, the colour which denoted areas of Empire – the British Empire. Most of this Empire had disintegrated before the 1980s, the period of this account. Nevertheless, Britain retained some considerable influence by reason of the remains of Empire, the unique geographical position of Britain and its importance during the Cold War, its common language with the United States and its prime status in aiding and abetting US foreign policy.

Even the United States valued the experience of Empire and the culture of secrecy. It is always useful to have a proxy to perform deeds which US Congress would never countenance, and better still to have a friendly state like Britain obsessed with secrecy and with an intelligence and security service which, though funded by the taxpayer at enormous cost, is totally unaccountable.

Our secret services have rarely distinguished themselves. They have produced traitors who have caused untold death and havoc and, administered by the Cabinet Intelligence Unit and the Joint Intelligence Committee at the heart of the Civil Service which processes their intelligence for highly selective distribution, they have made themselves the permanent and unaccountable government of Britain.

During the Second World War the most effective secret organisation was Special Operations Executive (SOE) – manned by 'amateurs' and betrayed out of jealousy by MI6. But now, these organisations and the shadowy people who run them are the real government. With their City and industrial favourites they control all – parties, ministers and elected governments.

With the communications eavesdropping service, GCHQ, nothing is impossible. Information is power. Laws can be circumvented for its US counterpart, which can perform the same service for permanent government in Britain.

So well entrenched is the covert establishment in Britain that the senior posts in all government departments can be controlled by placement, and the highly politicised army and naval units, like SAS and SBS, are on hand to do the cruder work – the dirty tricks which know no bounds. Through the part-time offshoots of the SAS run bridges to business, private security firms, and the less-publicised Thatcherite 'entrepreneur'.

Rules are indeed for the obedience of fools and the guidance of wise men.

In the 1980s the policies of Margaret Thatcher's government brought the activities of the covert establishment closer to the surface (particularly in the arms industry) than at any time. Mine was a 'privileged' glimpse of their activities in action. But anyone who believes that with Thatcher's passing they no longer have a forum, anyone who believes the election of Mr Blair and his party will make any difference to who runs this country, is indeed naive. Even the extremely unlikely success of the Liberal Democrats under Paddy Ashdown (former MI6 Controller, Geneva Station) will make not the slightest difference. *'Quis custodies custodiet?'*

I have written the tale of our life
For a sheltered people's mirth
In jesting guise – But ye are wise,
And ye know what the jest is worth.

RUDYARD KIPLING, *Barrack-room Ballads*

DIARY OF EVENTS

22 September 1980
Iraq invades Khuzistan, prelude to full-scale war with Iran.

1 October 1980
Gerald Bull, now widely acknowledged as creator of the Supergun, jailed for sanction-busting in South Africa in a deal set up by the CIA.

June 1981
Astra Fireworks acquired with Gerald James as chairman, whose strategy is to turn the company into a multi-million pound arms and munitions company competing worldwide.

1981
Prime Minister Margaret Thatcher signs first of Big Five multi-million pound government-to-government deals – this one with Oman – which includes a contract purportedly to build a university but allegedly for missile silos. Her son Mark's company, Monteagle, is paid a commission on the deal.

1983
Astra taken under wing of British Embassy in Washington, the crossroads at which US/UK Intelligence co-ordinated arms deals meet, many of which contravene UK guidelines and US congressional limitations on sales to Iran and Iraq.

On Embassy advice Astra move London offices in with MI5/CIA-related organisation in Regent Street.

Allivane, the company at the centre of UK government-sponsored

covert trade with Iran and Iraq, its ultimate owner the Chilean arms
dealer Carlos Cardoen, receives start-up grant from UK government.

December 1984
UK government draws up guidelines to limit sales of lethal weapons
to Iran and Iraq, and decides not to release them.

US Atlanta branch of Banca Nazionale del Lavoro (BNL) contacted
to underwrite first of many transactions with Iraq, totalling $5bn
worth of deals under the guise of 'agricultural credits'.

1985
Second of Margaret Thatcher's Big Five deals – the Jordan Defence
Package – signed with King Hussein of Jordan, a conduit for Iraq.

October 1985
UK government guidelines announced to Parliament.

1986
Alan Clark (DTI) visits Iraq to promote British business.

First part of Margaret Thatcher's £60bn Al Yamamah arms deal
signed with Saudi, another conduit for Iraq.

October 1986
Strategic infiltration into Astra of UK Intelligence-related arms cabal,
spearheaded by Stephan Adolph Kock (SAS/MI6), who joins as non-
executive director on recommendation of Midland Bank's secret
defence department, MITS.

December 1986
Mark Gutteridge, export manager for 'dual-purpose' machinery
manufacturer, Matrix Churchill, recruited to supply information to
MI5.

1987
Saddam Hussein directs Iraqi effort to the setting up of an indigenous
arms industry with help of Astra consultant Roy Ricks and 'dual-purpose' machinery manufacturers, including Matrix Churchill.

London-based Iraqi procurement company, Technology and Development Group, purchases Matrix Churchill from the TI Group, which helps Carlos Cardoen set up a missile factory near Baghdad.

Sir John Cuckney, ex-MI5, deputy chairman of TI Group, one of the creators of MITS, director of Westland, and sometime chairman of International Military Services, a government-owned arms company involved in the covert trade, becomes chairman of Astra's main shareholder, 3i Group PLC.

Trade Minister Alan Clark authorises £200m credits for Iraq. 200,000 shares in Astra purchased in the name of Clark's mistress, Valerie Harkess.

April 1987
UK government 'safe-sells' its arms manufacturer Royal Ordnance, involved in the covert trade, to British Aerospace.

20 May 1987
Gerald James acquires US Walters Group for Astra and learns that it is producing fuses for Iraq through American Jim Guerin's ISC, based in Britain to circumvent US congressional limitations and later merged with Ferranti.

June 1987
Gerald James arrested at Syracuse airport.

September 1987
London-based Iranian procurement office closed down. Henceforth Iraq to be Britain's main customer in the war.

1988
Second part of Margaret Thatcher's £60bn Al Yamamah deal with Saudi signed.

January 1988
Supergun creator Gerald Bull travels to Baghdad to meet Hussein Kamil, head of Iraqi procurement.

British Intelligence report massive breach of Britain's arms embargo to Iraq.

Alan Clark advises members of Machine Tools Technology Association to emphasise peaceful purpose of dual-purpose machines when applying to DTI for export licences to Iraq.

March 1988
Iraq agrees to finance Gerald Bull's Supergun.

UK government signs secret agreement (EPREP) with covert trader Royal Ordnance to perpetuate their 'special' and monopolistic relationship following RO's privatisation.

May 1988
Supergun project manager Chris Cowley approaches engineers Walter Somers and Sheffield Forgemasters to manufacture barrels of Bull's Supergun and prototype.

24 May 1988
On recommendation of MoD (Peter Levene), Gerald James acquires BMARC for Astra, unaware of BMARC's government-approved covert deals and uninformed of EPREP, which seriously limits BMARC's competitiveness in the UK.

Subsequently, James discovers BMARC's LISI contract with Iran and compiles dossier on regular covert arms deals via conduit countries both to Iran and Iraq, secret orders kept off the company books, and contracts in Astra's name never touched by Astra companies. Stephan Kock and BMARC management close ranks against exposure.

13 June 1988
Sir Hal Miller contacts DTI on behalf of Somers to ask if export licences are needed for covert Supergun deal. DTI consult MoD.

14 June 1988
MoD informed that covert Supergun contracts involve Gerald Bull through his company SRC.

17 June 1988

Supergun manufacturer Forgemasters phone DTI to discuss need for export licence.

22 June 1988

Supergun manufacturer Somers tell MoD that destination of covert contract is Iraq. MoD telephone the DTI.

Westland contacts Astra for bid to weaponise helicopters, part of Margaret Thatcher's Al Yamamah deal, bound for Iraq.

7 July 1988

MoD tell Forgemasters that it appears unlikely an export licence will be required.

8 July 1988

Covert Supergun contract signed by Forgemasters.

19 July 1988

Iraqi Air Force raids Kurdish villages using hydrogen cyanide and mustard gas. Thousands of civilians massacred.

20 July 1988

Khomeini accepts need to agree ceasefire with Iraq.

27 July 1988

DTI confirm no export licence required for Forgemasters' Iraq-bound contract.

28 July 1988

British government's secret agreement (EPREP) with Royal Ordnance announced.

August 1988

Gerald Bull invited to Saad 16, Iraq's top secret military-industrial complex engaged in missile production with nuclear potential. Factory fitted out with British machine tools.

Partly to counter the effects of EPREP on Astra, Gerald James approaches Belgian company SGB/Gechem to acquire their Poudreries Réunies de Belgique. James's approach initially stonewalled by SGB/Gechem.

Supergun manufacturer Somers telex DTI for urgent response as to whether contract needs export licence.

18 August 1988
DTI confirm to Somers no export licence necessary re: Supergun contract.

20 August 1988
UN ceasefire, Iran/Iraq War.

22 August 1988
Somers start forging.

September 1988
Margaret Thatcher's fourth big government arms deal, a £1.3bn contract with Malaysia on back of £234m aid incentive to build a hydro-electric dam at Pergau. Deal arranged independently by Astra non-executive director, Stephan Kock, and Astra consultant Richard Unwin.

Jonathan Aitken joins Astra's BMARC board.

1989
BMARC management enter into government-approved covert contract as partner-supplier in deal between Ordnance Technologies (Ordtec) and Gerald Bull's SRC for fuses bound for Iraq.

February 1989
Waldegrave (FCO), Clark (DTI), Trefgarne (MoD) approve licences for Matrix Churchill exports to Iraq.

Attempt by Stephan Kock to stem Gerald James's investigations into BMARC's government-approved covert trade by replacing James with Sir James Blyth, former head of defence sales (MoD), as Astra chairman.

Agent Kock threatens to kill a man in drunken scene at the Angel and Royal Hotel, Grantham.

Kock employs Tory Party lawyers, Trowers & Hamlins, to advise on more level-headed boardroom tactics to make Astra 'safe'. Suddenly SGB/Gechem pressure Gerald James to proceed with negotiations for PRB.

28 April to 2 May 1989
UK government (DTI) sponsor Astra and twelve other British arms companies to attend Iraq's arms fair in Baghdad. A model of Gerald Bull's Supergun is on show.

17 July 1989
Astra sign contract for PRB.

August 1989
MI5 and MI6 documents reveal Iraqi plan to extend range of Scud missiles with help of Matrix Churchill.

Gerald Bull promised grant from Industrial Development Board in bid to buy Lear Fan carbon fibre plant for manufacture of shell sabots and missile nose-cones in Iraq's nuclear missile programme. Grant rescinded after pressure from America and Israel. When Bull protests, Foreign Office threatens him with an imminent 'accident'.

Sir John Cuckney's 3i, Astra's main shareholder, dispose of 3m Astra shares prior to and despite recommending completion of Astra's acquisition of PRB.

4 August 1989
FBI agents raid Atlanta offices of BNL.

September 1989
Following completion of PRB deal on 11th, Gerald James and chief executive Chris Gumbley tipped off by friend in MoD to look closely at PRB contracts, subsequently discovered to include Supergun propellant contract and others bound for Iraq, some instigated by UK government.

Auditor General, Sir John Bourn, Deputy Under-Secretary at MoD when Al Yamamah was negotiated, refuses to publish results of official inquiry into Thatcher's deal.

Observer journalist Farzad Bazoft arrested at top secret Iraqi site, Al Qaqaa, where British machines are operating.

Foreign Minister William Waldegrave is lone voice in opposing fresh export licences for Matrix Churchill.

Foreign Secretary John Major meets Tariq Aziz, Iraqi Foreign Minister, in New York.

Britain's third-largest defence contractor ISC/Ferranti collapses, revealing three contracts to supply nuclear-capable PGM systems to Iraq (via UAE), Pakistan, and China.

5 October 1989
Trefgarne (DTI) tells Waldegrave (FCO) that arguments against Matrix Churchill export licences have 'weakened to the point of extinction'.

16 October 1989
John Wakeham, Energy Secretary, visits Baghdad courting new trade with Saddam Hussein.

26 October 1989
Astra's Gerald James and Chris Gumbley alert MoD to PRB Supergun propellant contract and others in PRB bound for Iraq.

Professor Roland Smith, chairman of British Aerospace, predicts that Astra 'will wither on the vine within six months'.

November 1989
Waldegrave (FCO) caves in to pressure from Trefgarne and Clark (DTI) and agrees to approve Matrix Churchill export licences provided Trefgarne answers any awkward questions.

3 November 1989
James and Gumbley meet Bob Primrose and Roger Holdness (MI6) to discuss Supergun propellant contract and are told to proceed with first delivery.

10 November 1989
Prime Minister Thatcher tells MPs, 'Supplies of British defence equipment to Iraq and Iran continue to be governed by the guidelines introduced in 1985.'

Astra chairman James meets Gerald Bull, who confirms Astra's offer for PRB was accepted in preference to much larger offers from outside the UK, including one from Bull's own company, SRC. Knowledge of the UK government's covert trade through PRB depicted as a potent political weapon.

14 November 1989
Stephan Kock arranges meeting with Gerald James and Roger Holdness (MI6) to discover what James may have gleaned from Bull.

20 & 23 November 1989
To safeguard their position, Astra provide further evidence to MoD relating to Supergun propellant contract.

December 1989
Astra chairman Gerald James meets Prince Mishari in Saudi and discovers a PRB contract for 155mm shells, part of Thatcher's Al Yamamah deal and bound for Iraq but withheld from PRB sale.

5 December 1989
Astra-PRB's Supergun propellant press at Kaulille in Belgium blown up.

January 1990
Agent Kock calls secret meeting at White Hart Hotel, Lincoln, attended by MoD/security services personnel, to set out final moves of Trowers & Hamlins-approved strategy to make Astra safe and to neutralise the threat of James and the Astra board.

Gerald James suffers death threat from agent Kock at the Berkeley Hotel, London.

Tension reaching a climax, Kock threatens the driver of a van outside his Scottish home, firing shots from an automatic pistol.

Astra's Chris Gumbley travels to Far East and Thailand and uncovers evidence of massive commissions paid on deals involving the British government and Astra's PRB.

February 1990

Gumbley discovers that Gerald Bull is amassing intelligence on a hidden agenda of the UK government in coercing SGB/Gechem to sell PRB to Astra.

2 March 1990

Kock with support of 3i chairman Sir John Cuckney forces James to resign from Astra chair. Roy Barber brought in as chairman.

11 March 1990

Astra chief executive Chris Gumbley subjected to investigation by MoD police. Kock saddles Gumbley with his own advisers, Trowers & Hamlins, for his defence.

15 March 1990

On Trowers & Hamlins' advice Gumbley resigns. Astra directors Guest, Miller and Anderson refuse to resign but with the help of members of the new board devised by Kock and, backed by shareholders Prudential and 3i, are suspended.

Observer journalist Farzad Bazoft executed in Iraq.

22 March 1990

Miller and Guest resign from Astra board.

Chris Gumbley travels to Brussels to meet Gerald Bull, who offers to help him mount case against government victimisation by exposing its dealings with PRB and various Astra companies and associated commission payments.

Bull assassinated one hour after Gumbley leaves him.

28 March 1990

Government 'PR' face-saving strategy goes public. Forty 'nuclear' capacitors shipped from USA by Euromac for Iraq seized at

Heathrow Airport. Managing Director Ali Daghir and Janine Speckman arrested. Deal later shown to have been a set-up by Intelligence, and Daghir and Speckman cleared.

31 March 1990
Defence journalist, Jonathan Moyle, with evidence of British involvement in equipping helicopters for Iraq, is assassinated in Santiago.

9 April 1990
Astra director Anderson resigns from the Astra board. Gumbley arrested by MoD police.

10 April 1990
Customs and Excise raid Middlesbrough port and seize Supergun shipment by Forgemasters.

12 April 1990
James forced to resign from Astra board.

18 April 1990
Secretary of State Nicholas Ridley claims in Parliament: 'The government recently became aware in general terms of an Iraqi project to develop a long-range gun based on designs by the late Dr Gerald Bull . . .'

25 April 1990
Supergun project manager Chris Cowley and Somers MD Peter Mitchell arrested.

1–2 May 1990
Arrests of six Forgemasters and three Somers personnel.

21 May 1990
Enforced resignation of Laurence Kingswood from Astra board completes Kock's clean-out of all board members with knowledge of and access to documents concerning PRB.

June 1990
Customs and Excise raid Matrix Churchill, leading to the arrest of three Matrix executives.

August 1990
Three directors of Ordtec and one executive of SRC involved in Iraq/Al Fao deal with BMARC arrested. No one at BMARC is touched.

2 August 1990
Iraq invades Kuwait, leading to Gulf War between Iraq and Britain.

16 August 1990
Kock and Roy Barber, in unprecedented move to discredit Astra directors, invite the DTI to conduct a public inquiry into Astra, the company they work for.

42 waggons leave Royal Ordnance's Chorley site carrying shells and anti-tank missiles, going via Hull Docks and Jordan to Iraq.

November 1990
Government 'clean-up' wavers. On orders from Downing Street all charges against Cowley and Mitchell are dropped for fear of exposure of government's involvement with Supergun.

Margaret Thatcher resigns.

January 1991
New Prime Minister John Major tells MPs: 'For some considerable time we have not supplied arms to Iraq.'

March 1991
Astra's Chris Gumbley sentenced to 9 months in prison.

April 1991
Lionel Jones, informant on EPREP and other illicit government deals, dies in strange circumstances.

July 1991
DTI Select Committee Inquiry into arms to Iraq begins.

5 July 1991
BCCI, the London-based bank involved in arms and drugs deals and generous gifts to Tory party funds, is closed down.

18 July 1991
Ex-Belgian Deputy Prime Minister, André Cools, investigating the sale of PRB to Astra, is assassinated.

31 July 1991
International Military Services, UK government arms company involved in covert trade through PRB to Iraq, ceases trading. All records destroyed.

August 1991
Peter Lilley (DTI) repeats Thatcher's assurance (11.89), to Parliament: 'Our examination of the record shows that the policy announced in parliament [in 1985] was adhered to both in the spirit and the letter.'

February 1992
Three directors of Ordtec and one executive of SRC convicted after Public Interest Immunity Certificates stymie their defence.

2 February 1992
Astra suddenly put into receivership as Gerald James gives evidence to DTI Select Committee.

May 1992
Euromac managing director, Ali Daghir, freed on bail pending appeal.

September 1992
Government attempts to compromise defence of Matrix executives by issuing Public Interest Immunity Certificates.

October 1992
Matrix PIICs thrown out, leading to collapse of trial.

November 1992
John Major orders the Scott Inquiry.

April 1993
Report of DTI Inspector's inquiry into Astra thrown out by the Serious Fraud Office.

September 1994
Following submission of synopsis of *In the Public Interest* to publishers, DTI institutes proceedings against all Astra directors except Kock for their disqualification as directors.

13 June 1995
Following five years' pressure by Gerald James, Michael Heseltine admits in statement to the House of Commons that BMARC's LISI contract may have gone to Iran.

17 June 1995
MoD police 'find' Astra documents not returned to the receiver in June 1993.

19 June 1995
Three-hour parliamentary debate on Astra's BMARC and exports to Iran.

HM Customs Inquiry announced and, after further negotiations, a new DTI Select Committee Inquiry into BMARC.

July 1995
Gerald James arrested in London for duration of HM Customs interview. Astra director John Anderson similarly dealt with in Glasgow.

7 November 1995
The four defendants in the Ordtec case (February 1992) acquitted.

GLOSSARY

ADI	Allied Defence Industries
AIG	Allivane International Group
Al Y	Al Yamamah (I/II/III)
BAe	British Aerospace
BBC	British Broadcasting Corporation
BCCI	Bank of Credit & Commerce International
BMARC	British Manufacture & Research Company
BNL	Banca Nazionale del Lavoro
BP	British Petroleum
BUI	British United Industrialists
CARDE	Canadian Armament & Research Development Establishment
CCC	Commodity Credit Corporation
CIA	Central Intelligence Agency
DEA	Drug Enforcement Agency
DESO	Defence Export Sales Organisation
DIA	Defense Intelligence Agency
DoD	Department of Defense
DTI	Department of Trade & Industry
ECGD	Export Credit Guarantee Department
EDP	European Defence Products
EMU	European Monetary Union
EPREP	Explosives, Propellants, and Related End Products Agreement
ERFB	extended-range full-bore
ERM	(European) Exchange Rate Mechanism
FBI	Federal Bureau of Investigation

FCO	Foreign & Commonwealth Office
FNLA	Frente Nacional de Libertação de Angola (National Front for the Liberation of Angola)
GCHQ	Government Communications Headquarters
HMG	Her Majesty's Government
ICFC	Industrial & Commercial Finance Corporation
ICI	Imperial Chemical Industries
IDB	Industrial Development Board
IMS	International Military Services
IOSS	International Ordnance Sales & Services
IRA	Irish Republican Army
ISC	Institute for the Study of Conflict
ISC	International Signals Corporation
JDS	Joint Disciplinary Scheme
JIC	Joint Intelligence Committee
KMS	Keeny Meeny Services
MI5	Military Intelligence, section five
MI6	Military Intelligence, section six
MITS	Midland International Trades Services
MoD	Ministry of Defence
MPLA	Movimento Popular de Libertação de Angola (Popular Movement for the Liberation of Angola)
MTTA	Machine Tools Technology Association
NAFF	National Association For Freedom
NATO	North Atlantic Treaty Organisation
NEC	ICI Nobel Explosives Company
NIDB	National Industrial Development Board
NSA	National Security Agency
NSC	National Security Council
Ordtec	Ordnance Technology
PGM	precision guided missile
PIIC	Public Interest Immunity Certificate
PRB	Poudreries Réunies de Belgique
PSBR	Public Sector Borrowing Requirement
PUS	Parliamentary/Permanent Under-Secretary
RAF	Royal Air Force

RO	Royal Ordnance
SAS	Special Air Service
SFO	Serious Fraud Office
SGB	Société Générale de Belgique
SIS	Secret Intelligence Service
SOE	Special Operations Executive
SRC	Space Research Corporation
STC	Standard Telephones & Cable
TDG	Technology & Development Group
TISC	Trade & Industry Select Committee
TSB	Trustee Savings Bank
UAE	United Arab Emirates
UN	United Nations
UNITA	União Nacional para a Independência Total de Angola (National Union for the Total Independence of Angola)
VSEL	Vickers Shipbuilding & Engineering Ltd.

CHAPTER ONE

HOT SHOTS IN AMERICA

It was June 1987 and I had arrived with our managing director, Chris Gumbley, and our US manager, Dick White, at Armex, the army equipment exhibition in Ottawa, Canada. Astra were very keen to make an impact, having just acquired a major US defense group, the Walters Group. We arrived on the Sunday evening, and the exhibition was set to run from the Tuesday to the Friday. When we came up to our stand, Dave Whysall, a pyrotechnic chemist in charge of our Canadian operation, was adding the final touches.

Now, in the normal way, Dave did a good job for Astra Canada; he had worked very hard, given everything to the company and I think came very near to burning himself out with the effort. But we were moving ahead rapidly and his perception of what was good enough for Astra at this exhibition did not, to put it mildly, coincide with ours. When we saw the stand, we were horrified.

We had seen that all the longer established companies like VSEL had tremendous exhibition presentations, but ours was little more than a trestle table with a tablecloth, a few posters stuck up on the wall behind, and some pieces of ammunition lying on the table. Gumbley went berserk and told Whysall in no uncertain terms that he had to do something about it, go out and get some of the craftsmen on the other stands and pay them to put things right.

Whysall seemed hurt. He pointed out that to put up the sort of stand we were after could cost anything up to $C20,000, that the Astra Canada account didn't have that kind of cashing facility, and that in any case there was no time, as the exhibition opened the day after tomorrow.

There followed quite a scene, Gumbley insisting that he get on the telephone and have some cash sent down immediately, Whysall digging his heels in and saying he planned company expenditure very carefully and didn't want to go bouncing into the bank and asking for that amount in cash; they would think it was for something funny.

Gumbley said that he didn't care what they thought or where he got the money but to go and get it, which, in the end, is what Whysall did. The money came down, and I put it in our hotel safe. There it remained, in fact, throughout the fair because it turned out that the work wasn't as expensive as expected and, as Whysall had predicted, there wasn't time enough to make the presentation we wanted, though thankfully some radical improvements were made.

Come the Saturday, after the exhibition, we were all set to fly direct to Washington in the evening to allow us a day's rest before meetings in Washington and moving off down to Santa Barbara in California to see a weapons designer/manufacturer by the name of Fritz Feldman of Patec Industries. That morning I got up in quite leisurely fashion, about 8.30, and went down to breakfast, returning to my room after the meal with a newspaper and nothing much pressing on my mind. Then, as I approached the door of my room, I heard the phone ringing; it was Gumbley in a state of agitation.

'Dick wants us all to go back right now,' he said. 'We can get on a flight this morning. It'll mean you and I can spend the whole day in Washington, which will be much more useful.'

I told him I wasn't very happy about that, particularly as I knew it meant a stop-over in Syracuse or Buffalo when we would have to leave the plane, take all our luggage off, go through Customs and then re-embark – an awful hassle. I told him that if he and White wanted to take this earlier flight, fine, but I would come along later. I hadn't packed my bag and, anyway, what was the rush? Why did Dick White want to go back especially? Gumbley replied that he wanted to ride his horse on the Saturday afternoon. I told him that Dick could do what the hell he liked but he didn't have to rearrange my life.

Then Gumbley said, 'You'll have to come because he's cancelled the flights already and you'll not get back on the original schedule.' Apparently ours had been one of the only through flights that day and the seats would have gone. I told Gumbley that I'd be giving Dick an earful when I came down, then put the phone down and set to packing my bag in a fairly ruffled frame of mind.

I suppose we had driven about 30 yards in the airport taxi when I remembered the money in the hotel safe. I had arranged for Whysall to pick it up from me when he had finished taking down the stand. So, round we turned.

After I had collected the money and left a message for Whysall, we got stuck in heavy traffic on the way to the airport. When we arrived, we had to stagger through hurriedly with heavy suitcases and all the rest of the tackle, before making the plane at the very last minute. I can tell you, I wasn't best pleased with Dick White by the time I sank into my seat.

Normally they give you your Customs and Immigration forms during the flight, but for some reason on this occasion the forms were handed out at Syracuse, and I found myself having to fill mine in as I was getting off the plane. I didn't think twice about the limit on funds declaration beyond assessing that there were three of us and we were well within the limit if the cash were divided between us. I ticked the various boxes, but never divided up the cash. Then, at Customs, and again unusually, they insisted on looking in everybody's briefcase.

The officer looked at the cash all packaged up in mine, and said, 'What's that?'

I said, 'I think it's $C20,000.'

'Is it on your form?' he asked, and I explained that we were together and that it belonged to all of us, indicating White and Gumbley.

'You should have put it on the form,' he said, but didn't dwell on it at that stage. He just turned to Gumbley and asked, 'Are you with him?'

Gumbley confirmed that we were together, and the man told us both to fetch our suitcases. The officer ignored Dick White completely, despite my having just indicated that he was with us. Gumbley and I brought our suitcases over to the table and opened them, and of course we had all the brochures from Armex with glossy pictures of Chinese rockets, missiles and Christ knows what, and, to make matters worse, Gumbley's case revealed a load of dummy fuses.

The officer almost ducked under the table in surprise and said, 'Are those real?'

Gumbley assured him that actually no, they were not real, but added rather too proudly, 'We are in the defence business; we do a lot of work with the American government and the Middle East.'

'Oh really,' the man said. 'Well, you two can just go over there and sit down. I don't think you'll be catching this flight. I plan to look into this a little further.'

This he then did in a huddle with his colleagues. When he came back he questioned us more and returned later to say, 'We have decided to send for a Treasury agent from Buffalo.' I asked him how long that was going to take, but he turned away and left us alone.

In the meantime White had come dancing back and asked me what the problem was. Gumbley told him to get lost, that if we hadn't caught this bloody flight we would never have got into this mess.

So Gumbley and I were left sitting on our own watching reserve pilots flying A-10 ground-attack tankbusters (black sinister looking planes, heavily armoured) in and out of Syracuse airport, wondering how on earth we could have got into this situation and what the hell everyone was playing at. I took the opportunity of reminding Gumbley that only a week before, a US ship – the *Stark* – had been hit by an Iranian missile in the Gulf. 'When you were telling that Customs chap we trade with the Middle East,' I said, 'I could see he was thinking he'd got a couple of arms dealers.'

The agent, a latter-day Elliot Ness figure, arrived four hours later. We were still sitting there innocently enough, when up he marched and produced this bloody great Magnum and banged it up against the wall above our heads. Then he dragged Gumbley off to be interviewed and left me alone.

On his return, Gumbley advised me that the scenario they seemed to be painting was that we were a couple of arms dealers going down to bribe Department of Defense officials on some deal with the Gulf States.

Unfortunately, despite what I had told him, Gumbley had played all open and cheerful, presumably in an attempt to dispel any suspicions, and when asked to explain exactly where it was we sold our arms, he had told the agent that we dealt with Kuwait, Abu Dhabi, Dubai, and so on.

Now this, to any intelligent American, would have been all right, but to a Treasury agent from Buffalo it had clearly been something of a red rag.

It was my turn next in the interview room and the agent went through the whole scenario again. He seemed to become obsessed in particular with the money and the literature. Apparently he had accepted that Gumbley's fuses were dummies, and there was no action to be taken over them, but the cash and brochures had convinced him that I was up to no good. Try as I might to explain, he concluded the interview by informing me that he was going to arrest me and lock me up over the weekend and I could explain my position before the court the following Monday.

I couldn't believe it. I said, 'Is it possible to get a lawyer or get to a phone and get bail?'

He said he couldn't help me on that. 'It's pretty hard to get a Federal judge to arrange bail over a weekend, and that's what you'll need. A local judge won't do; you'll have to get a Federal one.' He seemed set on locking me up.

All this was then explained to Gumbley, who said, 'What about me? I can't just go off and leave him. Can't you lock me up as well? At least we'd be in there together.' I was touched.

But the agent was firm. It was to be me and me alone. 'I suggest you take a room in a local hotel,' he said to Gumbley, 'and try and get some legal help for your associate.'

For once Gumbley was at a loss for words. 'You know you have completely disrupted our travel arrangements!' was the best he could manage, and the Treasury agent just looked at him hard.

Leading me out to his car, the agent told me he would treat me as a gentleman and not cuff me, but any relief I felt at this gesture soon disappeared when he told me that the local jail was one of the worst prisons in the United States for overcrowding; it had been built for 500 prisoners but apparently there were 1,500 at that time.

Before I joined them I was ushered into a special glass box in the reception room, my suitcase and briefcase left standing outside. The room was buzzing with action. People were brought in wearing leg-irons and handcuffs, and one by one they would look at me in my box and say something like, 'What's he in for?', and the local police would say, 'That's big stuff, that's a Federal offence.'

By the time anybody got round to processing my documentation, I had been in the box for three solid hours. I just sat staring into space, wondering what the hell I was doing there, and then finally an officer proceeded to type the entire contents of my cases on to a schedule, which took another hour. Afterwards they took me along to have a shower and get de-loused – they squirt powder on your head and up your arse – and then they issued me with prison clothes: denim trousers and some sort of blue shirt and shoes that didn't fit, so that I felt like a real spare part. Next I had my photograph and fingerprints taken, then back we trooped to wait for the next stage.

Meanwhile Gumbley had gone off to a hotel and telephoned Dick White in Washington, who had contacted Bob Martin of Leva, Hawes, Mason and Martin, a firm of lawyers that the defence department of the British embassy in Washington had recommended when first we had come over to America. Just about the time I was moved back to my box, a telephone rang and much to my amazement I was told there was a call for me.

'We've got a lawyer and we'll be along shortly,' Gumbley said, with no hint of what I had been through. 'I've spoken to Bob and everything will be all right. I'm not sure how long it will take to get hold of a Federal judge, so you'll probably have to spend a few hours in there.'

When I put the phone down they moved me up to this corridor, which was packed with people, from Puerto Ricans to laconic Americans. With the cells full, prisoners were being held in sealed-off, barred sections of corridor, areas outside the cells but within layers of security, each section sealed by hydraulic doors that came down behind me as I approached.

They gave me a bed in the corridor, no blankets or anything. There were no windows either, just this artificial light, which was always on, no matter what time of day or night. There was a television, but of course it was on too loud. If you wanted a pee, you had to get permission to go outside the secure system. I lay on the bed and people began coming up and asking me what I was there for, so that I had to explain my plight till I was blue in the face.

One chap I had a chat with was in for killing a man by hitting him over the head with a shovel. He told me he had been in there nearly two years and never been brought to trial. He didn't know what was happening, or even what time of day it was. Unbelievable. I tell you, when you have had that sort of experience you don't talk so glibly about prisons.

About 3 or 4 o'clock in the morning I was told my lawyer had arrived. I was led to a place with a line of grids that you looked through to whoever you were meeting on the other side. They had got me this lawyer called Emile Rossi. A tall dark chap, he arrived wearing a polo-neck sweater. He sat down opposite me, looked earnestly through my grille and said, like Edward G. Robinson in true B-movie style, 'We're gonna get you outa here.' Then, moving his head closer, he asked, 'Are you crumblin'?'

What could I say? It was all so absurdly unreal. He then said, 'Don't worry, it'll seem a long time to you, but it won't take much longer,' and went off to see the Federal judge.

Once back, I suppose I had to wait another hour, listening to my fellow prisoners say things like, 'Gee, you got Mr Rossi, he's the best lawyer in town! Who do you know?' and, 'Do you know, there was one of the guards shot here last week. Some guy got hold of a revolver and shot one of the guards and Mr Rossi's looking after the guard's family, so I don't know how you manage to come here, a total stranger, and get the best lawyer in town.'

I said I didn't know either.

Before leaving the prison, I had to go through the wearisome procedure of getting all my belongings back, everything ticked off laboriously. Once outside, Rossi told me that he was going to take me to the International Marriot on the outskirts of the town. 'It's pretty full,' he said. 'There's a lot of receptions going on here this weekend. Gumbley's got a room, but you'll have to put up on the bunk bed.'

When we got there, Gumbley, who is a short, powerfully built man, was sitting on this ocean of a bed and I had to take a kind of baby couch.

He said, 'This won't look very good in the papers, will it?' and then told me that it was Bob Martin that had got me Rossi. 'In terms of what goes on here, you shouldn't complain; you got out in no time. This Rossi must be connected with the CIA – we didn't even have to put any money up.'

It was a theme that we would return to the following morning. The arrest had begun to connect in my mind with the undercurrent of Intelligence activity that had attended the extraordinary facility with which we had been welcomed into the field of defence in America since Gumbley, a sometime production manager of Brocks Fireworks, and I, an accountant with City banking experience, had attended the Las Vegas Defense Exhibition four years earlier.

The Astra team, back in 1983, had been a very straightforward and rather unsophisticated bunch of people. Indeed, any success ever achieved, right up to the momentous events of March 1990, was gained by hard work, expertise and developing knowledge of the industry, coupled with determination. These qualities were to cause considerable upsets in an industry dominated by cartels, monopolies, inefficiency and clandestine politics.

At the start, in June 1981, when the purchase of Astra Fireworks was completed, we had moved straight into the pyrotechnics munitions business, using our capital to upgrade plant for military production. We had expected a lot of work from Malaysia in particular, but Margaret Thatcher had upset the Malaysians by stopping overseas student grants and they had adopted an official 'Buy British last' policy.

With Arthur Reed, our then managing director, I had made a trip to Asia and the Far East – to Malaysia, Korea, Hong Kong, Thailand and Pakistan – to quantify the situation and it was obvious that the Malaysian market was very sensitive and highly political. It was taken for granted that any military contract would have its price inflated 100 per cent or more for the purpose of 'commissions' or 'political donations'. The ability to sell to the Malaysian forces was in the hands of very few persons, in particular the military commanders and senior politicians. The position in Thailand we found very similar. Government orders and particularly military orders were perceived as being a routine method of topping up the coffers of political parties as well as those of politicians and military commanders.

So at the beginning we had struggled a bit, relying on the fireworks business and only a few military orders. Then, in 1983, we attended the Las Vegas Defense Exhibition in America and met Roger Harding, the Defence Counsellor to the British Embassy with two or three military attachés under him, and almost immediately the whole picture had changed.

Roger seemed to cotton onto Astra very quickly. There were all sorts of suggestions as to which direction we should develop in, and we became very close to the Embassy and were given to believe that they would do everything to help us get established.

I must admit that at the time I couldn't really understand why such a close interest was taken in us, because in the UK you get discouraged by everybody, nobody helps you. The City, where 'long term' means 'after lunch', battens on to a new company only if it can make money easily and quickly without any longer term involvement. But in America people seemed genuinely anxious to promote our position. I suppose I put it down to their different cultural attitude to enterprise.

Back in London after the Las Vegas fair I began thinking about our office facilities. At the beginning we had inherited a London office in a run-down building in Cleveland Street, near the GPO Tower, on a full repairing lease which didn't have long to run. Our manufacturing site was in Richborough, near Sandwich in Kent, and I felt we needed a London base for sales – the Ministry of Defence was in London, after all – but I was concerned that pretty soon the Cleveland Street building was going to cost a huge sum to put right.

Chris Gumbley must have mentioned the problem to Harding, because it was he who suggested we contact a friend of his in a building called Linen Hall in Regent Street, the same block that houses Mappin and Webb, the jewellers. His friend just happened to have three spare offices which we could have at a very reasonable rent. When we went over there we saw that it was a big space with corridors all round it. We were told we could have three rooms, a boardroom, my office on one side, and a secretary's on the other side. All round us were the offices of an organisation called the Institute for the Study of Conflict. Hearing the name of its boss, one Brian Crozier, gave me something of a surprise.

Brian Crozier had been a key element in the CIA/MI5 campaign against left-wing/communist elements in Britain in the 1970s, which had featured in the miners' strike of 1972, followed by Edward Heath's three-day week. The Institute for the Study of Conflict had come out of the CIA's Current Affairs Research Center in 1970.

Brian Crozier was also a leading member, alongside Dickie Franks, Maurice Oldfield's successor as the chief of MI6, of a Tory political group called the Pinay Circle, whose members were drawn from Intelligence and political circles on both sides of the Atlantic. Robert Moss, who worked with Crozier at Linen Hall, was one of Margaret Thatcher's speech-writers, and in the office next to mine, after we moved into Linen Hall was a man called Charles Elwell, formerly a Section head of MI5.

All this has since been confirmed in various books, one by Crozier himself. What it meant at the time was that Roger Harding had put us in a nest of spooks. But it seemed to do the trick.

As soon as we had moved to this office in Linen Hall we began receiving orders direct from the Department of Defense (DoD) in Washington; nothing very ambitious at first, just practice bombs and the like. But I was agreeably surprised that we, a small British company with a limited track record, were receiving reasonable orders from America.

In Washington we were assigned, again through Harding, this man, Dick White, whose change of flight plans had led to the trouble in Syracuse. Before he came to work full-time for us, White was with a company called Allied Defense Industries (ADI), run by Clifford Smith, a former Royal Navy nuclear submarine captain. The purpose of ADI was to enable British defence contractors to capitalise on the American arms market, to lobby for them.

White was Clifford Smith's right-hand man. His regiment was the Royal Ulster Rifles, but he had been awarded the MBE for his part in military Intelligence operations in Northern Ireland, setting up those special listening devices that can scan a whole terrace of houses for terrorist suspects.

White was an intense person, always living on his nerves. For his covert purpose he had developed a heavy Irish accent and had gone around like a scruff with long hair and jeans. As a reward, and because he was an obvious IRA target, he had been sent to the British embassy in Washington, where he became a major on the defence side.

There he had helped in Caspar Weinberger and Al Haig's defense strategy to help the British in the Falklands War. As it was told to me, they got round the limitations on support for the British, passed in Congress by the anti-British lobby of Jeanne Kirkpatrick and the rest, by arranging for weapons (notably the missile, Sidewinder 2) to be despatched secretly from American military depots and distributed in Ford transit vans to a variety of drop-off points for further transportation to Dulles airport, where they were put on RAF VC10s and flown to Ascension Island, and thence to the Falklands for use on British Harrier aircraft.

The crucial nature of this work to Britain's victory in the Falklands cannot be overstated. What enabled us to retrieve the situation there was the help we received from the Americans. They gave us satellite and other Intelligence, but crucially they gave us Sidewinder 2, which gave our Harriers air superiority over the much faster French aircraft used by the Argentinians. With Sidewinder 1 you actually had to get behind a target to bring it down, but with S2 you could fire from a position parallel to the target. Of course, now, systems are even more sophisticated and advanced. Instead of having to line the aircraft up on a target, the pilot wears a special helmet that allows his point of vision to target the enemy regardless of the position of the plane. All the pilot has to do is turn his head, look at the target, and press a button. The technology, as you might imagine, is very expensive and difficult.

But in its day Sidewinder 2 was tremendous. Before its deployment, the Argentinians bombed from 5,000 feet. After S2, they had to fly very much lower to avoid the Harriers and, as a result, because some of the Argentinian's bombs were fused wrongly (I doubt they had the know-how to re-fuse them all, which is a tricky business), they failed to explode when they landed on our ships.

Weinberger got his honorary knighthood for this work, and White had been very much part of the operation.

As time went on, Dick White, who was married with two young children, decided he wanted a more stable life and saw he could capitalise on his reputation as somebody who had given good service. So he left the army and became a consultant with ADI.

Whether he actually left Intelligence I doubt very much. It is a feature of the developing careers of former Intelligence officers, many of whom in Britain find a niche in the City, that their Intelligence connections are maintained and put to a purpose, often political.

As business grew, we asked White how we could get into a position to win the really big contracts. He and Harding advised us to buy a factory in Canada. Why Canada? Because, they said, it would be cheaper than in America and yet fell within the 'base mobilisation reserve'. Buying a Canadian company would be less expensive than buying an American one, but it would enable us to have an equal opportunity to win contracts from the US Department of Defense. (It is not widely appreciated that although it is very proud of its independence, Canada is not really separate from America. There is a great deal of overlap and privilege.)

I couldn't see anything wrong with this; I couldn't fault it. I had a very jaundiced view of Britain, as we really seemed to be in the last throes of a monopolistic economy, the same tired old companies, GEC, British Aerospace, Thorn EMI, Royal Ordnance, etc., soaking up huge chunks of the defence budget to the commercial detriment of our armed forces and defences. America really did seem the land of opportunity, especially to a young company, as Astra was at the time.

In Britain, if you want a defence contract, you must prove that you have the plant to service it. But it might take £500m at current costs to build a plant sufficient for a decent contract. In America, so it seemed, a company the size of Astra in the mid-1980s could compete with the likes of Martin Marietta, the US defence establishment making it possible by including the tooling cost in the contract price. It was an enterprising policy. What it meant was that the DoD agreed a more favourable price with Astra than, say, with Hercules or United Technologies or General Electric, who didn't need tooling at current costs.

Indeed, the whole emphasis seemed to be on helping us, the small company. How much better I thought than England, full of 'old boy' networks and tired monopolies and cartels. I didn't question any of it; I just thought this was the American way.

So we began looking around for a factory to buy, and who should make a suggestion but good old Dick White. He said we should go for a company called Aba Chemical, a manufacturer of pyrotechnic devices for the DoD and the Canadian government, situated near Toronto.

Due to internal problems, and after much difficult negotiation, we purchased only the manufacturing site and had Aba's contracts assigned to us with an option (never exercised) to purchase the company at a later date. As a result, Astra had a North American site and operation. We held it under Astra Canada, a new company, and manufacture commenced on 1 January 1986.

When our intentions were made clear, I suddenly found, to my surprise, that people started floating around the Canadian operation offering all kinds of help. Among the first was a former Canadian army major called Tom Morrice, who invited us to look over another site on the American–Canadian border that he assured us could be made highly profitable.

When we asked why we should want to see it, he simply said he thought it would be a good idea if we did. So compelling was he that we went down to this place in Highwater, which straddles the American–Canadian border. I was quite staggered. It was huge, over 1,200 hectares. There was this enormous gun in position, and while we were there Morrice began telling us a story about a man called Gerald Bull – how this man Bull had worked there at Highwater and had got arrested, selling shells to South Africa.

Then Morrice and others suggested that Astra would get a lot of work from the American and Canadian governments if we bought this site. I certainly felt that Morrice could make such a promise, that somehow he was more than army and was in a position to arrange it. Otherwise what were we doing there? Nevertheless, in the end, we told him that although we were impressed, we couldn't see how it would fit into our strategy at that time.

I met Bull some years later, and Chris Gumbley was with him only an hour or so before his assassination. The story of Gerald Bull, the brains behind the Iraqi Supergun, is now of course widely known. If you have seen the film they always show of him on television, where he is coming out of a building, hunched up against the cold with a file under his arm, his enormous test gun in the background, you will have seen part of this site at Highwater.

It is worth pausing for a moment to consider Bull's early career because it has a bearing on later events in Astra. Once again it demonstrates the dubious role of the Intelligence services in the defence industry, especially with young companies eager to do business.[1]

In 1951 Bull, still a PhD student of aerophysics, joined the Canadian Armament and Research Development Establishment (CARDE). He was just twenty-three and went to work on CARDE's top secret air-to-air guided missile project, aimed at Soviet attack aircraft and code-named Velvet Glove.

Velvet Glove was overtaken three years later by the development of intercontinental ballistic missiles, which meant that there was no longer any need for Russia to send aircraft to Canada. However, by 1959 Bull had been promoted to take charge of the Aerophysics wing of CARDE, and in response to the threat of intercontinental ballistic missiles, but still really against the run of developments (which was rocket and missile technology), he began to develop a gun capable of shooting a projectile at 12,000m a second.

Disappointed and dejected at the lack of interest shown in his project, the enigmatic Bull left CARDE in early 1961 and worked as an independent consultant, until one day Donald L. Mordell, the Dean of Engineering at McGill University, fell for the glamour of Bull's big gun technology.

It was at this point that Bull bought Highwater, and with Mordell worked on the so-called High Altitude Research Programme, ostensibly a high-altitude satellite launching gun, but financed to the tune of $500,000 by the DoD, who were persuaded, for a time, of its military potential. By 1969 he had built a 400mm smooth-bore gun that was 52m in length, but sadly for Bull it was never taken up by his political backers.

The turning point for Bull's company, Space Research Corporation (SRC), came suddenly in the spring of 1972.

The US navy, vulnerable to the superior firepower of the Soviet-supplied 130mm Vietnamese coastal guns, asked Bull to design a shell that could be fired from 125mm guns already in place on US navy destroyers but with an extended range of 10km. According to William Lowther, in *Arms and the Man*, Bull was given 120 days to complete the commission and he did it, with 5km to spare.

It was something of a breakthrough for Bull. His 155mm gun, the GC45 (almost 7m long), and the extended-range full-bore 155mm shells that he developed following that US navy commission, and which with further modifications would in the 1980s determine the fighting strategies of the Iran–Iraq war, opened up a way to balance the huge development costs of SRC's work, which had begun to bite.

In 1973 Joseph Severin, head of the Belgian explosives and munitions manufacturer, Poudreries Réunies de Belgique (PRB), a company that Astra acquired in the summer of 1989, flew to Montreal, toured Highwater and persuaded Bull to set up a Brussels-based firm, SRC-I, so that together they might market the technology internationally.

In Belgium, a centre for the arms trade for hundreds of years, PRB had a much freer hand in the international marketplace than Bull did from either the American or Canadian departments on the cross-border Highwater site. The unique cross-border location did, however, afford interesting opportunities. At Highwater, Bull could manufacture in either Canada or America, and chose which to utilise with an eye to the various and differing limitations placed on arms manufacture and export by both governments. It was a feature of Highwater that was recommended to us by our helpful government-connected advisers.

South Africa, a country subject to UN sanctions on arms, would be Bull's first undoing. The theatre of operations where his trouble was seeded was Angola.

Given its independence by the Portuguese in late 1975, the country's loyalties came to be divided between three guerilla groups – UNITA (with support from South Africa), the MPLA (with Soviet and Cuban support) and the FNLA (with support from the CIA).

The Russian 122mm rocket in the hands of the Communist-backed MPLA proved too much for the FNLA, and when battle commenced with UNITA, the CIA sought an effective deterrent. Bull's GC45 and extended-range full-bore (ERFB) 155mm shells filled the bill.

The deal, for 15,000 shells (the nose forgings to be manufactured and exported quite legally from the Canadian side of the Highwater site to Brussels, where they would be filled and fused by PRB), was done by the CIA via John 'Jack' Frost, an arms dealer in Brussels who had worked with the CIA in the past and was now placed by the CIA in direct contact with Armscor, the South African state-owned arms and munitions manufacturer which plays a key role in international arms trading.

In 1979 the South African government announced that it had developed a 155mm artillery and shell system. A year later Gerald Bull was sentenced to a year in prison, six months of which was suspended, and SRC was fined $105,000.

Gumbley and I were ushered around other places, too, first to a site called Camden in Arkansas, on the colossal former naval ammunition dump of Schumacher, now used by the 'majors' in the industry. The scale of this place was even more impressive than Highwater. It took us 20 minutes to fly round it in a light air-craft. Apparently it had been a naval ammunition depot used in the Korean War, and had had its own railway.

We were told that in the 1950s Eisenhower had closed the site down, with a consequent loss of 5,000 jobs, in retaliation for the Governor of Arkansas's opposition to Eisenhower's policy of racial integration in schools. Although the depot had cost between one and two billion dollars to build, it was sold eventually for a mere $10m to a company called Highland Resources, in which Lady Bird Johnson was a shareholder. A sale of the timber on site and the railway line alone raised more than the price they paid.

Then Highland Resources, wondering what to do with it, considered turning it into an industrial park, but came to the

conclusion that its position – situated out in the wilderness, with
forests all round it, inhabited by wolves – really only made it
suitable for its original use. So they began a campaign to encourage all the major manufacturers, United Technologies, General
Electric, General Dynamics, to come and build their dangerous
high explosive plant there and make use of its enormous storage
potential.

They showed us around, and on two or three occasions we
stayed the night in a guest-house, the former commanding officer's house. When I looked in the guest-book, I was amazed to see
the names of representatives of British banks, people I knew from
Clydesdale Bank, William and Glynns, Midland Bank. I wondered
what the hell they had been doing down there. It seemed odd that
these British banks should be interested, but no obvious answer
presented itself at the time.

Then we were taken to look at a high-explosives filler on the
same site, a company called Hi-Tec, which charged Maverick
missiles – an anti-ship missile fired from an aircraft, a colossal
weapon in destructive capability. Yet the plant was very simple,
almost absurdly so. All the missiles were lined up along each side
of a low building and there was a huge steaming cauldron on a
platform with a man in an apron and a pair of goggles. I was
reminded of the sorcerer's apprentice. Then I realised, as I looked,
that all the explosive for filling the Maverick missiles was coming
from this vat . . . coming down these pipes in front of me and running into the missiles. That was the plant! Like some cottage
industry, but each missile with the power to blow a ship in half.

We were told we could either set up our own plant at Camden
or buy one of these small existing companies like Hi-Tec. I could
see that it was a good concept because all the main contractors
seemed to be in there, and by this time they had convinced me of
the principle of acquiring an American company. But before we
could make up our minds, we were directed down to Florida to
look at yet more companies.

There was Maryland Assemblies, which made fuses, pyrotechnics and ammunition such as rifle grenades, and also Martin

Electronics, which was more in the field of sophisticated decoy and pyrotechnic devices. Of the two, Maryland was the better bet, I thought, Martin being more difficult to fit into our set-up. I even went as far as to get a report on both companies and a detailed report on Maryland by our London-based accountants, Stoy Hayward, which showed nothing basically wrong with the company. Only the man who owned it troubled me.

William Drum seemed incapable of negotiating a price and was rather a difficult person to get a precise fix on: for example, he employed his company's static water tanks as swimming pools. Our accountants advised us to steer clear of the acquisition.

Harding and White and our US government mentors – indeed all the various people who were expressing such an interest in Astra – were, meanwhile, patience personified. In no time at all they were suggesting that instead we might like to operate a Go-Co. We said we had never heard of a Go-Co, and they assured us that Rock Island and Piccatinny Arsenals would fill us in. They sent us over to see them, along with the main procurement officer for the US army.

We discovered that a Go-Co is a government-owned, contractor-operated plant that makes munitions. The American government actually owns the premises but, as a Go-Co, Astra would get a five-year government contract to make munitions. We were offered one of the big places in Longhorn in Texas. All we had to do was put in a submission. Admittedly this would cost us about $1m to prepare, but there was to be no risk – every help would be given.

The Go-Co idea looked extraordinarily attractive. But by now, although still unaware of the extent of co-ordination in a US/UK arms policy which, as I would learn, claimed Iraq and Iran among its real end-users and depended on the establishment of US/UK manufacturing channels to beat controls established by Congress and Parliament, I was more than privately concerned to know why we – a small British company – should be offered this virtual licence to print money by the DoD.

I asked whether any other British companies were operating

Go-Cos. The only one was ICI, I was informed; they were running two or three.

Then, out of the blue, at just the moment we were considering whether to take up any of these options that had been laid before us by the Department of Defense in Washington, an enquiry about a requirement for 81mm mortar proximity fuses landed on Chris Gumbley's desk from the Ministry of Defence in London.

The proximity fuse is a very sophisticated piece of equipment that can be set to explode at a fixed distance above the ground. It actually has its own doppler-style radar and sends out its own signal to the ground, being activated when the signal is at the desired level. It can be set to explode at 15 or 20 or 30 feet or at any other height above the ground, and turns a very basic weapon with a mere impact detonation into something wholly lethal with a force of explosion that is devastating.

During the Falklands War we lacked effective proximity fuses, particularly on mortar ammunition. A lot of the mortar bombs had impact fuses or target fuses that didn't go off properly or ended up in the peat bog and had no effect at all.

But Astra had no capability for making these fuses. The MoD in London were perfectly aware of that. Equally they were aware that the fuses depended on US technology. Taking on the order would necessitate our finding a company not just to work with, we discovered, but to acquire.

We went to Dick White to ask what we should do, and he steered us to Accudyne in Janesville, Wisconsin.

We arranged a meeting with Bob Mowris and his team at Accudyne, but when we arrived we were rather surprised to be met not just by Mowris but by Ed Walters, who for years had been making the metal components for Accudyne's fuses. We were even more surprised to learn that Walters had flown up from Chicago expressly to meet us. It then further transpired that Walters owned 80 per cent of Accudyne (the remaining 20 per cent belonging to the Accudyne management).

I began to think there was a misunderstanding about our visit, with all this talk of ownership, and I told Ed Walters that we only wanted to arrange a licence to make these fuses.

He replied that he didn't think we would get a licence because the fuse was designed by Harry Diamond Laboratories (one of the big US government research agencies). Accudyne had been approached by other people in fuse manufacture, like Thorn EMI, but no licences had been permitted. He then took us round the factory.

There were four or five different plants – a huge capacity – and they seemed to be making all sorts of fuses for all kinds of mines, artillery shells, bombs, and even the MLRS system and Gator mine, two very advanced systems. It was a fantastic operation. In the evening Walters took us out for a meal and told me about a very good friend of his called Jim Guerin.

Guerin, an American, had taken his company, International Signals (ISC), to England, and while it remained a US company, Guerin had managed, through Messels, to obtain a quote for it on the London Stock Exchange. His offices were out by London Airport. Sir Michael Checketts had helped set the company up, employing Tom Keays, whose sister Sara had a cosy relationship with the then DTI minister, Cecil Parkinson.

Walters had a terrific deal going with Guerin, he told us, making specialist fuse parts for ISC. If we wanted to make use of American technology, why didn't we raise the funds, buy his group, make use of the transatlantic channel for trade with Guerin that was already in place and set up a similar operation putting American technology through our own British company.

I had to admit Walters' idea was a good one, really the best possible deal for Astra in the context of our plans for an American operation, in that it gave us an immediate capability to channel US technology into the UK. International trade in arms technology across the Atlantic had to be a basis for real success for Astra, and the ongoing deal with ISC was, as Walters said, a terrific start.

The following day we flew to Chicago and inspected his equally impressive engineering operation that made precision parts mostly for munitions. He had rows and rows of Guildermeister machines, turning machines for metal components, fuses, shells and Christ knows what. It was a very substantial armament plant in its own right.

Our subsequent purchase for $35m, not only of Accudyne but of the whole Walters Engineering Group, was completed in April 1987 through an underwritten rights issue. It took us from about £1m profit in the UK in the year to 31 March 1987, to £6.5m pre-tax, and our stock rocketed in the market.

Roger Harding, Dick White, Brian Crozier, Charles Elwell, Tom Morrice and the DoD, all so eager to do business with us; then Schumacher, Hi-Tec, Maryland, Martin Electronics, the Go-Cos, and finally the plum, the Accudyne and Walters deal that had been inspired by that opportune and quite inexplicable request for proximity fuses from the DoD's opposite number in London. It was all a brand of assistance almost too good to be true, and now I began to worry that it might have a hidden price.

My arrest at Syracuse occurred just after we had made our big play for this major US defense industry acquisition, and the morning after, having grown used to my life being directed by Intelligence and defence departments, I woke up in my tiny couch bed after just a couple of hours' sleep and began to think that my problems might have more than their immediate significance.

It was a nervousness that had been building up over time. Besides my own direct experience of events and the people I was rubbing shoulders with daily, you heard remarks, people said things, you got the impression that every arms company was involved in some sort of covert dealings. But the overriding release had always been that I was very happy that we were making money.

It was a nervousness that would later be justified by what I would learn were the full ramifications of the Walters/Accudyne deal. Jim Guerin of ISC, the man with whom Ed Walters had such profitable dealings, had started his business in 1971 in a chicken shed in his back garden. He had previously worked at Lockheed Missile and Space Corporation in Sunnyvale, California, and for a

short time with Hamilton Watch, a Pennsylvania company bent
on diversifying into military electronics. Once again, as with
Gerald Bull, his business first thrived on the back of CIA operations in an area to which official US foreign policy denied supply.[2]

Project X, sponsored by the National Security Agency in 1974,
was an arrangement for ISC (with Admiral Bobby Ray Inman,
former director of naval intelligence on board) to supply electronic equipment illegally to South Africa through a front
company called Gamma Systems Associates, which gave the US
government the hedge of 'plausible deniability'.

Guerin also supplied Carlos Cardoen, the Chilean entrepreneur who became fabulously wealthy following President General
Pinochet's 'call to arms manufacturers' to put the Chilean economy right, and he did it in the main on the back of cluster bomb
exports to Iraq.

Cluster bombs are among the most devastating of conventional weapons and capable of destroying anything within a
ten-acre area. Cardoen, who has his own private army, is said to
have assets of some $400m. Like Guerin and Bull, Cardoen also
benefited from the patronage of the CIA. Howard Teicher, main
adviser on the Middle East to the National Security Council from
1982 to 1987, and assistant to Robert McFarlane, himself assistant to the chief adviser, William Clark at the NSC, filed an
affidavit in January 1995 that American Intelligence played a
direct part in Iraq's military build-up. Clark and the CIA director
William Casey were especially active in these covert operations –
'Bush knew about the covert operations,' Teicher has said, 'and
Casey felt he could trust him, with his intelligence operations and
all that.' Teicher's affidavit was filed in connection with the prosecution of two executives of Teledyne, who have pleaded guilty to
supplying 300 tons of zirconium to Chile for use in Cardoen's
bombs.[3]

The Intelligence services saw Cardoen as a useful offshore supplier to areas of strategic importance (Angola, Afghanistan) as
well as places that were off-limits, like Iraq in particular, where
Cardoen had contacts at the highest level. A great deal of money,

paid in commissions and laundered through banks such as BCCI and Castle Bank in the Bahamas, was then re-deployed in the massive costs of international Intelligence work.

Such strategies were not merely aberrations of the CIA working independently of the US government, but were co-ordinated by the Pentagon in defiance of Congressional controls. Teicher has said that shipments were sometimes made on direct orders from the White House.

In the three-year investigation into the collapse of Guerin's ISC, following its merger with the British company Ferranti (p. 132), Michael Baylson, the US attorney involved, was asked why Cardoen had been named merely as an 'unindicted co-conspirator'. He declined to comment, as he did also to questions about the role of the CIA.

In the 1980s Guerin's ISC exported to Iraq via China and also Fuchs electronics in South Africa, a business partner of the state-owned Armscor, and he relied on the technology and precision manufacturing of Astra's acquisition, Accudyne, along with Rexon and other companies. Accudyne shipped around two hundred million fuses from 1971.

What it boiled down to was that ISC had been set up in Britain with the tacit approval of the US and British governments and Intelligence services to get round US congressional controls on exports to South Africa and the Middle East (the result of pressure from the Jewish lobby); and our company Accudyne was in on the act.

Guerin's ISC offered a new kind of front for the CIA. Operating from Britain, technology and parts flowed from America and thence, as finished products, to countries banned by Congress.

The American Constitution is a written constitution. There are rules of public disclosure, public right to information, which we do not have in the UK. Moreover, the strict legal limitations on arms exports cut America off from the Middle East markets far more effectively than in the UK. But America could not afford to miss out on these markets, most lucrative during the Iran–Iraq war, and would later justify its supply in terms of maintaining the balance of power in the Middle East and deterring the real threat of the spread of Islamic fundamentalism.

This unofficial policy, which required the organisation and deployment of those most experienced in covert activities, depended upon friendly satellite countries with less stringent arms export laws. America's need was satisfied by Thatcher in particular, who celebrated her gratitude to America for its covert assistance to Britain in the Falklands War, in her special relationship with President Reagan, the fruits of which filtered down through business and Intelligence channels to encourage all kinds of sharing of mutual aims and information-gathering.

The British Embassy in Washington, where Roger Harding worked, was a main co-ordinating centre of this illegal business, the size of which few can appreciate, but which ran into billions of dollars. Others were the British Embassies in Bonn and Rome. When I first went to America, I could see that we were very active in something. Britain had as many as 1,000 military personnel in the USA, although at the time I failed to understand why.

After Syracuse, I would begin to ask questions about Accudyne's order book. I asked Ed Walters outright why we were exporting so many fuses to China. He said that the Chinese had placed, through Gerald Bull, a huge 155mm requirement and that we were in on the back of that. 'Yes,' I said, 'but they can't be firing all *this* ammunition.' 'Well,' he replied, 'I can assure you that that is what the DoD tell us.'

Then I began to listen to what others said to me as I went round the Accudyne plant. Charlie Shaff, the company director in charge of manufacture, was the first to come out with it straight. I asked him where he thought the fuses were going. 'The official story is that they are going to China,' he said, 'but everybody reckons they are going to Iraq.'

The Walters situation set the scene, and it became our policy in both America and Britain to make sure that all official documentation was in order and that when orders came in from the DoD in Washington or the MoD in London, we complied precisely with everything they demanded, that we didn't put a foot wrong with

the two bodies that supplied 90 per cent of our business, the
remaining 10 per cent being sub-contracts from other companies
for components, or fireworks. I didn't have any vocation to clean
up either country's foreign policy, not until, on the British side,
they began to take control of Astra from us. But there was always
this undercurrent of uncertainty that there might be repercussions,
that we might get left holding the baby.

Now, in our hotel room at the International Marriot on the outskirts of Syracuse, after a fitful sleep of an hour or so, these
concerns were uppermost in my mind, and Chris Gumbley was
no less anxious. I had woken at 7.30 a.m. to the faint sound of a
siren, and looked at Gumbley who was also awake. As the siren
got louder, his eyebrows rose and he said quite seriously, 'You
don't think they are coming for us?' The sound was definitely
approaching, and as it came towards us we both got out of bed
bleary-eyed and made for the window. By the time we looked
down into the street below, the siren was deafeningly near, and we
watched as two fire engines flashed past on the other side.

The relief we felt did nothing to temper our general concern,
which now focused specifically on Dick White's part in my arrest
at Syracuse. He was, after all, the reason I had even been in
Syracuse. There had been no proper reason for him to alter our
travel arrangements. The reason he gave was that he had wanted
to get home earlier so that he could ride his horse. But what, we
asked ourselves, had that to do with us?

In the whole context of the steering of Astra by the embassy
through ADI and Dick White, his reason for directing us via
Syracuse began to look very spurious, especially since he alone
had miraculously managed to avoid the attentions of Customs at
the airport.

Dick was used to Intelligence operations. Intelligence operations
traditionally include the blackmail tactic of the 'smear'. I had
heard of such things, as everyone has: MI5's 'Worthington file' on
Harold Wilson and files on other members of parliament and so
on. In the political arena it is what makes all-party Select

Committee inquiries so difficult. In 1971, the Franks Committee on the reform of the Official Secrets Act had revealed that MI5 had a programme of file-keeping on people who might pose a threat by virtue of their allegiances or what they knew. Its purpose was to find out anything they could to hold over or use against these people should they ever need to.

Years later, the ploy was used against one of our own directors. When, in 1985, we were trying to export hand-held decoy flares from Astra to Iran – purely defensive, quite above board – we had a whole debate in the company about how best to put the contract across to the government. In the end, we got Jonathan Aitken involved. He was our MP, as our original base near Sandwich was in his constituency. Aitken wrote letters and the deal went through with no problem. But some years later, when the political tide had turned *vis-à-vis* Iraq and they were hounding us, some people, allegedly from the DTI, went up to interview John Anderson in Scotland to gauge the extent of his knowledge about what the government had been up to through Astra. Suddenly, in the course of conversation, they produced photographs of Anderson, who had been handling the export aspect of the flares contract, coming out of the Iranian procurement office in Victoria, London. So even though they had approved the deal, someone had been covering it just in case it might prove 'useful' in another context.

The Intelligence services, you see, are above the law. In 1984 the House of Lords Judicial Committee heard Lord Fraser state the position clearly: 'The decision on whether the requirements of national security outweigh the duty of fairness in any particular case is for the Government and not for the courts. The Government alone has access to the necessary information, and in any event the judicial process is unsuitable for reaching decisions on national security.'[4]

Back in our hotel bedroom, Gumbley was making a call. At the end of it I heard him telling someone to mind their own business. He turned to me with an expression of alarm on his face. 'The receptionist chipped in and asked me what number I had been connected to.'

By this time we had become so paranoid about our situation that no thought occurred to us that the poor woman might have been concerned to bill us for long distance, and we determined to make all calls from booths outside in the street.

In fact we spent the rest of the morning doing just that. Then, in the afternoon, some young lawyer came by and took down a statement and filled us with more gloom. He said, 'You know, this town has awful problems. We had a mayor arrested for smuggling krugerrands just the other day. He got five years.'

That's all I need, I thought, a real Job's comforter on my side. Gumbley told him that he didn't think any of what had happened was normal, none of it rang true. I was concerned to bring everything down to the best line of defence against the charge and told the lawyer that I thought the crucial thing wasn't the money or the brochures or the dummy fuses, it was this business of having customers in the Gulf. That was why I was put inside, that was what made them think there was something funny going on.

The lawyer said they wouldn't think that much longer. 'We have got glowing references from Roger Harding, and Mr Rossi says he'll sort it out OK. But you are going to have to appear in court on Monday.'

After he left, Gumbley and I went for a walk in the vicinity of the hotel to get away from it all. We found ourselves walking towards the offices of Dresser Industries, a big American engineering company. We wandered near the back of the block and looking up I noticed video cameras moving wherever we walked, locked on to us, and then we peered in through a window and there, sitting accusingly on the sill, we saw a row of 105mm shells. I pulled Gumbley away and we walked back yet more disconsolately to our room.

The next morning we went to Rossi's office. He was dressed to the hilt with co-respondent shoes and a very flash light-coloured suit. He seemed very interested in my tie. He said, 'You get some nice ties in London.' He became involved in the reasons why – something to do with the stripes going the other way. 'You couldn't get me half a dozen ties when you get back?' Then he got to the point, 'Nothing to worry about here. I know the judge and the District Attorney, we all know each other very well.' Then Gumbley hit our mood with, 'Well, we don't.'

Eventually we went down to the court. It was the size of an old Odeon cinema with a huge eagle in attendance. There was a clerk of the court, a black man, and the judge, who was an old buffer, otherwise it was empty of people save for ourselves. A few moments later the Treasury agent turned up, rather obviously put out that I had been released.

Rossi said that he would tell me what to say, and then we marched up to the bench. The judge rabbited on for a while about what the case was about, and then asked me how did I plead.

Rossi, I am sure to this day, whispered into my ear, 'Guilty,' and I was so fazed by what was going on that I repeated it, thinking that perhaps it was some sort of technical guilty plea. The judge and the clerk seemed to rise out of their chairs as one. Then Rossi hissed at me, '*NOT* guilty, *NOT* guilty,' so I repeated that, and the officials subsided into their places once more.

The Treasury agent – I learned his name was Kaufman – was so peeved by the verdict, which fortunately concurred with my second plea, that afterwards he insisted on my accompanying him to a room below the court where he would take my finger-prints 'officially'. Down there we met a US marshal, and while the business was going on, he and Kaufman engaged in a conversation about the relative merits of being a Treasury agent or a US marshal. One of the main advantages apparently is that as a Federal agent you get a bigger gun. The result of this exercise was that the Federal authorities had my fingerprints, and for the next six months, every time I went to the United States I was searched by Customs, a reminder that the 'smear' was indeed permanently on file.

We had to leave the money behind. Rossi said he would try to retrieve it, but we never saw it again. He then said, 'We'll go back to the office, then I'll take you out and we'll have lunch at a hamburger place.'

I felt no great relief at the verdict, which seemed to me to have

little to do with the whole rotten business. As we came out of
Rossi's office to go to lunch, I noticed a real old-timer coming
along the pavement while we covered the sweep of the office
steps – Rossi in his co-respondent shoes and smart suit and
Gumbley and I in a couple of dark suits. As we came down, the
old man stopped, and looking up at us said, 'Aah, here come the
hot shots!'

That was the view from where he stood.

CHAPTER TWO

ROOTS
IN BRITAIN

It had all begun exactly as it should. I had come out of the army, where I had served as a paratrooper, and gone to visit my old school, Sedbergh, in Cumbria. I was walking in the grounds when I came across my headmaster, Michael Thornely, with Sir Hilary Scott, who was the father of a contemporary of mine and Thornely's father-in-law.

Sir Hilary was President of the Law Society and a senior partner in Slaughter and May, the legal firm. Naturally enough I was invited to lunch, and Sir Hilary asked me what I intended doing with my life. The upshot was that he introduced me to the accountants Peat Marwick Mitchell, where I came to be articled to Sir Ronald Leach, one of the star partners.

It always worked in those days; the 'old school tie' and the club survive today in different guises. I remember another young man benefiting from Sir Hilary's kindness and contacts. Bob Clark, who became chairman of the Mirror Group, was, like Sir Hilary, an old SOE (Special Operations Executive) man in the Second World War, where he won the DSC. Clark had been sentenced to death by the Germans in Italy. They had marched him out to be shot one morning and pulled the triggers, but the guns hadn't gone off. It was deliberate, a ploy to get him to answer their questions when they marched him back in. Bob Clark was about nineteen when it happened.

When he returned from the war, he went to Cambridge and

one day in the street met Sir Hilary, who asked him what he wanted to do, and then got him a job with Slaughter and May, where he qualified as a solicitor. Subsequently Clark became chairman of Hill Samuel and was, at one time or another, on the boards of a whole string of companies, including British Leyland.

Yet his whole career seems to have been punctuated with problems. He was at the Mirror when Maxwell dived (or was pushed) overboard, at Hill Samuel at the time of the TSB takeover, and he had been at British Leyland when it collapsed. But still he has managed to go from strength to strength.

In Britain some people can do no wrong. But the other side of this is that if you set yourself up as an independent in opposition and tread on the feet of the big monopolies, then they will bring the whole weight of the Establishment crashing down on you. In America they cannot understand this at all.

Peats has always been an international firm with practices all over the world, and has close links with other firms like Price Waterhouse. I had a good time there. I worked on the audits of companies such as Anglo-Iranian oil, Gillette Razor Blades, Champion Sparking Plugs, Crown Cork, many firms with American connections, the Greyhound Racing Association, Petrofina, and even BMARC, a company we eventually bought at Astra.

But I didn't particularly see the accounting profession as a long-term career, so when I finished my exams I went, through Bob Clark, to Hill Samuel, the merchant bankers, becoming involved in debenture and stock issues, takeovers and capital reconstructions. I stayed there until 1968 when I moved to Baring Brothers & Co. Ltd, a merchant bank with connections in pre-revolutionary Russia, which had been the purchasing agents for the Imperial Army and Navy. In fact, their coat of arms is reminiscent of the Imperial coat of arms with the middle taken out. Barings had huge amounts of money on deposit from those days from the Imperial Army and Navy and various people who disappeared in the revolution – none of it had been paid back when I was there.

It was a busy time. The heavy engineering industry – firms like John Thompson, Clarke Chapman and International

Combustion – were merging, and shipbuilders Swan Hunter, Yarrow and Upper Clyde Shipbuilders had their problems. It was while I was with Barings that Mersey Docks went bust. I worked closely on this disaster with a man called John Cuckney, a figure who would play a key role in my business life later. Cuckney's background was MI5. He had left the Security Service to become a director of Lazards, part of the Pearson Group, and was also chairman of a bucket shop they had at the time, a little investment bank called Standard Industrial Trust, where he interviewed me for a job, but I preferred Barings.

Cuckney is a very ambitious chap. He has no children and is committed to what he does. He left Standard Industrial Trust and Lazards to set up, through his Intelligence connections, a bank called Anglo-Eastern. Its backer was Davoud Allianz, an Iraqi Jew from a very wealthy family in Iran. Now Sir David Alliance, he is chairman of the textile company Carrington Viyella. With Alliance as sponsor, Cuckney was supposed to build up Anglo-Eastern Bank into a major force. But it didn't work out, indeed it was a bit of a fiasco, perhaps not helped by the property crisis of the early 1970s. When Cuckney bowed out, he really had nowhere to go until, that is, the crash of Mersey Docks.

Mersey Docks had been the most important port in the country during the Second World War with the bulk of goods from America going there. It was also a key link in the transport of passengers and goods to America, which was to be undermined by the advent of airlines as well as trades union activity. When it went bust it was regarded as one of the biggest financial disasters there had ever been. The old board was sacked and Cuckney was brought in by the government as chairman (with Sir Matthew Stephenson, former deputy chairman of the board of the Inland Revenue). The new Ted Heath government had wanted a man with Intelligence connections because there was a heavy left-wing/communist element in Liverpool and they needed someone to reorganise that and protect government interests, including the heavy investment in the new Seaforth docks.

Barings had advised the board previously and were retained as financial advisers, and I worked with Cuckney and Peter Baring on the capital reconstruction. Cuckney made his name at this time. After Merseyside he was given the Port of London to sort out, and then the shipbuilders and engineers John Brown, which became part of Trafalgar House, a company that crops up in my story time and again.

I continued at Barings until 1972, and might have stayed longer if Cromer, the chairman, had not been recruited by Heath as ambassador to the United States. That upset the whole balance of power at Barings. John Baring (Lord Ashburton today) became chairman and influence in the boardroom swung away from the more worldly and older directors close to Cromer (who was a Baring) to other members with Baring family connections. As it happened, at about the same time, I was offered a directorship at Henry Ansbacher, the merchant bank controlled then by Max Joseph, and I took it.

For the first time in its history Ansbacher looked as if it was about to go places. However, when fortune did not favour a merger opportunity with Johnson Matthey, and the 1970s property crisis set in, Max Joseph became disillusioned, sold out and left, and soon afterwards so did I.

It was 1977 and I was out of a job, when all of a sudden George Kennedy Young, a former deputy head of MI6 (actually head of MI6 in Vienna in the 'Harry Lime' days), whom I had met through the Monday Club, suggested I should meet Bill Baldock, who had been at Kleinworts with Young and who was then with Singer and Friedlander, another merchant bank.

Singer and Friedlander offered me a consultancy, which turned out to suit me quite well. I began to make use of the company connections that I had built up over the years and managed to consolidate my new independence with one or two non-executive directorships – with Norton Telecommunications Group, Belhaven Brewery, Ashpoint and Packbourne (both plastics companies), and VW Thermax, manufacturers of glass and precision engineers. I also became involved in several other situations, for example advising the Rawlings family, who first marketed Mateus

Rosé in this country and had wine cellars under Waterloo station, where the channel tunnel rail terminal now operates.

Then, to these clients I added a television manufacturing company owned by Derek Tyne, half of which I managed to rescue when it was forced into receivership. During this venture I met Sir David Napley, who was defending Jeremy Thorpe at the time, and Geoff Wilson, a public relations man and friend of Tyne, who was involved with a number of clients in defence work. He told me about one of them in particular, a company called Brocks the firework people.

A family-owned company, with its origins in the seventeenth century, Brocks had been co-opted on military production during the Second World War, returning afterwards exclusively to fireworks manufacture. They were doing moderately well when suddenly they received an offer from Ritblats for their factory site at Hemel Hempstead. The Brock family took several million pounds for the land and moved the company up to Sanquhar near Dumfries under a Scottish Development Agency grant, but it didn't prove easy in the firework field on a remote site with new workers. They plodded along around break-even, not really doing very well, until in the military boom of the late 1970s the Nigerian government placed an order with them to make thunder-flashes and smoke grenades. This immediately transformed the position. In a year or so they went from break-even to a profit of £850,000 and stood to make millions. It meant that they had to bring in new people with the necessary specialist experience.

Arthur Reed, the managing director, a former Home Office Inspector of Explosives, began to create a new management team made up largely of chemists and men from the army. Being an industrial chemist, Reed knew his explosives, but was somewhat autocratic and not commercially minded. This was why, when further military business materialised and he and his finance director, Jim Miller, realised they needed to raise capital to develop this side of the business, I and a business associate, John Anderson, a former bank manager with the Bank of Scotland, became involved.

Immediately, indeed in a matter of days, we justified our commission by realising for Brocks a debt of £2m outstanding in Malaysia. They had been told it could not be paid for about six months as they hadn't handled the Letter of Credit properly. Then I negotiated a long-term loan from Brown Shipley – about £4m at a very good rate.

Of course when the shareholders saw how 'easy' it was to raise capital and make money from military pyrotechnics, they suddenly wanted to become more involved in decisions. The management were on incentive arrangements geared to firework production, and when their salaries shot up as a percentage of the vastly increased profits from military sales, it caused resentment among the shareholders. Within the company there was a growing divergence of opinion over policy. Some wanted to make the company a real success – to raise money and go ahead; others – mainly the Brock family, and in particular a young man called Harry Smee, a chartered surveyor by training, a Brock on his mother's side – wanted to benefit from the new position but at the same time stay in control.

Smee's father had been kept out of the company, I was told, which understandably had left him with a bit of a chip on his shoulder. When he saw the company was becoming a success he persuaded two aged aunts, who owned about 40 per cent of the shares, to part with them for £40,000. As a result of military sales, the value of these shares was very significant. Advised by Hambros Bank and Sir Ian Morrow, former chairman of the Scottish Institute and Hambros, Smee, from his new position of power, started to dominate the boardroom and came into conflict with Reed and the new management.

The upshot was that Reed was fired, and the team of young military specialists he had brought in walked out as well, partly in protest and partly because they feared that Brocks would renege on their contracts over profit-linked bonus payments. I believe they thought that Brocks would have them back on their terms, but they didn't.

At about the same time I was asked to find a purchaser for

Astra Fireworks, a company formed in 1947 on a 12-acre site at Richborough, near Sandwich in Kent. Cowan's Camp, as it was known, had been a main First World War embarkation point from Richborough docks and subsequently in the next war it had been used to house Eastern European refugees.

It was owned by a charming Jewish gentleman of Russian extraction called Bernard Yelin, and a Czechoslovakian refugee, also Jewish, Dr Gregory Lax, who I believe had been interned at Cowan's Camp during the war. The fireworks factory was decrepit and run down, but in the right hands and with military business on its licensed explosives site, I felt it had considerable potential. I alerted a German company called Feistel, and they expressed an interest in buying it. They could see the advantage of a UK explosives site from which they could sell, more easily than from Germany, to places like Malaysia and Nigeria, as Brocks were doing. In Britain there would be minimum government interference and relatively cheap labour.

So a report on the Astra site was needed, and the only people I could think of who were qualified to do this, from an explosives point of view, were Arthur Reed and his sometime research manager at Brocks, Martin Guest, both of whom were out of work.

When the report was produced I met Reed and Guest at the Bell Hotel in Sandwich to discuss it. Christopher Gumbley, the former Brocks production manager, was also present. The report the three men gave me was positive, so much so that they suggested that they would like to consider making an offer for Astra. I explained that that was impossible because of Feistel's interest. However, over the following week or so, Yelin and Lax rejected the German offer of £500,000, Feistel withdrew, and Anderson and I joined forces with Reed and his men. I organised with the 3i Scottish office in Glasgow the formation of a new company called Astra Holdings and made Yelin and Lax our offer, which included consultancy arrangements for both of them.

Astra Fireworks was bought in June 1981, nine months after the start of the Iran–Iraq war, as it happened, by an injection of £102,000 equity by ex-Brocks personnel Arthur Reed, Chris

Gumbley, Martin Guest, John Park, former contracts manager, and Atholl Mowbray, former sales manager, and by myself and Anderson. The ex-Brocks people had to sell their houses to fund it. ICFC/3i injected £40,000 of preferred ordinary shares and a £600,000 loan at 17 percent per annum interest. So when we started, we had a large debt to deal with, and initially, during the purchase phase, Anderson and I had to raise the cash to fund office facilities.

We created Astra almost from nothing. In the eight years from 1981 we raised turnover from £1,165,000 to £96,223,000, and profit before tax from £81,000 to £9,512,000. In the same period, company assets grew from £264,000 to £53,852,000. When I resigned from the chair in March 1990, I left the company with an order book approaching £300m.

In summer 1989 we had acquired the Belgian explosives and ammunition manufacturer Poudreries Réunies de Belgique (PRB) from Gechem, its holding company, itself owned by Société Général de Belgique (SGB), a company so large that it was equal to one-third of the Belgian economy. All the talk at that time in British industry was for a drive into Europe, and PRB made especially good sense strategically to Astra for another reason. We had discovered that the US government had authorised a secret contract, described to us by Brian Peet, an assistant in Peter Levene's Ministry of Defence procurement department, as the Explosives, Propellants and Related End Products (EPREP), which guaranteed their recently privatised company, Royal Ordnance, 80 per cent of the UK government market and the ability to compete for the remaining 20 per cent. Integrated with Astra's other companies in England and America, PRB was an opportunity to produce a sales potential far greater than PRB had on its own, and at the same time to make us less vulnerable to this monopolistic UK government policy. The potential of PRB would be proved a year later during the Gulf War, when it became clear that what the British army lacked on the battlefield was precisely what PRB produced – 155mm, 105mm artillery ammunition, and tank ammunition. Unfortunately, it was a potential never to be realised,

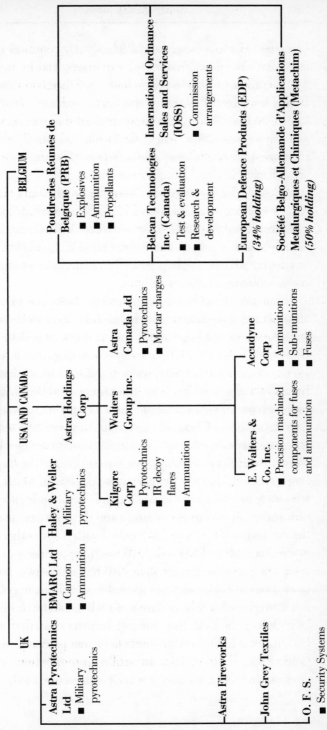

ASTRA HOLDING PLC

UK

Astra Pyrotechnics Ltd
- Military pyrotechnics

BMARC Ltd
- Cannon
- Ammunition

Haley & Weller
- Military pyrotechnics

Astra Fireworks

John Grey Textiles

O. F. S.
- Security Systems

USA AND CANADA

Astra Holdings Corp

Walters Group Inc.

Kilgore Corp
- Pyrotechnics
- IR decoy flares
- Ammunition

E. Walters & Co. Inc.
- Precision machined components for fuses and ammunition

Astra Canada Ltd
- Pyrotechnics
- Mortar charges

Accudyne Corp
- Ammunition
- Sub-munitions
- Fuses

BELGIUM

Poudreries Réunies de Belgique (PRB)
- Explosives
- Ammunition
- Propellants

Belcan Technologies Inc. (Canada)
- Test & evaluation
- Research & development

European Defence Products (EDP)
(34% holding)

Société Belgo-Allemande d'Applications Metalurgiques et Chimiques (Metachim)
(50% holding)

International Ordnance Sales and Services (IOSS)
- Commission arrangements

and the MoD had to buy stocks from NATO countries at three or four times the price PRB could have supplied them.

Two months after the purchase, in September 1989, Chris Gumbley and I discovered that a PRB contract for propellant worth around £38m to the company, and thereafter about £50m a year for about five years, which was purportedly bound for Jordan with the official approval of the Belgian government, was in fact part of Gerald Bull's Supergun project, Project Babylon, and bound for Iraq. We had been tipped off by our old friend Roger Harding, who had moved from the defence department of the British embassy in Washington to deputy head of defence sales at the MoD in London, that we should look carefully at any contracts in PRB that might possibly be connected with Iran or Iraq, or were in any way peculiar.

After the Iran–Iraq ceasefire (mid-1988), the government, fearful of its own vulnerability to criticism over its covert policy to supply, at various times, both Iran and Iraq, and its role in the building up of Iraq's own indigenous arms industry (in particular in the development of its missile capability), hatched a new strategy of 'damage limitation'. In the spring and summer of 1990 the strategy would entail crushing the relatively small independents (Ordtec, Matrix Churchill, Euromac, Walter Somers, Sheffield Forgemasters and Astra), companies which had been used for these covert purposes and knew too much, leaving the big boys such as Rolls-Royce, British Aerospace/Royal Ordnance, ICI (through its subsidiary Nobel Explosives Company) and others who were more closely bound in with government interests, untouched.

We had taken the decision to report the existence of the PRB propellant contract not for any moral reason, but to safeguard our own interests, to ensure that we were not left holding the baby.

We reported it to the MoD in London, and we had meetings with MI6. Amazingly, they did not order us to cancel the contract. At a meeting at Stuart House in Soho Square, Chris Gumbley and I were told specifically to continue with it. Weeks later, in early December 1989, our explosives press at the plant at Kaulille, which was processing the requirement, was mysteriously blown up.

The immediate financial impact on Astra, which we had of course weighed up before reporting the contract, was to wipe out up to £38m of projected turnover for 1990. It was a major blow, but it was not terminal. The Astra turnover, profit and asset figures quoted on p.38 do not include the benefit of PRB business. I believed that we could bear it and that, following the integration of PRB and Astra's other companies in America and England, we could ultimately have solved the PRB problem.

However, our reporting of the Supergun propellant contract came on top of other internal investigations I had made into Iran- and Iraq-destined, UK-government approved and covert contracts being put through our UK subsidiary BMARC and our US interests, Walters and Accudyne. Also, Chris Gumbley had discovered fantastic commissions being paid to officials on PRB contracts engineered abroad, in particular in Thailand. Those in power had got wind of this and now reacted ruthlessly to protect their own interests.

As a direct result of these investigations, and in line with the government's new strategy, an agent with Intelligence, government and City connections, who had been infiltrated onto the Astra board, in March/April 1990 engineered my removal from the chair and the arrest by the MoD police of Chris Gumbley, and 'pressed the button', as he would later boast, on the remaining original Brocks/Astra directors, before entering into a deliberate strategy for Astra's break-up and piecemeal disposal.

These are events which will be described in detail later. For now it is enough to point to the transparent flaw in the financial reasons that were used to justify Astra's break-up.

Such was our underlying strength that the company managed to survive until 1992 with absolutely no new sales made by the new 'management' team. Indeed one contract worth £1.5bn, in which Astra would have been the lead contractor, which Gumbley had negotiated and which was due for signature in April, one month after I was removed, was never concluded by the new team.

And yet, turnover to 31 March 1991, a year after I had left the company, was £86.6m on the basis of orders won in 1989 by the original sales team under Chris Gumbley. The group had managed to sustain itself from 1990 to 1992 solely from orders left by the original management and in spite of ludicrous asset write-offs by the new management.

That this conspiracy against the directors of Astra was politically motivated is the nub of the following pages. But first let's look at the nature of the political animal that devoured our company and whence it came, for it will become clear in my story that in Britain the performance of our elected politicians is little more than a media mirage of what goes on beneath the surface, and that the forces which really drove Margaret Thatcher's foreign policy and the 'strategy of damage limitation' that followed were spawned by the very forces that had brought her to power.

One key development in the long lead-up to Thatcher's coming to power was the shift from a manufacturing-based economy to an economy centred on the City. Prime Minister Edward Heath's term of office in the early 1970s saw the rise of companies like Slater Walker, which, in chairman Jim Slater's own words, was 'a maker of money, not a maker of things'.[1]

This revolutionary shift in the economy of Britain was not made without stout resistance by the trades unions, who added a political dimension. Following the 1972 miners' strike, which brought Heath's government to its knees in the three-day week, the battle-lines were clearly drawn. Dire warnings about the 'new growth industry' of subversive groups in Britain that had been published in pamphlet form by Brian Crozier's Institute for the Study of Conflict (ISC), spawned in 1970 by the CIA's Current Affairs Research Center, suddenly appeared justified, and the threat of communist insurgency in Britain focused the agenda of a number of Tory political groups.

Simultaneously, and increasingly through Wilson's second term in office (1974–76) and Callaghan's term from 1977, Tory groups marshalled support in the City for an economy free of restraints –

free enterprise and a free market. One of these groups was the Monday Club, so named because members met on a Monday. I joined it because, as a qualified accountant since my late twenties, I had spent a lot of time looking into companies and had begun to feel that Macmillan politics were betraying business and our overseas interests.

Also, as a child, I had spent quite a lot of time with older people like my grandfather and his friends, who had fought in the First World War, and when I grew up, the British empire was the great thing. Britain was a power that was respected; we were supposed to be superior in attitude, in everything. This was the ethos when I was brought up.

It may sound strange, but it is true, that throughout my life betrayal has been the main theme, right from the beginning – betrayal of this country. I am talking about what has happened to British industry, to the fishing industry in the context of the EEC, what has happened to the agricultural industry, what has happened to the British army, navy and air force. We have been dismantling our empire, and all the institutions that were in my opinion the best part of Britain have gradually been destroyed.

Throughout my lifetime there never has been a time when we were moving forward in this country. Always, it seems, we have been on the retreat, always apologising to other people, always saying we got it wrong, always being fed the most appalling nonsense by politicians, including Churchill, saying one thing to the British people and at the same time betraying them, getting them to work for nothing and give thousands of lives.

Suez was appalling, the way we backed out of that, as was Cyprus after all the sacrifices, also India, Africa, the Middle East and recently (and unnecessarily) Hong Kong – what deals have been going on there? For years it was the same thing in Ireland. I don't think it is so much a question of what is right or wrong as that people are never told the truth by government. In the 1980s I watched a select band of people, who were apparently above the law and superior to everything, living the good life while everybody else went down the drain, whereas in America the positive attitudes I found produced an entirely opposite result.

The real purpose of the Monday Club, as I saw it, was to push the Conservative Party back on course. A lot of people who belonged to it would be called reactionary or right wing, but that doesn't mean that they were bad people.

The Monday Club was very influential and people tried hard to undermine it – Ted Heath among them. Why? What was there to be afraid of? What did 'right wing' mean? Those who supported the Monday Club were not all very rich or even people who had a lot of influence. They were people who were deeply concerned about the direction of the country.

Macmillan was a totally amoral man – one of those people who looked the part but whose whole life was all betrayal. When he was saying one thing, he was actually doing the opposite – no substance, he just looked the part. 'You've never had it so good' was a pretty meaningless phrase for a British public that had nothing to compare it with, that had been through a war and suffered rationing right through into the 1950s.

As I saw it, the Monday Club was a return to values that had some honesty, some substance. It may have been said that some of the MPs who were connected – John Biggs-Davison, Paul Williams, Ronald Bell, etc. – were a bit extreme or naive, but they were basically honest people. People like Douglas Bader, and latterly, Colin Mitchell, and even the old Lord Salisbury, who has been vilified, were very decent men. I thought the Monday Club might put a bit of integrity back into the Conservative Party. I thought it might arrest the betrayal.

There I met George Kennedy Young, who had retired as deputy chief of MI6 in 1961 and joined Kleinwort Benson. He had joined the club in 1967 at the invitation of John Biggs-Davison.

George Young didn't tolerate idiots. He was a brave man and forthright, not at all the typical Intelligence man. What I took from Young was a realisation of how things were actually done rather than how people thought they were done, and it stood me in very good stead in the years to come. He was one of the people involved in the strategy to restore the Shah to the Iranian throne.

He told me openly how, with the CIA, they had totally undermined the Iranian state under Mossadeq with disinformation and
by organising riots, even down to the detail of how they eliminated
a key minister by sending him an exploding shaver.

Young had encouraged the proliferation of Monday Club
groups throughout the country, but when he was defeated in 1973
by Jonathan Guinness in a bid for the chair, he left. Some that left
with him resurfaced in the Selsdon Group, which became the
breeding ground for many of the ideas that were said to have
constituted Thatcherism.

I was an early member of the Selsdon Group, a lot of mainly
idealistic young men, named after a policy meeting by Heath at
the Selsdon Hotel. It still goes on. There were other groups, too,
such as the Freedom Group, where Ross McWhirter was active,
and the Institute for Economic Affairs (IEA), all dedicated to promoting private enterprise and free-market, laissez-faire economic
traditions which would be loudly trumpeted in the 1980s, while,
at the same time, abused by Thatcher's government when it came
to privatising their own state-owned defence company, Royal
Ordnance, which, to the detriment of our armed forces (and not
a little to the detriment of Astra), turned out to have been a sham.

I became involved with the IEA while I was working at
Ansbacher, through a self-effacing man called Anthony Fisher,
who had made a bit of money but felt very worried about the way
the country was drifting. Fisher subsidised the IEA to research into
a lot of the economic policies which Harold Wilson was pursuing.

By way of a contribution I got Ansbacher, through the group
managing director, John Cowen, to sponsor a book called *Failing
the Nation* – the title was taken from a phrase used by Wedgwood
Benn in the context of private enterprise – which was in fact the
very first economic study of the nationalised industries. Believe it
or not, Central Office had never previously bothered to analyse
the economic performance of the nationalised industries. I went to
the IEA to find the best economists to research it, and then gathered some practical industrial examples of the sorts of things that
had been going on.

The now Lord Harris was the executive in charge of the IEA, and they produced an excellent economist, the late George Polyani, to write the draft.

When we published, we supplied a copy to every chairman of every major company, to every MP and to every member of the House of Lords, and sent a press release to the national papers. The book demonstrated how the state-controlled industries had written off capital, how their accounts had been cooked to ensure their continuance, and how these industries had in fact bled the British economy for years and years.

As a result, they put me in charge of the Economic Committee of the Monday Club. This didn't amount to very much, but through the book's publication and my membership of the Selsdon Group I became involved with Ross McWhirter and George Young in a project that might have made something more of a splash.

Before George Young and I went to see Airey Neave in the House of Commons with our idea, which concerned Wedgwood Benn's proposals to nationalise the aircraft and shipbuilding industries, I had had an amusing meeting with Lord Weinstock of GEC over the same issue because of his particular vested interest in the aircraft industry. Michael Richardson, deputy chairman of Fraser Ansbacher (the holding company of Ansbacher, the bank) and I, had sat in Weinstock's office and witnessed what I can only describe as a re-run of Charlie Chaplin's *The Great Dictator*.

There was pint-size Arnold Weinstock striding up and down the carpet with his hands behind his back inveighing against politicians in general, while a gaggle of senior directors from major companies, all Weinstock's friends, sat on the sofas and chairs around his office sycophantically egging him on. He kept exclaiming, 'This is very serious! We own 50 per cent of the British aircraft corporation with Vickers – and Vickers are no fucking good! Here we are, left to shoulder the burden . . . useless management! The government is going to nationalise the aircraft industry and the shipbuilding industry, and it'll take another great slice off Vickers, and they hardly dare say boo to a goose!'

Whenever he paused for a moment, all the clowns that were sitting around the walls chipped in with, 'That's right, Arnold, I quite agree, Arnold' – really quite nauseating examples of senior levels of British industry.

Weinstock had been attracted to Ansbacher because he had seen our book and wanted to know what else we might do to help him. But, as I would later learn in an altogether different context, when it comes to the crunch, few who are reliant upon government contracts want to put their head above the parapet. Weinstock wanted to stop the nationalisation programme, but he preferred someone else to do it, which was, I am afraid, rather typical. Lord Weinstock has always been managing director of GEC, never really anything else, preferring to have some figurehead like Jim Prior for the job of chairman to shoulder much of the media attention.

It was after this that I went with George Young to see Airey Neave at the House of Commons. Neave was probably one of the prime people behind Thatcher's appointment. One of the first tasks he set himself was to sort out the Intelligence services, to clean out the crooks and amalgamate MI5 and MI6. Things would have been a bit different for Astra if he had. But he made the mistake of saying this publicly, and he was killed by a bomb in the House of Commons car park. The crime was laid at the door of the IRA, but bomb experts have since said that it couldn't have been an IRA bomb because it had a mercury fuse, tripped on the angle of the car, a type that was available only to the CIA at the time.

Neave was going to appoint Christopher Sykes at The Hague as head of MI6 and Christopher Tugendhat, who was on the *Financial Times* for many years, as head of MI5. But Sykes was machine-gunned on his doorstep in The Hague to make sure that never happened, A similar attempt was made on the life of Tugendhat, but he survived because when he came out of the house he realised that he had forgotten his briefcase and walked inside again just as they opened fire. Unfortunately, with Neave's passing, the whole Thatcher charabanc went in a totally different direction.

When we met him in the House we told Airey Neave that we had decided to act over this business of nationalising aircraft and shipbuilding, that it would be a disaster economically, place a big burden on the Exchequer, reduce efficiency to zero and so on, and that from a public relations point of view we had decided to do something that had not been done for more than a hundred years – organise the impeachment of Wedgwood Benn. It wouldn't require more than a handful of MPs to put down a motion, and it would draw the whole issue into focus to be debated before the House. Neave didn't sound worried about it, but he said he wasn't a legal expert, and we should go and see Ivan Lawrence.

Unfortunately, when I went to see Lawrence, this time with Ross McWhirter, and we put the same proposal to him, he nearly wet his trousers. Looking furtively over his shoulder, he appeared frightfully worried and ushered us down to some room in the depths of the House of Commons, slammed the door, and said, 'Right, now what is all this?' We repeated that we wished to organise the impeachment of Benn and explained why and how we could go about it. He said, 'Ooh, I don't think we could ever do that!'

When Lawrence didn't perform, we went to see Ronald Bell QC, a member of the Monday Club, but he was terrified as well. We found it all very strange, but after that, tragically, Ross McWhirter was shot and the whole scheme rather ran out of steam, as did the Freedom Group.

An interesting footnote about Ivan Lawrence is that a decade later he served on the Foreign Affairs Committee inquiry into the shortcomings of the Falklands campaign. Ammunition shortage was a key issue and one that was of no small interest to me. Nothing damaging about the Falklands War would ever have been uttered by the loyal during Thatcher's time, of course. The committee didn't disappoint her, and shortly afterwards Ivan Lawrence received his knighthood.

Meanwhile, after his defeat at the Monday Club, Young had re-emerged in a new and clandestine group called Unison, an organisation interlocked with Intelligence, which Young described as 'an anti-chaos organisation', and which first went public in 1974, when Chapman Pincher described it in the *Daily Express* as 'a formidable vigilante group to help protect the nation against a Communist takeover . . . organised by former Service chiefs, senior ex-members of the Secret Service and MI5'.[2]

I also was a member of Unison. The idea was that should things fall apart, if you can maintain communications, you can always win. That was the motto, and Young was basing it on his Intelligence background. It was all about maintaining communication between the key people. In practice it meant having people on the ground in different places, people who could drive cars and take messages, and a system in operation to replace the telecommunications and postal system if they should fail.

It may sound absurd now, but in those days there was a fear of chaos that was tangible. The threat was communism, evinced by confrontational scenes between the Communist NUM leader, Mick McGahey, and the government.

In their book, *Smear!: Wilson and the Secret State*, Stephen Dorril and Robin Ramsay quote Heath Cabinet member John Davies saying to his wife and children, when he went home to celebrate Christmas 1974, 'that we should have a nice time, because I deeply believed then that it was the last Christmas of its kind we would enjoy.' By 6 January there were tanks at Heathrow airport. 'Heathrow is being defended by rings of Police and the army with tanks,' recalled Wedgwood Benn in his diary. 'The rumour in the press is that there might be a SAM missile attack.'

People forget that all this happened. Seven years earlier, the threat had been economic chaos, and I had witnessed the effects of it for myself. When I was at Hill Samuel in Wood Street, I watched articulated lorries queuing up at the Bank of England, all the way up Gresham Street, down Wood Street and down London Wall, to take the gold out of the Bank because total confidence had gone in Harold Wilson's government. They flew it out from RAF Mildenhall, an American base, to Switzerland. We watched the first leg of its journey. Experiences like that – the physical effects of lack of confidence – make you want to do something.

In 1975, Young also organised with Airey Neave a group called Tory Action, to raise support in the constituencies for Margaret Thatcher. Then, all the various groups that were formed during this intense period following Wilson's re-election seemed to find their focus in the launch of the National Association for Freedom (NAFF) at the end of 1975.

Sponsored by the construction firms McAlpine and Taylor Woodrow, supported by the Tory Party and welcomed by the City and various Intelligence-related agencies like Crozier's ISC, NAFF embodied all the elements – Intelligence, right-wing Tory, business interests and the City – that would fall in line behind Margaret Thatcher as prime minister for the 1980s, although only after Edward du Cann and then Keith Joseph had eliminated themselves from the race.

Now I am not of course blind to the fact that I was part of the swell in Tory ranks that made this happen, that created precisely the group which would turn on Astra ten years later. On the face of it, it is the great irony of my story. But despite what has happened, my own beliefs have not changed. Two of my sons have served in the army, one has seen active service in Ireland and the other in the Gulf and Ireland; my younger son is still in the army, and I am proud that they have served the country. What I do feel is that I and indeed all of us have been betrayed, not by George Kennedy Young or Airey Neave, who laid the groundwork for Thatcher to come to power, but by those who rode in on their coat-tails.

The difference between Young and the people who came after lies in their motivation. Here is a circular sent out about 1955 by George Young, when he was still deputy head of MI6:

In the press, in Parliament, in the United Nations, from the pulpit, there is a ceaseless talk about the rule of law, civilised relations between nations, the spread of democratic processes, self-determination and national sovereignty, respect for the rights of man and human dignity.

The reality, we all know perfectly well, is quite the opposite

and consists of an ever-increasing spread of lawlessness, disre-
gard of international contract, cruelty and corruption. The
nuclear stalemate is matched by a moral stalemate.

It is the spy who has been called upon to remedy the situation created by the deficiencies of ministers, diplomats, generals
and priests.

Men's minds are shaped, of course, by their environment
and we spies, although we have our professional mystique, do
perhaps live closer to the realities and hard facts of international relations than other practitioners of government. We are
relatively free of the problems of status, of precedence, departmental attitudes and evasions of personal responsibility, which
create the official cast of mind. We do not have to develop, like
the Parliamentarians conditioned by a lifetime, the ability to
produce the ready phrase, the smart reply and the flashing
smile. And so it is not surprising these days that the spy finds
himself the main guardian of intellectual integrity.

This is a picture that is wholly unrecognisable in the context of
the Intelligence services today. Young, like Graham Greene, had a
sense of the difference between what is Good and Evil and what
is right and wrong, and took for granted that in the political arena
the public interest is not the self-serving interest of the powerful
writ large.

After Young's death, a friend wrote: 'Although generally
described as "right wing", commentators were often puzzled by
his membership of such groups as the South Place Ethical Society.
There was no mystery or contradiction. Young remained very
much a Scottish borderer of Calvinistic stock on both sides of the
family, with a strong tradition of dissent and independent thinking combined with a deep attachment to Dumfriesshire hills and
dales and the Solway merseland.'[3]

It has been said that George Kennedy Young did more than
anyone to create the political culture out of which Thatcherism
grew. I was part of that culture at the beginning and what I saw
at the end of the 1970s was that as these groups started to have

some real influence, all the parasites started climbing aboard. It was quite clear that these groups were used by certain people as vehicles for their own self-interest or in the interests of other scenarios that were alien to their constitution.

The people I came upon working in clandestine areas behind Thatcher's government in the 1980s, when the national interest became muddied by the interests of those in power, were, as I will show, doing things for reasons quite other than the good of the country.

CHAPTER THREE

THATCHER'S MILITARISED ECONOMY

Government has a role in the story of every British arms manufacturer, and yet it is precisely the government's role that has
been deliberately ignored or suppressed both in court (by the
government itself wielding Public Interest Immunity Certificates)
and in all the various inquiries that have been published to date,
such as the Public Accounts Committee Inquiry into Margaret
Thatcher's Al Yamamah deal with Saudi Arabia (which was suppressed altogether by the Auditor General, Sir John Bourn), the
Foreign Affairs Committee's Inquiry into her Malaysia/Pergau
Dam deal (which omitted to interview key witnesses and publish
vital evidence), the Department of Trade and Industry (DTI)
Select Committee Inquiry into the whole arms-to-Iraq saga
(where witnesses to government involvement in the trade were
'visited' prior to giving their evidence), and the DTI Inquiry into
Astra, where in the opening pages of their report the inspectors
declared that all evidence concerning government involvement
had been ruled out as immaterial.

Since then, the Defence Committee under Sir Nicholas Bonsor
has consistently refused to investigate Astra properly, even though
Bonsor himself has acknowledged in a letter to me that Astra was
the victim of 'underhand policies'.

Now, in June 1995, with the Scott Report apparently imminent and forced into a corner by allegations about Jonathan Aitken and Astra's BMARC, and by the recent release of documents (after intense legal and political pressure which I have helped to co-ordinate since Astra's collapse) Michael Heseltine has had to admit to the House of Commons that my 'allegations' about government involvement are indeed relevant.

It seems that official policy now, as I write, is to minimise the fall-out by admitting what they hope can be explained away as ineptitude stopping short of connivance. Heads will roll (as Aitken's seems to have), but not those of the guilty ones who hold real power.

My book is written to show who these are and that the conspiracy runs deep into the very fabric of government. The Aitken case is relatively superficial, usefully so for those who would conceal that government involvement in the illicit arms trade of the 1980s was no less than the 'magic' at the black heart of Margaret Thatcher's economic miracle.

Unlike in other manufacturing industries, in arms the government has a key ongoing role to play. It is in effect a participant. Nothing goes on – no deals, no contracts – in which the government is not principally involved. Ninety per cent of our contracts at Astra were drawn direct with government – the MoD in London or the DoD in Washington. All of them were submitted to government for their approval.

So, the government was involved and remains involved in both the home and export trade in arms. Up to its neck, one might say, for, specifically in the 1980s, in the sphere of my own particular experience at Astra, government was not only involved but actively trading, openly and covertly, in arms through its own companies, which included (up to 1991, when it ceased trading and part of the business was sold to British Aerospace) International Military Services (IMS), a 100 per cent government-owned company which was established from the Crown Agents to assist Royal Ordnance (RO) in the 1970s during the heyday of arms exports to the late Shah of Iran. RO was at this time and up to April 1987 also wholly government owned, after which it was sold to British Aerospace (BAe), but it is now still so tightly linked to government that its security is undertaken by MoD police (also, it has offices in the MoD).

How was government involved in the day-to-day business? Contracts came to us in different ways. The Ministry of Defence Export Sales Organisation (DESO) in Soho Square monitors potential export deals from around the world. Information is gathered by DESO and then passed to major British arms manufacturers. DESO relies for its information on MI6, military attachés in foreign countries and arms dealers.

So, often we would be guided in the right direction by way of a memo from DESO informing us, say, that the government of Abu Dhabi were looking for ammunition or whatever, and would we like to pursue it. The person to contact would be our desk for Abu Dhabi at the MoD, who would put us in touch with the military attaché in the country concerned.

Alternatively, you might literally find that an Arab or African came in off the street saying he was the agent for a certain Government and Astra's name had been given to him by the MoD. Or perhaps he says he likes what we are up to or has seen our name in the British army or navy equipment catalogues and could we give him a quote to supply him.

He is the accredited agent. There are very many agents and facilitators in the arms business. They build in commissions 5, 10 or 30 per cent, whatever it is, keep some of it for themselves and disperse the rest as appropriate – they will never say who it is for. Sometimes there would be two commissions to be paid to different agents. You may even have a situation where the foreign agent is introduced by a British agent who will require a payment as well. Arrangements differ.

There is nothing illegal about an agent taking a commission of course; that is his livelihood. Bribes are something different. When the Organisation for Economic Co-operation and Development set up a working party to draft an agreement among the main industrialised nations to outlaw bribes in foreign countries to secure lucrative contracts, it found, interestingly, only two nations in opposition: Britain and Japan.

All British defence exports, even down to rifle slings, require the submission of an official very detailed application to the MoD, which leaves no doubt as to the project itself, how the order was obtained, who for, and at what price. If approved, the shipment will also require a valid end-user certificate from the DTI, and if there is any doubt about granting it, the DTI can refer it to the Foreign and Commonwealth Office (FCO), the MoD, and/or the military attaché of the country concerned.

The feeling in Astra was that it was up to the government to decide what was and was not permissible in a volatile market. The system was set up for the purpose. That is not to say that we abrogated total responsibility to government, but our concern was never to do anything to upset the MoD or DoD, who were our main clients.

From the MoD there is a monthly list of requirements open to tender, perhaps for 155mm shells or 30mm ammunition. Having picked that up, we would put in a tender. If it was a MoD order, you wouldn't necessarily know where it was going to. You would deliver it direct to one of the MoD depots, unless they wanted you to ship it abroad, when normally it would go into Nato army or navy stocks. When the MoD sell their stocks on, on a government-to-government basis, there is no export licence required. It just goes.

The key civil servants appointed by Margaret Thatcher to look after this set-up are worth noting because they crop up time and again in my story: Peter Levene, Chief of Defence Procurement from 1985; James Blyth, Head of Defence Sales from 1981; Colin Chandler, Head of Defence Export Services from 1985; and John Bourn, Deputy Under-Secretary for Defence Procurement from 1985. All were knighted for their service to Thatcher's Middle East arms policy.

The government bent over backwards to help the industry by creating a system whereby prompt payment to the UK manufacturer of arms exports was insured by taxpayers' money. The man very much responsible for this was Sir John Cuckney (knighted in 1978), whom I had worked with on the collapse of Mersey Docks. Cuckney masterminded the Midland Bank's extraordinary role in the arms trade in the 1980s. Alone of the High Street banks, Midland had a department dedicated to defence. It was so highly secretive that its top executives claim not to have known what was going on. In 1982 Cuckney set up Midland International Trade Services, within which was a defence sales unit, the Defence Equipment Finance Department, which employed 'consultants', highly experienced 'negotiators' in the arms trade. As we shall see, it is in this context, which includes businessmen and financiers in the City with links to government and the Intelligence services, that the real secrets of the covert arms industry are to be found.

The government's insurance scheme for the commercial funding of the arms industry by Midland worked like this. The Export Credit Guarantee Department (ECGD) is an official credit body offering credits to insure up to 80 or 90 per cent of the value of a manufacturer's risk in exporting. In addition, in 1986, IMS offered a financial service to manufacturers where deals could not be covered by the ECGD. IMS would arrange for the supplier to be paid 85 per cent of the value of a contract and when the full money came in, the supplier would pass 100 per cent over to IMS. Cuckney was chairman of IMS from 1974 to 1985 and a director of Midland Bank from 1978 to 1988.

With Iraq (and in the case of Iraq-related contracts like those going via Jordan) the government sought to establish a country credit rather than a deal-by-deal credit. So they would let the Midland Bank set up a credit for Iraq of, say, £275m (the figure agreed by Thatcher in Amman in 1985 with the Jordanians), which would be guaranteed by ECGD. This meant that if the Jordanians didn't pay up, which is indeed what happened, the shortfall was covered by taxpayers' money. Of course Midland and others – Morgan Grenfell was the other big player in the Iraq credit scheme – were very happy to stump up the cash to go in to bat on that sort of wicket. In the event of default, they were paid within three months normally, from taxpayers' funds.

In the Matrix Churchill trial over their sale of machinery to Iraqi arms factories, it came out that ECGD had bent the rules to enable more than the stated 20 per cent of a country's credits to be spent on arms. There was talk of a secret fund that could be used, say, if Iraq had exceeded its 20 per cent quota. How this was administered remains shrouded in secrecy, as does most of the ECGD paperwork. The BBC Television investigative reporter Graham McLagen has suggested that there was a certain amount of mathematical obfuscation, the 20 per cent arms quota on a country's medium-term loans (most arms contracts are medium-term) being applied also to its quotas of long- and short-term loans, thereby setting a ceiling of some 60 per cent of a country's loan quota via ECGD for arms exports. When at the Scott Inquiry Margaret Thatcher was told, 'We understand that 20 per cent of the export credit for a country can go for arms purposes', she was understandably happy to agree to 20 per cent.

A more traditional obfuscation technique, a stratagem to which we would fall victim at Astra, is receivership or sale. In the case of ECGD, part of its business was hived off to NCM Credit Insurance and, as a result, there is today even less material available than there might have been about its deals. Proof of payment on this or that arms deal is available for inspection at the bank which fronted the deal, but whether the taxpayer ultimately picked up the tab remains hidden.

This lack of information has already been utilised to advantage by the government. In January 1995 £83m of taxpayers' money was reported to be missing from ECGD. Payments had apparently been made 'erroneously'. Robert Sheldon, chairman of the Public Accounts Committee, said that the total missing from ECGD coffers could be much higher – no one could be sure, 'as the relevant paperwork was missing'. No blood-letting would result, for, as the ECGD chief executive Brian Willott declared rather mysteriously, 'All those responsible are deceased, retired or no longer employed by the ECGD.'[1]

We shall return to the missing £83m+, which is wholly relevant to my story. For now it is enough to understand the mechanism, sponsored by the taxpayer but clandestine in its management, which underwrote the massive trade in arms with the Middle East and elsewhere during the 1980s. In the end, because so much of the trade went unpaid, the glamorous economy of Thatcherism was reduced to feeding off the nation's fat by means of ECGD.

The Italian Banca Nazionale del Lavoro (BNL) played a role not dissimilar to the Midland in both America and Europe. In America it supplied some $5bn 'agricultural credits' to manufacturers in that country's efforts to participate in the great Iraqi arms bonanza, which was of course strictly off limits as far as Congress was concerned. BNL helped finance the French company, Luchaire, and the British company, Allivane, that were at the centre of a cartel that included NEC, British Steel and BAe among other British companies, in the shipment of arms and propellant to Iran. It became involved, too, with Matrix Churchill, and it had a hand in the financing of a shipment of $200m worth of land-mines to Iraq, arranged by Casalee, probably the busiest agents in the world at fixing deals with Iraq and Iran, and closely linked, as we shall see, to the Tories.[2]

Eximbank, the Export-Import bank affiliated to the US government, wisely resisted the 'opportunity' of taking on the guarantee role of ECGD in Britain, claiming that it had written into its constitution that it was not allowed to deal with countries harbouring terrorists. So the government cast around until they settled on the Commodity Credit Corporation (CCC), which was affiliated to the Department of Agriculture. The great advantage of doing it through CCC was that it provided such marvellous cover. When Chris Cowley, the project manager of Gerald Bull's Supergun project, visited the Baghdad arms fair in 1989 he saw 'US-made helicopters, fitted with air-to-ground missiles and labelled "For Agricultural Use"'.[3]

But the subterfuge did not stop at fraudulent packaging. Agricultural goods could be shipped to the Jordanian port of Aqaba and be bartered for arms with the Jordanians, who were in receipt of vast quantities from Britain and other places. A telex, one of many documents available, confirms that this system was used even to supply Iraq's nuclear missile project, which involved Gerald Bull, Carlos Cardoen and the British machine tool company, Matrix Churchill. 'Please notify,' the telex from the Rasheed Bank of Baghdad to BNL reads, '. . . we establish our irrevocable letter of credit for account of Iraq Atomic Energy Commission Baghdad up to the aggregate amount of USD 5400000/– USDollars five million four hundred thousand only . . . Shipment of the following goods: 300 tons worsted yarn . . .'[4]

BNL's role as commercial funder of the operation began, we are told, one day late in 1984 when Christopher Drogoul, manager of an obscure branch of BNL in Atlanta, Georgia, received a telephone call from Continental Grain. '[They] called to inquire whether we might be interested in handling a $13m transaction to Iraq involving a shipment of wheat and flour,' Drogoul later recalled.

Subsequently Drogoul was pointed by Continental Grain in the direction of Sadik Taha, director-general of loans at the Central Bank of Iraq. They met at the Sheraton Hotel in New York, Drogoul apparently unaware that Taha was a key player in Sadaam's arms procurement network.

Then, in 1988 and 1989, Drogoul began dealing with Hussein Kamil, head of the Iraqi procurement agency based in Stratford Place, London W1, which is when he began lending BNL money, apparently off his own bat, to the tune of $2.1bn eventually, unsecured by any CCC guarantees. But we know, as indeed the Bank of England knew at the time, that BNL was in fact being backed by the Bank of Credit and Commerce International (BCCI) based in London, with loans fixed at the extraordinary rate of 0.5 per cent.[5]

BCCI, which was closed down in July 1991 following a report commissioned from Price Waterhouse, was a laundering operation for drugs and arms money and it had a special relationship with Iraq. Kickbacks from over-priced arms deals, assigned to BCCI accounts, were funding further arms deals, including BNL-fronted deals. It was one method by which the Intelligence services greased the mechanism of arms sales worldwide. The key section of L.J. Bingham's report (an appendix) on BCCI was suppressed by HMG and the Bank of England to the annoyance of US Senator Kerry.

On 4 August 1989, a year after the Iran–Iraq war ended, when both British and American governments were adopting a strategy of 'damage limitation', the offices of BNL in Atlanta were raided.

It has been said that in Margaret Thatcher's time the British economy was militarised, that the arms industry was the key to her economic strategy for the nation. Little has been said about its failure or the fact that there was other than national interest in its implementation.

After the dismantling of much of Britain's traditional manufacturing industry, she believed that the only way to stir the economy was to help the defence industry, Britain's single major exporter. Because of the huge sums involved, arms deals would have the most immediate effect upon the balance of payments and unemployment.

Pursuant to this policy she drew up a series of defence-related, government-to-government contracts. The chief five contracts were with Oman (1981), followed by the Jordan Package (1985 and 1987) and Al Yamamah with Saudi Arabia (the first of three contracts was signed in 1986), followed by the Malaysia/Pergau Dam deal (1988 and 1991); already in development before she left office in November 1990 was the Indonesian Package. These deals have been shown to be riddled with corruption of one sort or another – goods ending up in Iraq, huge commissions and backhanders, trade-offs with aid packages, and so on, which will be dealt with in more detail later.

The Oman deal, made famous by the exposure of £50,000 commission paid to Mark Thatcher's company, Monteagle, was in fact effected by Margaret Thatcher on the coat-tails of the United States. It was an early example of how Britain could help the US participate in weapons deals that would otherwise have been impossible owing to Congressional arms export controls. Although it was for weapons and other military goods, they dressed up all the expenditure to make it seem that Margaret Thatcher's part in it had to do with building a hospital and a university.

In fact, as J. Martin-Martin has confirmed – he was the first person to finger Mark Thatcher on television and really started the whole investigation into his arms 'facilitating' activities – the nub of the deal was the building of weapon silos to store American PGMs (precision guided missiles), the result of US strategy in the early 1980s, which was to stop a thrust by Russia into the Gulf, using Afghanistan as a springboard from which to control the world oil industry.

The Al Yamamah deal is in three parts. Initially 132 Tornado aircraft and Blackhawk helicopters were due to Saudi. Al Yamamah II was signed in 1988 but not proceeded with until 1992. More Tornado strike aircraft, BAe Hawk trainer jets, Sandown class mine-hunters and Blackhawk helicopters were to be sold. Al Y I and II together were worth some £40bn. Al Y III, yet to come, is valued at a further £20bn. Part II called for a £1.5bn down payment in cash, the rest in oil, a deal designed by Peter Levene of the MoD calling for payment of as much as 500,000 barrels of oil per day, which were then to be traded by Shell and BP. There are various question marks hanging over Al Yamamah that concern the real destination of the goods, and the commissions allegedly up to £12m to Mark Thatcher and around £240m in total to his group.[6]

The Indonesian contract is going on now. The government sold Indonesia £500m of British Hawk military training jets and God knows how much other military equipment just two months after the Foreign Secretary Douglas Hurd visited Jakarta to announce a 'soft loan' for a power station to be built by a British company.

The pattern had been set in September 1988 by Margaret Thatcher's £1.3bn arms deal with Malaysia, with its 'sweetener' attached – £234m to build a hydro-electric dam at Pergau, again by British companies such as Trafalgar House/Cementation, who were also involved in Oman and a number of other arms-related deals through Cementation and their South African associate company Blockberg.

What then of the economic bonuses to the nation that were supposed to have flowed from these contracts? Can you see them? Thatcher was certainly aggravated that in the arms industry we were being outsold everywhere, by the French in particular, and determined to put that right, which she did. From being about No. 4 or 5 in the world she made us No. 2 to the United States. But that this effort benefited the nation is not so clear. I don't think a single penny has been paid on Thatcher's Jordan defence package. IMS played a central role in managing the initial Jordan Package of £75m in 1985–6, but by 1989 King Hussein had already defaulted on payments and many companies on all these deals had to resort to ECGD for settlement. Jordan is in hock to us for hundreds of millions and the debt is being rolled over by issuing fresh credits to pay the interest.

It is not widely realised that Thatcher's economic miracle was largely a conjuring trick that turned North Sea oil revenue into cash dispensed by ECGD to the City (and fat commissions) for arms deals that had essentially failed. In a memo to the government Foreign Affairs Inquiry into the Malaysian Pergau Dam aid-for-arms affair, Mr K.H. Harrison, a former industrial technical manager in the oil industry (BP), pointed to the concept of linking overseas aid to arms deals as but one strand, an inducement that proved necessary, in an economic strategy that was based upon the investment of North Sea oil revenues overseas and the plundering of these to finance Thatcher's various defence packages when customers didn't pay up.

In 1988 Lord Young boasted to a government Select Committee that with £120bn of North Sea oil revenue invested overseas, bringing in £5bn dividends, and with City and service industries similarly poised to bring in dividends from overseas, we no longer needed the traditional economic base of manufacturing, shipbuilding, etc.

Mr Harrison corresponded with the Treasury on this subject, and was informed in a letter written by Mr David Lawton of the Public Sector Finances Division on 14 December 1992, that Lord Young's boast related to the figures for 1986, 'when the identified level of overseas net assets reached a peak'. Lawton then provided figures from 1988, which showed an extraordinary diminution of our position to a minus figure in 1990 (see Table).

	£bn net overseas assets	£bn interest and dividends
1988	73.7	4.4
1989	64.6	3.5
1990	− 0.4	2.1
1991	16.1	0.3

The diminution of our net overseas assets coincides precisely with the period when ECGD was most pressed, the time that we were supplying and/or settling huge credits to Malaysia and elsewhere.

With our net overseas assets reduced in proportion to the artificial stoking of the City and the defence industry, and with privatisation revenues exhausted to meet unemployment in manufacturing, what these figures show, as Harrison pointed out, is that 'by 1990 when we joined the ERM . . . every penny of those North Sea oil overseas investments had disappeared! . . . We had actually entered the ERM under "false" colours when she [Mrs Thatcher] was Prime Minister and John Major Chancellor . . . The UK had introduced a "designed flaw" into the ERM as an eventual means of producing "Black Wednesday" and destabilising EMU.'

They thought they could hide it, they thought they could get away with it, but the figures are astronomic. This is what worries me about the Scott Inquiry. He is in a position to expose the whole scam, and he may not do so. He has not got to the root of the matter, the connivance of the government and the banks and the City. He has not called the right witnesses.

The whole of our foreign reserves were expunged between 1986 and 1990, and when you realise that the idiot team of Lamont and Major come on top of that, backing up the ERM on this platform of insolvency, you can believe that they have bankrupted the nation. They claim to have lost only £5bn over the

ERM fiasco, but there are commentators who reckon it was nearer £50bn. That is the reason why we are getting all these cuts in the health service and in the defence area and other government services now.

The big government-to-government deals were celebrated in the media, but Iraq was always 'the big prize'. Saddam Hussein had it in his power to become the world's second biggest oil producer, and oil was the best capital asset to be found anywhere.

'I doubt if there was any future market of such a scale any-where where the UK is potentially so well placed if we play our diplomatic hand correctly, nor can I think of any major market where the importance of diplomacy is so great on our commercial position,' said William Waldegrave, Minister of State at the Foreign and Commonwealth Office in 1989, adding just one month after the *Observer* journalist Farzad Bazoft was arrested in Iraq (later to be executed), 'a few more Bazofts or another bout of internal [Iraqi] repression would make it more difficult.'[7]

The moral dilemma of selling arms to a murderous dictator was dealt with pragmatically by anybody who thought it needed to be. 'Arms will continue to reach the people who want them,' wrote John Reed, editor of *Defence Industry Digest*, paraphrasing Alan Clark's view that if a lot of nig-nogs want to beat hell out of each other and pay us for doing so, why should we complain.

The other justification was given as political expediency. By arming Iraq we were containing the great threat to the West of Islamic fundamentalism. It was arguably better to arm Iraq than to put our own troops in the field.

Unfortunately, the government conspired to supply arms to both sides in the conflict, and the threat of fundamentalism, which is real, has, as a result of the government's duplicity, increased one hundredfold. Thatcher's policy, which amounted to a betrayal of trust involving the most purist regime in the world by one of the most duplicitous, may yet be assessed, though I hope not in my lifetime.

At BMARC's Faldingworth plant in Lincolnshire, in the early

part of the war, Iranian Air Force officers were being trained how to use Skyguard air defence weapon systems developed by Oerlikon Buhrle of Zurich, from whom Astra bought the company. From 1985 no Iranian military were allowed to be trained in Britain, only Iraqis, whom BMARC also trained up until 1990. In September 1993 the *Observer* reported that 'in the summer of 1988, British-trained Iraqi air force pilots were heard on British-made radio sets (by American listeners) bombing the Kurds with chemical weapons.'

The Iranian procurement office in Victoria in London closed down in 1987, by which time the Government had made it plain whose side it was on. 'In a playground full of bullies,' wrote Stephen Dorril, 'Saddam Hussein was the biggest of all. But he held the keys to the tuck-shop, so we had to stay on his side.'[8]

But did siding with Saddam Hussein, 'the butcher of Baghdad', in 1987 turn out to be politically wise even in the short term? Britain was supplying Iraq up to and after its invasion of Kuwait in August 1990, which led to the Gulf War, when British soldiers – my son Christian among them – were capturing crates of Royal Ordnance ammunition from Iraqi positions.

'Pragmatism and economic interest blinkered us to reality,' recalled Mark Higson, former Iraqi desk officer at the FCO. Just one year after Saddam Hussein had employed chemical weapons to massacre thousands of Iraqi Kurds, David Gore-Booth, Assistant Under-Secretary in charge of Middle East affairs, was enthusing with the dictator over the 'working relationship between our countries'.[9]

The policy brought British diplomacy to the lowest depths: 'There was never any question that we wouldn't try to play cricket with him,' says Higson. 'Always preceding any top level diplomatic talks we made it absolutely clear that we had problems with Baghdad's record on human rights. Briefings with the Iraqi Ambassador in London would always begin with our concern for Ian Richter [the British businessman serving life for alleged corruption since 1986]; later Daphne Parish and Farzad Bazoft were added to the unpleasantries. Then, when we'd cleared the air on that, we'd go straight into bat for Britain . . . The whole system of

checks and vetting was half-hearted . . . They had people working here on civilian nuclear installations, how do you vet that?'

Saddam's oil was tempting indeed, but Iraq's only resource is
oil, their only significant currency is oil, and the requirement for
military purchases was such that although they physically had it
they could not physically release it and meet their debts to Britain
without completely devaluing its currency.

In the three years from 1980 the price of oil fell dramatically on
world markets. Earnings from crude oil, which was 99 per cent of
Iraq's exports, fell from $28bn to $8bn.

Iraq had to be given time to pay, which was why the British
and the Americans, along with other countries, were persuaded by
Iraq to issue them with credits, effectively promissory notes.
Gullible Western governments saw this as a major strategic error
by Iraq. Huge loans would make Iraq beholden to them. After the
war with Iran was over, we would have a stake in the oil-rich Gulf.
With oil the single most important commodity in economic terms,
what this meant was a transfer of world economic power from the
Middle East. But it didn't quite work out that way.

The figures which ECGD are prepared publicly to admit show
that between 1980 and 1990 they supported £2.377bn plus more
than £1bn medium term, and a spokesman admitted that 'it
would be prudent to assume that recovery will be a difficult and
extended process.'

By 1990 the size of Saddam's debt to Britain to which our
government was prepared to admit totalled £1bn, a figure greatly
magnified when credits to conduit countries for arms destined to
Iraq are taken into account. Trade Secretary Nicholas Ridley
named the figure to the Overseas Policy and Defence Committee
in June of that year. At that stage, nearly two years after the end
of the war with Iran, it was every government for itself, and
Britain found that its boast that it had treated Iraq so well during
the war cut no ice with Saddam on payment day. Mr Ridley
warned that Iraq's continued default on payments would 'clearly
be extremely serious for ECGD and would have implications for
the PSBR [Public Sector Borrowing Requirement].'

Iraq declared that if new credits were not forthcoming, old debts would not be paid and they would find others to service their orders. It was the combination of a declining oil price and insurmountable debts which drove Saddam Hussein to invade Kuwait in August 1990. Thanks to Western governments, he had the weapons and ammunition to take what he wanted from Kuwait and run.[10]

Now we boast that we have got them by the balls by not allowing them to sell their oil. But I dare say they are smuggling it out; and British sanctions on Iraq, which cover everything, food, medical supplies, the lot, mean only that the ordinary people in Iraq are suffering. What can we possibly hope to gain from them?

You just might find someone in Whitehall who would tell you honestly, though I doubt it. The only reason for sanctions on Iraq is to make them so desperate that they will come back and actually pay us for more. There is no morality in it at all.

In this light it is interesting to speculate what is augured by the recent defection of Saddam Hussein's son-in-law, Hussein Kamil, who, as head of the Iraqi procurement agency in the Iran–Iraq war, knows all about the British government's involvement with arms to Iraq. If Saddam Hussein's overthrow is the next point on the West's agenda, will Kamil then return to take up the reins and resume 'normal' trade relations with the West? It is a plausible strategy certainly, for the resumption of trade betweem Iraq and the West is clearly essential to both parties.

The government set up its own code for the Iran–Iraq war some four years after it had started. 'The main apparent constraint on exports to Iraq,' the Trade and Industry Committee on Exports to Iraq: Project Babylon and Long Range Guns reported in March 1992, 'was a set of guidelines, introduced in December 1984', but not published until the following October. They were drawn up by Geoffrey Howe and went like this:

Criteria for exports to Iraq
   (i) We should maintain our consistent refusal to supply any
        lethal equipment to either side;

(ii) Subject to that overriding consideration, we should attempt to fulfil existing contracts and obligations;

(iii) We should not, in future, approve orders for any defence equipment which, in our view, would significantly enhance the capability of either side to prolong or exacerbate the conflict;

(iv) In line with this policy, we should continue to scrutinise rigorously all applications for export licences for the supply of defence equipment to Iran and Iraq.

On the meaning of 'lethal' equipment, the committee was told by the Foreign Office, 'There is not a precise definition which is used by all governments and accepted as such. We defined "lethal" equipment . . . as equipment designed and likely to kill. It is a matter that requires judgement case-by-case.'

The utility of the government's guidelines was obvious to everyone. According to Alan Barrett, the former MoD official responsible for monitoring arms sales, 'You can use them when you want to, you don't use them when you don't want to, and all the time you can change [them]'. According to Alan Clark (DTI), they were 'imprecise and so obviously drafted with the objective of flexibility, of elasticity'. According to the notorious Chilean arms dealer Carlos Cardoen, they were one significant means by which the legality of trade to Iraq was greased by Tory policy. 'On behalf of the Iraqi Government,' he said, 'we acquired Matrix-manufactured machine tools [manufactured in Coventry] and then re-exported them to Baghdad. All this was done in keeping with all legal documentation demanded by British law.'[11]

The granting of export licences, rubber-stamped by Lord Trefgarne and Clark at the DTI, and William Waldegrave at the Foreign Office, was the area where 'flexibility' lay. Export licences, as I have explained, require the nomination of an end-user. False end-user declarations were the means by which much of the traffic to Iraq was let through. An example of this in Astra was when we were approached by the Ferranti chairman Sir Derek Alun-Jones, the company with which Jim Guerin's ISC merged in 1988, to fill the Paveway bomb.

ISC had received the principal contract from the US government and Alun-Jones approached us, as an explosives filler, to fill it, ISC Ferranti having no filling capability of their own. The Paveway is a 1,000-pound bomb dropped by aircraft up to 100 miles away and steered on to its target. The destination for the consignment was supposed to be Abu Dhabi but it was clear that it was destined for Iraq because the Paveway needed an aircraft at least as big as a Mirage to carry it – Abu Dhabi didn't have such a carrier, but Iraq did.

Evidence to the Scott Inquiry has made clear that the Foreign Office and the DTI were wholly conversant with countries which were being put up as false end-users for Iraq.

As early as 1983 the FO had known that Jordan was used as a conduit for arms to Iraq. In that year, 200 Sterling machine guns were seized at Greenwich dock, leading to the 1985 trial of the arms exporter Reginald Dunk, and Alexander Schlesinger (of Atlantic Commercial, a company based in Cuckney in Nottinghamshire).

The guns, with Jordan marked as end-user on the government export licence, were in fact going on to Iraq. Dunk was forced to plead guilty after Foreign Office officials put 'diplomatic pressure' on witnesses from the Jordanian and Iraqi embassies in London whom Dunk's lawyers had intended to call as witnesses for his defence. When the murky business was aired at the Scott Inquiry, Sir Richard Scott said that the collusion was 'disgraceful'. Sir Stephen Egerton of the Foreign Office agreed that it was 'a bad show'.[12]

The shipment was hardly an isolated occurrence, as James Edmiston, managing director of Sterling Armaments, described at the trial. A zone was actually fenced off to take in arms 'from Britain, Germany, Spain, Italy, America, Holland, Belgium, Switzerland and Austria . . . Squadrons of lorries carried the arms . . . along the road to Amman, and from there to Baghdad. So great was the traffic that parts of the road were expanded into a dual carriageway.'[13]

Jordan was so popular a conduit for Iraq that it became known as 'Jorq' or 'Joraq', and Alan Clark himself admitted to the Inquiry that 'there was a tendency for the trickier items to be consigned to Jordan. Nobody ever seemed to do anything about it. [It was] simply accepted.' He even quantified it — 'more than half the British military equipment bought by Iraq in the 1980s had been assigned to Jordan.'[14]

Margaret Thatcher of course denied having any idea about Jordan being a conduit for Iraq. She said that she had found out about it in August 1990, whereupon she had 'had a word' with King Hussein.

The admission by Clark makes the list of thirty-three suspect countries drawn up in December 1991 by Trade Minister Tim Sainsbury, a list which omitted Jordan, seem something of a retrospective whitewash. The Scott Inquiry heard 'irrefutable evidence' that Jordan was diverting arms to Iraq and the omission of Jordan from the list was described by Sir Richard Scott as a 'glaring loophole'.

Abu Dhabi and Jordan were only two of the conduits for sales to Iraq. Saudi Arabia was used for at least part of Thatcher's Al Yamamah deal, as I discovered when I flew to Jeddah in December 1989 and met Prince Mishari, half-brother of King Fahd, who was eager to get involved with the weaponising of Blackhawk helicopters — an aspect of Al Yamamah that we at Astra had been offered by Westland — and a huge 155mm artillery project, again part of Al Yamamah and organised by Gerald Bull with PRB, the Belgian company that we had just acquired. Both contracts, I discovered from Mishari, were bound for Iraq.

Kuwait and certain other Gulf states were also recognised conduits, as were Egypt, Hong Kong, South Africa, Portugal, Cyprus, China, Singapore, Thailand, and many more, variously for Iran and Iraq.

In 1986, the year after the Dunk trial, Egerton became ambassador to Saudi Arabia and found himself in trouble once more. During his appointment, questions were asked in Whitehall about a consignment of 15,000 long-range artillery shells shipped by Allivane (a company we will deal with in more detail later) to

Saudi. Egerton said there were 'suspicions but no proof' that they had gone on to Iraq.[15]

Lieutenant-Colonel Richard Glazebrook, a MoD armaments expert who advised on the granting of export licences, tried and failed in 1985 to prevent the export of rocket parts to Egypt, suspecting that the assembled rockets would be sent to Iraq. After the Gulf War, UN inspectors found the same model of rocket – fitted with nerve gas warheads – in Iraq.[16]

Timothy Renton (former minister at the Foreign Office) told Scott that when Iraq was using chemical weapons against Iran in 1986, the FCO agreed, after pressure exerted by the DTI, to sell Egypt chemicals that could be used to make chemical weapons even though it had intelligence reports that Egypt had earlier the same year bought substantial quantities of hydrogen fluoride on Iraq's behalf. Hydrogen fluoride is used in the manufacture of nerve gas.[17]

The evidence of government-approved trafficking via false end-users to Iran and Iraq is, as we shall see, endless and the only conclusion any sane person could reach is that the fictional end-user was recognised by government as a device to further its covert arms policies on Iraq.

The Intelligence services certainly knew where the goods were going. GCHQ monitors all overseas telephone calls, faxes and telexes, and has the ability to trace the movement of goods by satellite. In a letter to the *Observer*, James Rusbridger, author of *The Intelligence Game*, wrote, 'All communications entering and leaving Iraq are monitored by GCHQ from Cyprus and the NSA (GCHQ's US equivalent) from their geostationary satellites, and, as soon as the first orders started being placed, the companies in Britain would also have had their communications tapped.' Again, transfers of more than £5m are monitored automatically by GCHQ and the Bank of England.[18]

There is no hiding behind a screen of ineptitude, either, since it will be seen that the trade was encouraged openly and indeed deals were instigated by the government through the MoD.

One well-publicised occasion when direct trade with Iraq was apparently openly encouraged by the government occurred in January 1988, when Alan Clark (DTI) advised representatives of the Machine Tools Technology Association (MTTA) to emphasise the peaceful uses of their dual-purpose machinery when applying for licences to Iraq. There can be no question that the true purpose of the machines was known, and Sir Richard Scott was quick to stamp on any attempt to say otherwise – 'Obviously they were going to be used to make arms, given the state of war . . .'

In December 1990, after Clark was accused in the press of giving MTTA a 'nod and a wink' for exports to Iraq of machines that were clearly for making weapons, John Major called an urgent meeting with Sir Robin Butler, the Cabinet Secretary, to agree precisely what it was that Clark had told the MTTA companies.

Sir Robin's original record of that meeting was that Clark told MTTA 'to downgrade specifications so that they could not be used for military purposes', but afterwards Clark persuaded him to change this to the effect that MTTA companies should submit specifications 'so that they would not be seen as suitable for military purposes'.

As director of the DTI unit responsible for issuing export licences, Tony Steadman was also at the original MTTA meeting and told the inquiry counsel, Presiley Baxendale, QC, 'I assumed people were acting in good faith.'

This is all a war of words with, at best, a certain pathos attached to it. More interesting, because it points to where Tory policy actually led, is the confidential conclusion to the original January 1988 meeting that gave MTTA the green light. The minute reads: 'The Minister [Lord Trefgarne – Defence Procurement, 1986–9] advised that the advice given during the discussion was based on the current state of play. *If the political overtones of the Iran/Iraq conflict change* [my italics] . . . then the current order may change.'

The Iran–Iraq ceasefire occurred six months later, and there is no doubt that policy did change from mid-1988, but not in the way that Trefgarne, Clark and Waldegrave have been accused in the Scott Inquiry and in the press of changing it – relaxing the guidelines after the ceasefire in July. This accusation, which seems set to bestow on these three junior ministers inordinate power and convenient blame, ignores the fact that encouragement was given to members of MTTA during the war, and it seeks to muddy the real issue which, as the *New Statesman & Society* pointed out on 17 June 1994, 'is not that the 1984 Howe guidelines were relaxed after the war was over, but that they were knowingly and repeatedly breached while the war was on.'

Waldegrave has consistently maintained that the Guidelines were not relaxed, and he is right. As the war came to an end, if anything they were more rigorously respected. In fact, policy shifted to and fro according to fears about the economy which had been put on the rack by payment defaults, notably by Iraq, and fears about what would be made public about the government's active involvement in covert traffic without the benefit of the cover of war, and conversely the difficulty in stopping the runaway train and otherwise satisfying the apparently insatiable levels of greed.

When the truth did begin to come out, the powerful realised that something more had to be done than merely applying the brakes. What was needed was an effective strategy of damage limitation.

The solution was a public relations operation, a strategy of disinformation so bold that the government managed for a while to avert the public gaze from its involvement in the trade at the cost of ruining a few businessmen's lives, and, on the back of it and apparently open-handedly, to launch a Public Inquiry by Scott with a brief that almost made it impossible for him to get to the real truth.

For example, initially Iran fell outside Scott's remit altogether. Only recently (June 1995), after some five years of my pressing the DTI, the MoD police, and Coopers & Lybrand, the administrators of Astra, for the release of pertinent documents, has the government been forced to admit that arms were also sent to Iran. Since then correspondence between myself and Scott has

escalated, and of course Jonathan Aitken has been the first minister to fall. Why did they want to steer Scott away from the Iran
question? Because before 1987, the year the Iranian procurement
agency in London closed down, after which Britain dealt principally with Iraq, it was the government's own companies (IMS and
RO) and those establishment companies close to government
which I will shortly name as members of the propellant and arms
cartels, whose business with Iran was critical, that would be put in
the inquiry's frame. With Iraq only as the focus of inquiry, post-
1987, they could point the finger at companies wholly
independent of government (Euromac, Forgemasters, Somers,
Matrix, Astra, etc) and attempt to exonerate themselves from anything worse than sloppy administration of Howe's guidelines in
the government's export licensing departments.

The outrageous show trials of the Euromac, Matrix Churchill
and Ordnance Technology (Ordtec) executives almost achieved
their end, and the celebrated arrests of Christopher Cowley, project manager of the Supergun project, and Peter Mitchell,
managing director of Walter Somers, the company which manufactured the barrels for the Supergun prototype, looked all set to
provide the icing on the cake.

In line with the government's co-ordinated strategy to cleanse
itself in the blood of others, the arrests all occurred in 1990 around
the same time – Ali Daghir and Janine Speckman (Euromac) on
28 March, Christopher Gumbley (Astra), Christopher Cowley
(SRC), Peter Mitchell (Walter Somers), two other Somers executives and six Sheffield Forgemasters executives in April–May, the
Matrix Churchill executives in June, and the Ordtec executives a
few months later.

Only Chris Gumbley, whose case we will look at later, and
Janine Speckman served full sentences (with remission), the lat-
ter completing her eighteen-month sentence before both she and
Daghir were cleared.

Euromac

Euromac was possibly the most transparent frame-up of them all. The nuclear triggers trial, as it came to be known, was the result of an eighteen-month joint UK-US Intelligence operation literally to persuade managing director Ali Daghir against his better judgement to export capacitors/detonators to Iraq, allegedly for Saddam Hussein's nuclear programme.[19]

Crucial to the prosecution's case was evidence given by Peter Gall, former senior executive at the export licensing unit at the DTI. 'An export licence would not be granted for the supply of any equipment which would significantly enhance the military capability of Iraq,' he said. It transpired that not only had Daghir resisted the deal and been pushed into it by his US supplier Dan Supnick, acting in concert with the CIA, but that the capacitors were below standard for detonating weapons, nothing more than might be used by a professional photographer to power his flash-lights.

Before the truth was made public, Margaret Thatcher had shown her approval of the way her team had gone about its business in a letter to Brian Unwin, chairman of British Customs: 'May I ask you to pass on my warm congratulations to all those engaged in the operation to prevent the illegal export to Iraq of components for a nuclear weapon. It must have required the highest professional standards, as well as great patience and skill, and the whole nation has reason to be grateful to those concerned.'

Supergun

Gerald Bull's 1,000mm Supergun, presented in the media as a comic-book concept worthy of Jules Verne, was bound to catch the public imagination. For the government it provided a fantastic smokescreen behind which they sought to hide the billions of pounds of weapons, technology and machinery arriving in the war zone in almost daily shipments, and the rip-offs and back-handers that were dealt out in the name of patriotism.

It is important, however, to realise the devastating effect of the Bull technology in the war between Iran and Iraq. At our PRB artillery range at Matagne in Belgium, we had six 130mm artillery pieces imported from Yugoslavia for testing Bull's 130mm ammunition. Through the Belgian company, which we acquired in 1989, Bull developed improved shells and extended-range ammunition for 130mm heavy artillery. This weapon, standard Russian heavy artillery, was used by the Iraqis, as well as by the Egyptians and Malaysians.

But Bull's GC45 and 155mm 'extended range, full bore with base-bleed' shells could outstrip anything in NATO by six miles. The Iran–Iraq war was largely fought on the ground and, in the second half of the 1980s, when more than 500 guns based on Bull technology found their way to the front, they proved critical.

Base-bleed was a new feature added to the ERFB specification which, in the late 1970s, had so endeared Bull to the South Africans. In April 1981, following his release from prison, Bull had been invited to travel to Beijing, and as a result of discussions over China's requirements, he had developed the base-bleed mechanism. Base-bleed, a way to reduce drag as a shell passes through the atmosphere, was not new, but Bull first perfected it. The mechanism released a gas to fill the vacuum left behind the shell as it moved forward, and so dramatically improved the flight of his 155mm shells.

However, in the aftermath of the South African business, in much need of finance for SRC, he had sold the technology of the GC45 to Voest-Alpine, the government-owned Austrian arms company, for a modest $2million fee, no royalties. Voest-Alpine then modified and marketed the gun under the title GHN-45.

Now Bull was in a position where he desperately needed to make money – hence the trip to China. All the time, however, he still yearned to have the opportunity to develop the big guns that had failed to appeal to the US government when he worked for CARDE and then independently at Highwater. In January 1988 he got the opportunity when he accepted an invitation from Amir Saadi, deputy to Hussein Kamil, Saddam Hussein's son-in-law and chief of Iraqi Intelligence.

During the course of his stay in Baghdad, which included discussions about the GC45 and a 210mm self-propelled gun (the Al Fao project, with which Ordtec and BMARC, a company owned by Astra, became involved), he visited the top secret explosives site, Al-Hillah, where the Iraqis were involved in trying to harness the power of five Soviet Scud missiles as the first stage, Saadi apparently told him, of a three-stage space rocket capable of launching a satellite into space.

When Bull and Saadi talked of satellites, they were speaking in riddles. Back in 1957, when the Russians had launched Sputnik, the first satellite, into space, Bull had been among the first to recognise that the same gun technology could equally well be used to launch inter-continental ballistic missiles, and there is no doubt that Saadi was endeavouring to get Bull's help in the Iraqi missile programme.[20]

William Lowther, in his book *Arms and the Man*, clearly written with the special knowledge and co-operation of Bull's son Michel, who worked at SRC, tells us that it was at this point in Bull's discussions with Saadi that Bull suggested developing a supergun that could 'litter the skies with satellites' at a fraction of the cost of the three-stage rocket which would be spent at each launching; further, that a smaller prototype gun, which would be required in the development of the Supergun, could be used to test the rocket nose-cones of Saadi's project.

Back in 1973 a brilliant German rocket scientist called Lutz Kayser, who as a teenager had worked under Werner von Braun, came to me at Ansbacher with a similar proposal on behalf of his company, Otrag, to create a rocket system capable of launching a heavy payload. Like Bull, the emphasis was on cost cutting, in Kayser's case achieved by using standard components from the aerospace and automotive industry. GEC Marconi turned the project down, but later it appears Kayser got support to build a multi-million pound rocket range in Zaire, which caused the

Russians concern and became the subject of a BBC Panorama programme.

When Bull first mooted the Supergun, which would have a range of 700km, it appears that it was as a complementary project to the Iraqi missile project (named Project Bird) and he believed that in the end Supergun would have a similar capability to the Project Bird rocket system, which included the despatch of biological, chemical and nuclear weapons.

No commitment was made by Saadi to the Supergun (or Project Babylon as it came to be known) until March 1988 when Saadi approved Bull's first calculations for Project Bird. After which, with a total budget of $25m, Bull entered Project Babylon into the SRC production schedule as Project 839 and commissioned Bristol-based Dr Christopher Cowley to manage the project.

In late May 1988 Cowley offered the British company Walter Somers the contract for the barrel of Baby Babylon, the prototype, saying that it was for a petrochemical pipeline. A few weeks later the contract for two sets of the Supergun barrel was offered to Sheffield Forgemasters. This time Cowley said that it was for 'the polymerisation of polyethylene' at an Iraqi petrochemical plant.[21]

Following the seizure by Customs and Excise of crates of steel tubes made by Sheffield Forgemasters at Teesport near Middlesborough on 12 April 1990, Nicholas Ridley, Secretary of State for Trade and Industry, announced in Parliament: 'The Government recently became aware in general terms of an Iraqi project to develop a long-range gun based on designs by the late Dr Gerald Bull . . . The Government are entirely satisfied that the tubes form part of a gun.'

One member present, Sir Hal Miller, rose to his feet in astonishment: 'Since, more than two years ago, I made an offer to [the DTI], to the MoD and I believe to a third agency [MI6], on behalf of Walter Somers, to withdraw from the contract, to meet the contract and to enable it to be traced, or to carry on with the contract, and as I repeated that offer 12 months later, does [the Secretary of State] share my surprise that there can be any

question of prosecuting the company for any contravention of
regulations or lack of good faith in the matter?'

In the same month, Douglas Hurd, who as Foreign Secretary
was supposedly in close touch with MI6 reports, wrote to Gerald
Kaufman, Labour's foreign affairs spokesman, 'we did not learn of
the involvement of British companies in supplying tubes for the
Iraqi long-range gun (or supergun) project until 30 March 1990.'

Leaving aside the fact that Chris Gumbley and I personally
informed two MoD officials, Roger Harding and Bob Primrose, and
Roger Holdness, pure MI6, back in October and November 1989,
about the Supergun project, for which we, through our Belgian
subsidiary PRB had been contracted to supply the propellant, Bull
himself had informed MI6 in 1988, in the presence of Chris Cowley.

Bull was of course constantly involved with the intelligence
services of America and Israel, as well as Britain, which is what
makes any protestations of ignorance on the part of the British
government so patently absurd. Particularly as, far from being
ignorant, the government was actively encouraging his progress,
even to the point of encouraging his purchase (with the Iraqis as
50 per cent financial partners) of the bankrupt Lear Fan carbon
fibre plant in Belfast. Carbon fibre is critical in the manufacture of
missile nose-cones and sabots for shells.

I am in possession of a letter, dated 31 October 1989, from
Gerald Bull to Philippe Glibert, sales director of PRB, in which
Bull describes how the Industrial Development Board sponsored
and organised his first survey of Lear Fan.

'They devised a schedule to visit both Queen's University and
the University of Ulster, as well as the former Lear Fan Plant,' Bull
wrote. 'At the University of Ulster they had formed a "Composite
Technology Group" to absorb the key engineers that were made
redundant by the Lear Fan bankruptcy. The former Chief
Engineer of Lear Fan was Mr Jim Brooks, who, by chance, had
worked for me on the Canadian guided missile programme from
1955 to 1960 at CARDE.'

We should be clear what we are talking about here: the sponsorship by the Industrial Development Board of a trip to a plant

that specialised in technology and manufacture critical to missile nose-cone manufacture, by a man known to MI6 to be engaged, in participation with the Iraqi government at the highest level, in the proliferation of systems with a biological, chemical and nuclear capability.

The government encouragement went further than sponsorship of that first trip to Lear Fan, however. 'On Friday August 11 at 4.30 pm, Michel [Bull's son] received on the SRC telex at Highwater, Canada, a telex from the IDB saying that a grant of 2.2 million pounds had received approval from all UK authorities. They wished to close by mid-week and asked Michel to travel on the weekend to ensure all matters were in order for a Wednesday morning closing . . .'

In the event Mossad [Iraeli Intelligence] and the US National Security Agency, who knew as much about Bull's activities as the British security services, put pressure on Britain to withdraw the NIDB offer of a grant and put a stop to the purchase.

'Monday morning at 9am (UK time) Michel received by hand the letter attached . . . Ultimately I found out that a "Mr Levine [sic], former head of United Technologies [actually Scientific Holdings, Alvis], now the Czar for all UK defense buying and selling" had intervened. Mr Levine is Jewish . . .'

The Foreign Office then engaged in their strategy of 'damage limitation' by running, as Bull put it, 'a press campaign through "leaks". The utter nonsense they spread was beyond belief . . .'

It didn't stop there. 'I addressed a blunt memorandum to the Foreign Office on the whole matter. Through publicity, they were making me a target of terrorist groups. I was advised in a letter of an imminent "accident".'

Bull responded with characteristic dry wit: 'The Foreign Office was advised about the curious fact that accidents often happen in series.

'After the memo was delivered, the matter was dropped from the press. Also we were assured that the action was by "a few irresponsible juniors and did not reflect the Foreign Office views of myself, our companies, the past, etc."'

So there we have the true picture of the government with which we are dealing, a government capable of aiding the proliferation of nuclear supplies to Iraq, capable of turning under pressure on those they were tied up with in this enterprise, a government then capable of threatening their partner with an imminent "accident", and finally disowning the threat and finding a few junior officials to blame for the whole thing. It is a picture that fits time and again as we examine the real facts of Margaret Thatcher's government.

Both the Somers and Forgemasters executives did all they possibly could to inform the government about Supergun. In June 1988, the DTI was asked by Sir Hal Miller on behalf of Somers whether export licences would be needed, and the MoD was informed that the contracts involved Gerald Bull. Separately, on 17 June, Forgemasters phoned the DTI to discuss the need for export licences. Five days later Dr Rex Bayliss, managing director of Somers prior to Peter Mitchell, told Mr Bill Weir at the MoD (a senior officer on the Defence Intelligence staff) that the destination of their contract was Iraq. The MoD then consulted the DTI, and Forgemasters was informed by the MoD (on 7 July) that it was unlikely that an export licence would be required.

Nevertheless, Phillip Wright, chief executive of Forgemasters, remained so concerned that the tube specifications were too precise – Lowther tells us that the fit of the pipes had to be within 0.5mm – to be for anything other than a gun barrel, that he sent the DTI the specifications anyway. They even made a video stressing the importance of the fit and the fact that the pipes were more than twelve times more resistant to pressures and temperatures than was required in the manufacture of polyethylene.

On the strength of the DTI's continued approval of the contract, Forgemasters signed the contract on 8 July, ten days later seeking written confirmation from the DTI that no export licence was required, which the DTI then supplied on 27 July.

The project initially envisaged the building of two 1000mm

guns 156m in length, made of tube sections bolted together, and one prototype gun, 350mm by 30m in length. Forgemasters' contract called for, in Chris Cowley's words, 'two sets of 26 five- and six-metre long sections of flanged tubes made from alloy-steel, and varying in weight . . . from 136,000kg to typical weights of 95,000kg, reducing to 80,000kg in the lower sections of the barrel. The wall thickness of the barrel varied from 250mm in the high pressure region to 50mm in the muzzle area, where the pressure would be lower. Studs, each with two nuts, were to be used to fasten the flanged ends of the tubes together. To lift the largest of these bolts required two men . . . [It] was a gun on an enormous scale.'

On 17 August Somers telexed the DTI for an urgent response as to whether their tubes needed licences, and the DTI complied the following day, adding, 'no need to send faxes of drawings'. Five days later they commenced forging, and delivered the first consignment of five tubes by Iraqi military plane from Manchester airport on 8 March 1989.[22]

Between 28 April and 2 May 1989, a 1.5m-long scale model of the gun was on open display at the Baghdad military fair. Astra had three representatives there who saw it, Ken Wingad, Steve Yates and Alan Clark (no relation to the minister). Astra was one of seventeen UK companies sponsored by the DTI to attend the fair. The DTI had paid 25 per cent of the cost for us to represent Britain at an arms fair being held in a country supposedly off limits to British arms exporters. We had a gun on display and ammunition items. All this occurred a year before Ridley announced to Parliament that the government had only recently become aware of Supergun.

Seven months later, in November 1990, on orders that came from 10 Downing Street (to which Customs and Excise had reported directly throughout), charges against Cowley and Mitchell were suddenly dropped.[23]

In the same month, Margaret Thatcher resigned.

Ordtec

After Thatcher's resignation in November 1990, a new tactic emerged in the government's strategy of disinformation. Public Interest Immunity Certificates (PIICs) would, in theory, gag the accused and prevent them telling about the government's involvement. It is interesting that they were employed only after the more barefaced, cavalier attempts on Cowley and Mitchell under Mrs Thatcher had failed.

In the first case the tactic worked, for a while. In the second, the trial of three Matrix Churchill executives, Judge Smedley could not resist Defence Counsel Geoffrey Robertson's arguments, threw out the PIICs and the floodgates opened.

In February 1992 three directors of Ordnance Technology, Paul Grecian, Bryan Mason and Colin Phillips, also of EC Transport, a shipping agency, and Stuart Blackledge of SRC, were convicted of accepting a contract, part of Bull's Al Fao project drawn up with SRC Geneva to equip the Iraqis with fuses for shells for his 210mm self-propelled gun. The contract went to Iraq via Jordan.

Paul's father John Grecian was a former executive of a company called Allivane, which, as we shall see, was bound up with covert government business to Iran and Iraq and was never the subject of an inquiry. The Grecians had set up Ordtec with Stuart Blackledge, a former MoD and SRC employee after the collapse of Allivane, and began pushing business through BMARC, an Astra subsidiary bought in 1988. Our part in the Al Fao contract was for the supply of a £300,000 order for booster pellets for the shell fuses. The names of Ordtec or SRC were originally nowhere to be seen on our contract, however, which was initially drawn with B. & J. Industries, a suitably innocuous company in Sleaford, now defunct.

By March 1990 BMARC had imported 15,000 shell fuses from Rexon and from one of our companies, Accudyne, in the US. Their job was to make the explosive booster pellets and fill them and onward-ship them to an 'Al Fao organisation c/o the Jordanian Armed Forces'. The export licence supplied by the DTI was marked destination 'Al Fao organisation, c/o Jordanian armed forces'. Al Fao, I learned, was a Baghdad arms factory.

Paul Grecian claimed constant communication with Special Branch over the principal contract, but the judge refused to overturn PIICs issued by the Home Secretary Kenneth Baker and Peter Lilley (Secretary of State, DTI), which prevented Special Branch officer Stephen Wilkinson from revealing that he had all the time been working with Paul Grecian on Al Fao, apparently to gather intelligence on Iraq's arms build-up.

Without Wilkinson, Ordtec's lawyers claimed they could not mount a satisfactory defence. A deal was done. The defendants pleaded guilty, Phillips was fined £1,000, the others received suspended sentences. Later, Andrew Collins QC, the H.M. Customs' barrister for the prosecution, was summoned by Sir Richard Scott to give evidence in private session to his Inquiry, and, on appeal, on 7 November 1995, Lord Taylor, the Lord Chief Justice, acquitted the four defendants on the 'material irregularity' of withholding Whitehall documents relevant to their case.

Matrix Churchill

In 1987 Saddam Hussein began directing his efforts to develop an indigenous arms industry. An important aspect of this factory build-up was the so-called dual-purpose machinery produced by such companies as Matrix Churchill which, like other members of the Machine Tools Technology Association, would be shown how best to assist the dictator by Alan Clark and Lord Trefgarne at that MTTA meeting in January 1988 which I have already described.

A key figure in the build-up was Roy Ricks, whose company, MFA, we had taken under our wing in 1986. Ricks, who had high-up associations in British Intelligence, including Sir Brian Tovey, a former head of GCHQ, with whom he entered into some lucrative partnerships, worked at this time with the Iraqi engineer Waddi Anees Mansour to establish an Iraqi network of machine-tool companies in Britain, West Germany and Switzerland. From Britain, TI Machine Tools, BSA Tools Ltd (also later prosecuted by the British government), Wickman Bennett and other hi-tech companies were contracted to satisfy Iraq's main preoccupation as the war came to an end, namely to establish their own arms industry and to pursue the development of a nuclear capability.

Ricks also helped in the formation of Technology and Development Group (TDG), a subsidiary of the state-owned Baghdad-based Al-Arabi Trading run by Hussein Kamil, Saddam Hussein's brother-in-law and chief of SSO, the Iraqi secret service. By the time TDG had become established as the world-wide headquarters of the Iraqi procurement network, Ricks and Waddi had serviced some £40m worth of orders with British companies alone.

On the Board of TDG were Fadel Jawad Kadhum and Dr Safaal-Habobi, both senior members of Iraqi Intelligence. Its offices were originally in Chiswick, West London, but its registered office was that of Baileys, Shaw & Gillett, Astra's lawyers, a fact which was never revealed to us but was not without significance.

With Iraqi money, TDG, through one of its subsidiaries, TMG Engineering Ltd, in 1987 purchased the Coventry-based company TI Machine Tools Ltd from the TI Group. The director of TI behind the sale was none other than Sir John Cuckney, the company's deputy chairman. Subsequently TI Machine Tools Ltd was renamed Matrix Churchill Ltd.

On the sale, Baileys, Shaw & Gillett acted not only for the Iraqis but for Matrix Churchill. They sent a representative out to Chile, where finance through Dresdner Bank was organised.

By the following year (1988), Matrix executives were actively involved with the millionaire Chilean arms dealer Carlos Cardoen in the setting up of the Nairawan missile factory near Baghdad. Ricks had first come to Astra about this deal. The substance of our discussions was an Iraqi requirement for fuses and 155mm shells, but they opted instead for a deal with Cardoen, valued at £37.5m, who made an arrangement with them to construct and equip an entire factory, Matrix Churchill providing the machine tools required in the manufacture of the artillery ammunition. The factory was up and running by the middle of 1990. Most of the

Matrix machinery going to Iraq ended up at Nairawan.[25]

In the very same year, 1987 (the year before the Iran–Iraq ceasefire), Alan Clark authorised £200m credits for Iraq, and, according to the investment broker Gerald Morse, urged him to buy as many shares in Astra as he could, introducing Morse to Valerie Harkess, Clark's then mistress, in whose name 200,000 shares were subsequently purchased. This was no idle punt, for 1987 was the year when, specifically encouraged by the MoD, we began serious negotiations with Oerlikon-Buhrle of Switzerland to acquire BMARC, a company with which the ministry had long enjoyed a fruitful relationship in the covert arms business. This company was so tight with the MoD that its executives even managed to avoid prosecution over the Ordtec Al Fao contract, though they too were involved.[26]

1987 was a pivotal year. There was no longer any pretence as to whose side in the war the government was on. The Iranian procurement office in London closed down and Iraq became Britain's main customer, with Matrix among those at the centre of procurement operations. Two years later, in September 1989, following the FBI raid on BNL Atlanta, which turned up large loans being made to Matrix Churchill, the CIA sent a report to the National Security Council and copied it to MI6, naming Matrix Churchill as 'the UK's leading producer of computer controlled machine tools that can be used for the production of sophisticated armaments', and warning that 'Baghdad has created a complex network of holding companies to acquire technology for its chemical, biological, nuclear and ballistic missile development programs.'

A confidential International Atomic Energy Agency report revealed that fifty Matrix machines had been discovered by inspectors at nuclear sites, twenty-nine of which were used to make parts for a centrifugal uranium enrichment cycle – a vital part of the process to produce materials for nuclear warheads.

A UN nuclear inspector said, 'I saw a Matrix Churchill CNC multi-access milling machine at the Nassr Establishment in Taji, where it was involved in the gas centrifuge programme . . . also at

an engineering complex in Salahuddin that was used in the production of gas centrifuges . . . and at a manufacturing site in
Badr, Matrix machinery was involved in the production of
calutrons . . . If the British government was doing what it ought to
have been doing, we shouldn't have found that equipment in
Iraq.'[27]

There can have been no doubt in the minds of the British
security services that Matrix Churchill's exports to Iraq were being
used to manufacture weapons that could threaten our national
security. Nor had there been for some time. As early as May 1987
Mark Gutteridge, Matrix's export sales manager, had shown MI5
drawings of machines they were selling to Iraq that could be used
to manufacture conventional 122mm, 152mm and 155mm shells.

Indeed, so obvious was the purpose of the Matrix exports to
Iraq that Scott was moved to comment on claims to ignorance,
'How could you not have been suspicious given the state of the
war, that's what I don't understand; it almost beggars belief.'[28]

One route by which government received information was
through Gutteridge. His MI5 handler was one 'Michael Ford', a
qualified engineer and expert in technology transfer with a special
interest in Iraq. When Ford was himself transferred to MI6, a new
handler, 'Ian Eascott', took over.

Managing director Paul Henderson also claimed to have been
used by the Intelligence services quite willingly for years, and in
1989, with intelligence on Iraq rather than the Soviet bloc being
the order of the day, he was given a new MI6 controller, who
went by the name of 'John Balsom' and who provided Henderson
with a contact in the Foreign Office to facilitate applications for
export licences.[29]

All went well even up to June 1990, a month before the start of
the Gulf War, when Customs and Excise raided the company's
Coventry offices and suddenly Matrix's friends in Intelligence were
nowhere to be seen.

In an attempt to parcel Matrix up and despatch it out of sight
(and be seen to be doing so), the government, in the persons of
Home Secretary Kenneth Clarke, Foreign Office Minister of State

Tristan Garel-Jones, Defence Secretary Malcolm Rifkind and President of the Board of Trade Michael Heseltine signed Public Interest Immunity Certificates to withhold information from the defence that Whitehall and government ministers knew and approved all that Matrix Churchill had been involved with in Iraq 'even though,' as Michael Meacher MP put it, 'they knew that would lead to three innocent men then on trial being jailed'.

After the judge overruled the PIICs, Heseltine argued that he had had no alternative but to sign, but it is now known that the Trade Minister Richard Needham successfully refused.

On 12 January 1994 Kenneth Baker, former Home Secretary, also admitted (at the Scott Inquiry) that he had signed a PIIC suppressing information that Henderson had been working with MI6 and making illegal exports with the government's knowledge and approval.

The law governing PIICs is that government documents can be withheld on grounds that revealing them would damage the public interest. But in whose interest were the PIICs? Were they in the public's interest or, rather, in the interest of those in a corrupt government?

A Gallup poll in March 1994 showed where public interest lay: 77 per cent of those questioned described the arms-to-Iraq scandal as very or fairly serious, only 4 per cent thought that government ministers were telling the truth; and 83 per cent thought it was 'always wrong' for innocent people to go to prison to protect state secrets (6 per cent thought it right).[30]

But the issue is not only a moral one. What made the government do it?

Eric Beston, the DTI official responsible for export controls, confirmed to the Scott Inquiry that export licences had been granted to Matrix Churchill in order to keep open Intelligence communication lines with Iraq. If that were true, and the Matrix executives were performing such a valuable service to the nation, why prosecute them? If the answer is, to stop the proliferation of weapons in Iraqi factories, why not simply stop dishing out export licences?

'It does seem very peculiar,' admitted Alan Clark at the Scott Inquiry concerning a similar prosecution of BSA Tools of Birmingham. 'The machinery of government was put into play to make a particular exception . . . and they were later prosecuted. It is Kafka, really.'

The answer of course is that the Matrix trial was an attempt to shut people up and to show the public that the government was doing something to clean up the defence industry, and by implication, therefore, that its own hands were clean. Nevertheless, it was a risky operation so soon after the government had been forced to drop the charges against Cowley and Mitchell. No doubt the government will have examined the downside of such a risk, namely what the fall-out would be if the PIICs were thrown out and the government's involvement made plain.

There were two get-outs. Three junior ministers organised the rubber-stamping of the Matrix export licences. Alan Clark (then Trade Minister) and Lord Trefgarne (then Defence Minister) persuaded William Waldegrave at the Foreign Office against his better judgement, Waldegrave only agreeing provided the DTI would handle any 'presentational problems'.

They were dispensable; they could be blamed.

This get-out was in fact employed at the Scott Inquiry by Margaret Thatcher, whose overall performance on 8 December 1993 at the Inquiry was described by Matthew Engel in the *Guardian* as, 'part Nixon, who took the responsibility but not the blame, part Reagan, who remembered nothing, and part Ceausescu, who regretted nothing and how dare they.' The 'tilt' to Iraq, Mrs Thatcher said, had been the province of William Waldegrave, Alan Clark and Lord Trefgarne. Yet, as repeated in the *Guardian*, Sir Charles Powell, her private secretary, told the FO on 2 September 1988 that 'the prime minister wanted to be kept closely in touch at every stage', and in November 1988 Alan Clark told Waldegrave that 'whatever is agreed between us will require the prime minister's approval'.

Dr David Clark, shadow secretary for defence, was moved to comment, 'To blame your employees for your own failure is symptomatic of a morally bankrupt political party.' Powell, incidentally, was not interviewed by the Scott Inquiry, nor was he interviewed by the inquiry into Thatcher's Malaysian arms deal. Powell is now a director of Trafalgar House, whose involvement with Thatcher's arms dealings has already been alluded to.[31]

The second excuse, grown tired in the mouths of civil servants, was that the licences were granted in order to keep the security services' lines of communication open. That, besides blaming each other, was Alan Clark's and William Waldegrave's angle.

These were excuses, not explanations, not credible even in their utterance to the people making them, for they ignored the avalanche of arms and munitions that had swept into the battle zone from Britain.

By the time of the Scott Inquiry, Thatcher herself had long left Downing Street and confidence had disappeared in her strategy of damage limitation even before her passing, when it was seen how it would backfire if Cowley and Mitchell revealed all of the government involvement in Bull's Supergun. At this stage, as I will show, Bull himself had enough material to blow Mrs Thatcher's government out of the water, and he was in a mood to use it.

I believe she was sacrificed for the good of the Tory Party, which the powerful thought might just stagger on for a while in the face of increasing investigation and accusation by the media, and the suspicion of the British people under a low-key replacement, John Major. The PIICs were a poor substitute for an outrageous brand of leadership which had ultimately proved too dangerous for the party.

That then was the real downside. Why did she risk it? Why did she risk her own position in order to show the British people that 'by Jove we don't stand for what these companies were up to'? Why did she not go to the Scott Inquiry and say, 'I am very sorry about this, but we have certain interests in the Middle East which we want to preserve. We had to create disunity in the Middle East, to divide and rule, otherwise we would have lost our oil interests.' I believe it would have been totally accepted by the British people.

Why didn't she? Because there are personal interests involved. They are still terrified at what will come out. The journalist Richard Norton-Taylor described the decision by Customs to raid the Matrix Churchill offices in June 1990 as sending 'shivers across Whitehall'. But the cold wind brought worse than the threat of exposure over a few export licence approvals.

The first layer of conspiracy that they wish to hide is direct government involvement in the trade with Iran and Iraq through its own companies, IMS and Royal Ordnance.

A defence industry report has maintained that 'Whitehall has often made use of IMS to purchase ammunition from Belgian manufacturer PRB . . . to meet the needs of countries which it has not been practicable or politically advisable to supply direct from the UK.' Documents came to light, after our takeover of the Belgian arms and explosives company PRB in July 1989, disclosing contracts between PRB and IMS for the provision of ammunition (mainly 155mm) to Iraq in 1984, 1985 and 1986. PRB had been contracted by IMS to carry out the manufacturing side of contracts entered into between IMS and Iraq.[32]

In September 1989, following our purchase of PRB, Chris Gumbley commissioned a report on illicit contracts in the company. Among them were contracts for shells going to Jordan, Portugal, Zambia, Morocco, Singapore, Cyprus and Thailand, none of whom had the guns capable of firing them or any particular military requirement. The report concluded: 'PRB have reliable information that ordnance hardware has been cast in the UK, machined by Royal Ordnance, and exported with UK approval to the Kingdom of Jordan to Iraq.'

Christopher Cowley has testified to the Scott Inquiry that Royal Ordnance was involved in contracts licensed to PRB, which made munitions to Bull's design. 'Royal Ordnance made complete shells for PRB (105mm and 155mm calibre, for instance); on others the Belgian firm assembled parts supplied by RO. PRB then sent shells to Iraq via Jordan.'[33]

A photograph of a box of 81mm mortar bombs was taken by

my son Christian while serving in the Gulf. It shows an ammunition case found north of the Saudi border inside Iraq in a captured Iraqi gun position. The markings, 'MOD RO IRAQ, L/C NO. 86/1/450', indicate that the RO contract was licensed by the MoD for export to Iraq in 1986 and that it found its way to the battlefield for use against our troops from the Ammunition and Supply division of the MoD. The L/C NO. 86/1/450 refers to Letter of Credit dated January 1986, batch 450. In all probability this was part of the Jordan Defence Package, where the export was organised by IMS.

When I gave the photograph to investigative journalist Kevin Cahill, he confronted a senior Customs and Excise official with it on my behalf. The official reported: 'We have hundreds of photographs, too. We know all about that stuff going direct to Iraq. We have prosecuted no one because we cannot prove that there was an intention to evade the law in relation to military exports.'[34]

Why can't they prove it? Because the paperwork concerning all direct sales by the government through IMS was destroyed when the company was wound up and sold to British Aerospace in 1991. Equally, it is difficult to discover the true extent of IMS dealing because they had offices abroad which looked after their projects in Thailand, Iran, Jordan, Saudi, Belgium and elsewhere, which did not necessarily go through a British arms manufacturer at all.

In 1994 there was a court case in Rottweil in Germany in which Walter Lamp, managing director of Heckler & Koch, was alleged to have breached German arms exporting laws with the help of the British government-owned Royal Ordnance for a period of nearly ten years prior to RO's privatisation. In one instance in 1987, at the time of privatisation, machine guns were exported via Britain, the destination the United Arab Emirates. En route from Liverpool the ship was detained by Italian police, who discovered Iraqi naval officers on board. Iraq had been its real destination. In 1991, when the British government was trying to lock up any evidence of its covert deals, Royal Ordnance bought Heckler & Koch and integrated it into its 'security systems'.[35]

At the Scott Inquiry it was disclosed that in April 1989, RO had supplied 900 tubes of ethyl cellulose (a chemical used to build up pressure as a projectile moves up the gun barrel, suited to Bull's Supergun) to a British businessman, who sold it to a German client, who sold it to Iraq.

Ian Woodward, director of public affairs at BAe, who now own RO, exonerated the company with the industry's accepted excuse: 'As a responsible manufacturer we always strictly abide by the export requirements of Her Majesty's Government. No supplier can guarantee the end-use of his products. We naturally do everything to check up.'

As late as August 1990, when Britain was preparing to send its soldiers against Iraq, a train of forty-two wagons laden with anti-tank missiles and shells guarded by British soldiers travelled from RO's Chorley factory to Hull docks to be unloaded on to a Yugoslav ship bound for Jordan. It was halted by Customs and Excise, who had reason to believe that the real end-user was Iraq. On 14 September, the ship was quietly allowed to slip away to Aqaba, the arms still on board.[36]

By 1990, Royal Ordnance had been privatised, of course, and sold to BAe, but as will become plain, this privatisation was a cosmetic distancing of the company from the government. RO is tightly bound to the government to this day.

I have in my possession documents emanating from Swedish Customs and sent to the Scott Inquiry, which show that long before its privatisation Royal Ordnance was part of a European explosives cartel which traded with Iran, Iraq, Argentina and South Africa when arms exports to those countries were banned.

Besides RO, among the companies involved in the cartel were ICI Nobel of Scotland, Muiden Chemie of Holland, SNPE of France, PRB of Belgium, Bofors Nobel of Sweden and Rio Tinto of Spain. The documentation goes from 1983 to 1987, which was when the Customs investigation stopped. The trade still continues.

Minutes of the cartel's meetings, obtained by Swedish Customs from Bofors name senior executives, including Trevor Truman, the then Director of Royal Ordnance's explosives division, and show that ICI chairman Sir John Harvey-Jones, who was aware of what was going on, gave the order that the head of ICI Nobel should no longer attend cartel meetings in Paris, Geneva, Oxford, Brussels, etc. The relevant minute reads: 'Harvey-Jones forbids continued participation in our meetings and therefore Frank cannot participate, but wants individual contacts with the members. Someone will contact Frank before each meeting. (Luns/Nye before next meeting).'

'Individual contacts' were in fact made on the telephone before cartel meetings and by getting hold of the meeting minutes, and the trade continued. The Customs report reads:

> NEC is a member of the cartel and thus has participated in many of the discussions that have taken place concerning the deliveries of powder and explosives to Iran . . .
>
> Of the Italian company Tirrena's huge order for 5300 tonnes powder, NEC was to deliver 900 tonnes at a value of SEK 53.5 million. These deliveries were to take place to Yugoslavia from where the goods would be taken over by the Swedish arms dealer Schmitz for delivery to Iran . . .
>
> FDSP in Yugoslavia placed a number of orders for various types of war materials with several suppliers in Europe. Schmitz lies behind all these orders. A good number of the orders were placed with Bofors in Sweden, who, in its turn, placed orders with other companies, among them NEC.
>
> NEC received an order from Bofors for 100 tonnes after the latter had received a tender from NEC dated 25 October 1984.
>
> NEC representatives had participated in cartel meetings on several occasions at which the Iran business had been discussed. So it is not unreasonable to assume that NEC had throughout been aware of the ultimate destination . . .

These are just some aspects of ICI Nobel's involvement in the trade with Iran. 'In conclusion it can be named that NEC invited the Swedish arms dealer Schmitz to visit the company in early 1986. Schmitz, one of Iran's most important intermediaries in the arms market, came to NEC with a long shopping list . . .'

When I talk about this, people find it difficult to believe that ICI
was involved, but I don't really see why. On Desert Island Discs,
Harvey-Jones denied ICI were involved in armaments. Of course
they are; they were the only British company running Go-Cos in
the United States. At Nobel, they have one of the most sophisticated research establishments into propellants and explosives in
the world – scientists, computers, and research into how explosive
performs under different environments. There is nothing new in
this. The British government actually considered shutting ICI
down during the Second World War because so much of the explosive dropped on London had been exported by ICI to Germany
from the USA. The only reason the government didn't act was
because they realised they wouldn't have anyone to make explosives for them.

When we bought the Belgian explosives company PRB, I had
no idea that we at Astra had joined this exclusive club. It was quite
amusing. Suddenly, after the acquisition, I was surprised to receive
an invitation from ICI to the golf championship up in Troon in
Scotland. They hired a house, and the managing director of RO,
Peter Kenyon, was also there, ever so hospitable. I couldn't understand it, because it was such a complete change of heart from
RO's hitherto cavalier attitude towards Astra. As our competitors
and at the same time so 'in' with the government, they had always
been hostile to us, a too successful independent, even making it
difficult for us when we had to use them as sub-contractors if they
had a cheap line because of their monopoly on a particular manufacturing capability. We had the same experience with ICI Nobel
on items such as initiators. It was always such a difficult business
to get RO's end of a deal efficiently and cost-effectively completed, and I know that they resented our being in the driving seat
on a deal in which their role was as sub-contractor. But now,
suddenly, we were great pals.

The cartel was not involved only with propellants. They had a
multi-source international production line, shell casings from one
place, propellants from another, fuses from another, cartridge

cases, initiators and so on from others. All the bits and pieces would then be shipped off somewhere else (sometimes PRB) to be assembled.

At first Portugal often appeared on export licences as the favoured (false) end-user. But sometimes ships' manifests were actually changed en route. For example there is one manifest that shows the shippers as Royal Ordnance, Bridgwater, and the shipment going from Ridham in Kent to Piraeus in Greece, and another manifest for the same shipment showing the final destination as Bandar Abbas in southern Iran.[37]

The cartel began doing business in 1981 with a consignment of 155mm shells. The French arms company, Luchaire, contracted, on behalf of its Italian associates, Società di Armamento and Consar, to supply Iran with the consignment.

A year or so later, when the business with Iran was developing and Luchaire's list of sub-contractors was growing to include Gea-Remie of Italy, Muiden Chemie of Holland, NCS Pyrotechnie Technologie de Survilliers of France, Indep of Portugal and its own parent company in France, SPEL, Jim Guerin of ISC offered to help set up his friend and associate, Terry Byrne, in business in a new company, Allivane International, to become part of the action. Allivane was first registered as a company in 1983 and was awarded a £147,000 grant from the Scottish Office.[38]

Allivane's ultimate owner, however, was Lagan Investments in Panama, a company controlled by Carlos Cardoen, the man to whom Jim Guerin supplied cluster bomb technology, the mainstay of the Chilean's business with Iraq. So Allivane began life with some interesting connections. Terry Byrne had worked for Rexon and for Jim Guerin at the fuse production company, Hamilton Watch.

At first, Allivane had no production capability and sub-contracted to companies such as Royal Ordnance, then still wholly owned by the British government, ICI Nobel and British Steel, before shipping parts out to Greece, Austria, Spain, and to Portugal where the shells were actually assembled by SPEL before onward shipment to Iran.

Allivane's special relationship with the MoD goes right back to the inception of the company. In the early days of Astra, in 1984 and 1985, Chris Gumbley was steered by the MoD towards Allivane, which appeared to us to have an extraordinary export licensing capability. It was suggested that Astra might like to participate in one or two small orders to assemble products being imported by Allivane from Holland, which were then being exported with UK government approval to Singapore, now a known false end-user for Iran and Iraq. These orders came as a direct result of our dealings with the MoD, and would be the beginning of our own involvement with the cartel.

Before long Allivane opened up a small production facility of its own in Cumbernauld in Glasgow, managed by Gerrard Heneaghan, ex-Ferranti and later ISC, Jim Guerin's company. The plant had previously had connections with Honeywell, the US defense manufacturer. Big companies like ICI were still part of the picture. In fact ICI's wholly-owned subsidiary, the Nobel Explosives Company, was situated just twenty-five miles away in Stevenston, and from 1985 to 1988 it was a regular supplier to Allivane of fuse components, although sometimes – twice in September 1986 – Nobel was bold enough to ship fuses direct to Radmer, Austria, where Noricum, later involved in a court case for selling $300m worth of arms to Iran, stockpiled goods for onward shipment to the Middle East.

British Steel was another essential sub-contractor that remained very much in the team. Through its Glasgow-based subsidiary British Tubes Stockholding, it was commissioned to produce 20,000 parts (including 'thick-walled seamless tubing') each month for six months in 1987.

In this period Allivane began its move into the centre of international operations, taking on as much as 50 per cent of the cartel's business. European members preferred to deal as a subcontractor to Allivane than get involved further down the international production line in the riskier shipping of finished items. In France, Luchaire had had some bad publicity in the press over suspect shipments uncovered in Cherbourg, and Muiden

Chemie, quarter owned by the Dutch government, had by this time been forbidden to export arms to Portugal, obviously suspect end-users. Shipments of components to Britain were certainly safer, and Allivane, with its close ties with the MoD, DTI and FCO, found no apparent difficulty in handling that end of the business.

This, however, presented Allivane with a new problem: storage. With explosives coming in from Holland, France, Italy, Spain and Yugoslavia, storage space had to be greatly enhanced to cope. It was for this purpose, as I would later discover, that our company BMARC's huge storage facilities at Faldingworth were commissioned.

Secrecy was Allivane's particular forte, and secrecy had always been the key principle of the cartel's operations. With that in mind, the company invented a spurious English associate company, called Allivane International Group, through which hundreds of millions of dollars of covert arms deals were processed but which had no legal existence whatever.

Llew Smith MP, in a letter to the *Guardian* in December 1993, claimed that the company had been set up as 'a creation of the MoD/MI6 to act as a conduit providing "plausible deniability" when uncovered.' Allivane was to the British government what Jim Guerin's Gamma Systems had been to the US government.

In August 1991, a search undertaken by the Registrar of Companies for England and Wales certified that 'a search made this day of the Index of Limited Companies, including Overseas Companies, registered during the last 10 years, has failed to reveal any trace of a company registered in the name of Allivane International Group Limited.'

Allivane International Group, the 'company that never was', banked with the Midland, Victoria Street, SW1, where Astra, IMS, the Iraqi and, previously, the Iranian procurements offices had accounts. AIG had an office in Horseferry Road within walking distance of the DTI, the MoD, the FO and the government military services company IMS. Regular meetings were held at the MoD to discuss Allivane's business requirements, details of supply and shipment and the licences that would be needed.

Frank Machon, whose haulage company carried shipments for Allivane, has described the extraordinary measures taken by the MoD to safeguard the shunting of components from one stage of the production line to another. One job, overseen by the MoD and involving Royal Ordnance, was to move 1,000 tons of fuses and high explosives destined for Saudi Arabia between two factories in Glenrothes and Cumbernauld and the RO factory in Bishopton. It took seventeen weeks to complete, with Machon's lorries running twenty-four hours a day.

'The Ministry of Defence was overseeing everything,' said Machon. 'They were paranoid about anything going wrong and the Saudis being upset . . . We were having to ferry high explosives all over the country, finding safe storage for it while the order was being put together.' Machon's lorries, loaded with explosives, drove from Bishopton to Glenrothes, where the charges were assembled, and from Bishopton to Cumbernauld, where the fuses were made. Then back to Bishopton, where the 155mm charges were stored. At one point the M6 was closed in the early hours to allow seven of his lorries to speed through. Police, Special Branch and army logistics were involved.

'At first the loads were the maximum legally allowed per vehicle . . . Then the instructions came . . . load the lorries to the limit. So we were shuttling 15-ton loads, nearly three times the legal limit.'

As reported by the *Guardian* journalist Richard Norton-Taylor in June 1993, Machon warned Mrs Thatcher to no avail in December 1988 about such shipments to Iraq, one shipment being for 'three times the quantity specified in the contract'.

When in 1990–1, in the course of the DTI Inquiry into Astra's purchase of PRB, I pointed out to the Inspectors that the UK government had supplied export licences for munitions to Portugal sufficient to enable that country to participate in all-out global warfare, it was never followed up. Only the Dutch government ever took any action after the Swedish Customs investigation – against Muiden Chemie.

In September 1988 Joost de Graaf, managing director of

Muiden Chemie in Holland, gave evidence in the investigation into shipments to Allivane of explosives and igniters for use in GHN45 and GC45 howitzers. Contracts ran into millions of pounds for onward shipment, once assembled, to Portugal. Investigators' documents, and Graaf in interviews, name Astra as a supplier of one large Portuguese order totalling £90m. The contract was drawn in 1986, although it came as news to us and, as we shall see, is but one example of the way the government-coordinated covert trade was unofficially run through our company; a trade which, when the DTI launched its official government inquiry into Astra, the Inspectors chose to ignore completely.

A little-known fact about Joost de Graaf is that he was one of the founder shareholders of Allivane. And who do you think now owns Muiden Chemie? Royal Ordnance.

So close was Allivane to the British government that in 1987 it was co-opted into supplying 155mm ammunition as part of the Al Yamamah deal with Saudi, but before Allivane could deliver, it went bust. In desperation George Younger, then Secretary of State for Defence, told the MoD to take the order over.

There were two raids by Customs on Allivane's Scottish offices. The first, in 1987, occurred following the seizure of documents during a raid on Muiden Chemie in Holland; the second after the Allivane managing director Gerrard Heneaghan alleged in an Edinburgh court that Terry Byrne had embezzled £2.2m. In neither case was any subsequent action taken by the Crown Office in Edinburgh. The Secretary of State for Scotland at the time was Malcolm Rifkind. In 1992 it was reported in the *Guardian* that Customs officers alleged Whitehall interference with the case. Malcolm Rifkind was subsequently appointed Secretary of State for Defence.

Frank Machon informed not only Margaret Thatcher a year before she resigned as prime minister, but John Major in January 1991, that he had documentary proof that Allivane in conjunction with Royal Ordnance and other companies had been arming Iraq. No action was taken by either government.

*

Another aspect of the British government's policy concerns its relationship with Chile. It is interesting that the name of Carlos Cardoen crops up consistently. It is linked with Gerald Bull, Jim Guerin, Matrix Churchill, Allivane and a host of other companies and arms facilitators (including, as we shall see, Mark Thatcher), all of which were engaged in the traffic of weapon-making machinery and arms to the Middle East.

Cardoen's freedom to roam and incredible success is due not a little to the Tory government's relationship with his country, Chile, the consequences of which are demonstrated particularly nastily in the tragic case of Jonathan Moyle.

Margaret Thatcher's policy was forged during the Falklands War when arrangements were made with General Pinochet for Britain to use bases there in return for which the UK would press the UN – where our representative described Chile as a 'moderate and stabilising force' – to lay off Chile on their appalling human rights record. There followed a big sales effort by the DESO in Whitehall to sell weapons to the Chilean government, which came to a head when Jonathan Moyle, a twenty-eight-year-old British journalist, was found crammed in a 5-foot wardrobe, hanging by his shirt from a clothes rail. His head was covered with a pillow case, and over two pairs of underpants he was clothed in a towel and polythene bag, which has been said to have been placed there to stem the flow of body fluids and delay discovery.[39]

Only a few years later we would be astonished by a similar scene in a kitchen in Hammersmith. Again the victim would be connected with defence (he was an assistant to Jonathan Aitken, the then Minister for Defence Procurement at the MoD) and had also been an investigative journalist. As with Moyle, the case would be explained as the consequence of some sort of bizarre sexual practice. The victim's name was Stephen Milligan.

The connection of Moyle with Cardoen is that he interviewed the arms dealer the night before he was killed, looking for corroboration of information he had received that Cardoen was selling fifty Bell helicopters to Iraq. Nothing so astonishing in that – Cardoen was among the world's biggest arms exporters to

Iraq. What is relevant is that Moyle had discovered that these helicopters were to be fitted with Britain's electronic guidance system for TOW anti-tank missiles, known as Helios. The journalist's own notes make this clear, and there is also evidence that Cardoen was involved in the marketing of Stonefish (or a copy), NATO's naval mine developed by GEC Marconi.

Moyle has, however, thanks to the energies of his father, been morally vindicated, although his murderers have not yet been identified. The judge co-ordinating the original inquiry complained that his investigation was 'obstructed by the unwillingness of the British authorities to co-operate'.[40]

Britain did everything it could to wash its hands of the incident – the rumour of strange sexual practice is said to have emanated from a party in the British embassy there, where, of all people, the Archbishop of Canterbury had been a guest. It is an indictment indeed when this seedy hush-up is put beside the action taken eventually by the Chilean courts, following pressure on the equally corrupt Chilean government by Moyle's father.

Once again, truth and justice fly in the face of greed. In May 1991 Pinochet (by then deposed but still commander of the military in Chile) visited Britain in connection with an Anglo-Chilean arms project, in which Royal Ordnance was to license Chile the technology to produce their own missiles.[41]

The second layer of conspiracy they would like to hide concerns government-related commissions and kickbacks. Allegations have been rife in the press since the story began to unravel.

It was revealed in 1984 that in Oman, when Cementation, a subsidiary of Trafalgar House, was awarded the £300m 'university' project, Margaret Thatcher's son Mark's company, Monteagle (set up with his friend Stephen Tipping, best man at Mark's wedding), was paid a commission on the deal of some £50,000.

Following the scandal, Margaret Thatcher, beset with questions about whether she was 'batting for Britain' or for those closer to home, met with two of her close advisers Sir Tim Bell and Sir Gordon Reece, and together they decided that the best answer was to despatch Mark to Dallas, away from the limelight, where he started work as a car salesman for Lotus Cars and British Car auctions, then run by David Wickens, a family friend. Wickens was until 1986 principal shareholder in Attwoods, the waste disposal firm where Sir Denis Thatcher was deputy chairman from 1983 and which has been rumoured to have Mafia connections.[42]

Tipping meanwhile was set back on his feet in a new career as arms facilitator with the help of powerful people in the Thatcher inner circle of businessmen and senior Defence Ministry officials, including Colin Chandler, then chief of defence sales at the MoD. There is every reason to believe that the Stephen Tipping/Mark Thatcher double act never faltered during the Thatcher years.

In February 1993 in *Business Age* magazine Kevin Cahill published an analysis of Mark Thatcher's finances: 'On 14th December 1992 Mark Thatcher had 93,142,139 Swiss francs in 11 bank accounts deposited at 3 different Swiss financial institutions. £41,581,312 in sterling. In addition he has unidentified shareholdings in South Africa and substantial personal assets worldwide. Estimates of the total value of his fortune vary from £50million to £100million, putting him amongst Britain's super rich and approx 80th richest man in the UK.'

Tipping has been named as a facilitator in part of the £1.3bn defence deal signed by Margaret Thatcher and Dr Mahathir Mohamed, the Malaysian prime minister, in September 1988. He helped to fix the sale of laser-guided British Starburst anti-aircraft missiles, worth £70m, to the Malaysian defence ministry, and was also involved with a Malaysian company in the supply of parts for Hawk aircraft from British Aerospace.[43]

It is further alleged that Mark Thatcher was rewarded with a commission of some £12m in the biggest deal inspired by his mother, the £60bn package destined for Saudi Arabia and known as Al Yamamah.[44]

Although this allegation was made by the *Sunday Times* in 1994, it first appeared in an extraordinary document received anonymously five years earlier by Jeffrey Rooker MP, who was involved in a Public Accounts Committee inquiry into government use of public money in the financing of Thatcher's big defence packages. It is extraordinary, because over the years its astonishing claims have proved increasingly correct.

The document, dated 2 May 1989 and marked 'Classification: Restricted', is in the form of a memo to the chairman of a company whose name has been blacked out, as has the sender's. It is set out under the headings of Thatcher's three largest defence packages – Jordan, Saudi Arabia [Al Yamamah] and Malaysia [Pergau].

Inter alia, the memo is concerned with the overpricing by British Aerospace of Tornado fighter-bombers up to 112 per cent more than the going rate to the RAF (in the case of the Jordan Package) and 120 per cent in the case of the Saudi Arabia Package.

Commissions reaching 'over 45 per cent' are said to go some way to explaining the inflated price, but in the case of Al Yamamah the mark-ups are described, apparently by an executive of BAe, as 'proper profit margins on unprofitable business in the past'.

The system of payment, however, makes this seem at best unlikely. The Saudis were invoiced by Colin Chandler of Defence Sales, and Defence Procurement under Peter Levene were invoiced by BAe, the principal contractor. If BAe were issuing inflated invoices to Levene, he would know that they were inflated because the MoD were buying basically the same aircraft from BAe for RAF use.

Further, since it is known that the lion's share of payments from Saudi are in heavily discounted oil (as much as 500,000 barrels a day have been flowing into Britain on Al Yamamah II), which must then be traded through Shell and BP, there is another hidden profit margin, no mention of which has ever been made.

The memo suggests that this profit area from the crude oil arrangement was of particular interest to Margaret Thatcher. 'There are constant phone calls between Mrs T and King Fahd and Sir Peter Levene [MoD] and Prince Sultan.'

So commissions of 45 per cent were coming from the inflated

price paid by the Saudis and there was yet more slack in the sell-on profit margin from the bartered oil. The memo is not the only evidence of these payments. In November 1994, Sir Colin Southgate, chairman of Thorn EMI, revealed a 25 per cent commission payment on a £40m Al Yamamah contract to supply bomb fuses for the Tornado bombers.

What became of all this money?

The Rooker memorandum alleges that Mark Thatcher, in conjunction with a man called Wafiq Said, is administering 'a huge sum', later fixed at £240m by *Sunday Times* sources, and that a 'sizable payment' was bound for Conservative Party funds.

'The additional financial benefits to Mark T. [presumably that which was later fixed by the *Sunday Times* at £12m] and his friend Wafiq Said and other middlemen, all non-tax-paying residents of the UK and to the Conservative Party are absolutely enormous, according to the BAe executive.'

Wafiq Said is another interesting player. His father, an eminent ophthalmologist, helped found the Syrian University in Damascus. After attending school in Lebanon, Wafiq came to London in 1959 to study at the Institute of Bankers, during which time he met two Saudi princes Bandar and Khalid, nephews of the Saudi King Fahd. The princes' father, Prince Sultan ibn Abdul-Aziz, was later to become King Fahd's Minister of Defence, while the princes themselves became ambassador to Washington and commander of the Arab forces in the Gulf War respectively.

Following jobs in Geneva in the 1960s for Union de Banque Suisse and then the Banque Commerciale Arabe SA, Said returned to England and in 1967 opened a couple of restaurants which, according to investigative journalist David Pallister, were rendezvous points for visiting Arab businessmen and officials. Two years later Said linked up with a man called Akhram Ojjeh, the Saudi financier and Middle East arms broker.

Akhram Ojjeh is the common denominator between Wafiq Said and Mark Thatcher. Mark met Akhram's son, Mansour, more than a decade later in the context of motor racing. Mansour Ojjeh would become chairman of McLaren International. In the early

1980s, when Mark and Mansour met, Wafiq Said, as Akhram's business partner, was setting up a company called Sifcorp in London, an investment and finance corporation based in Bermuda but ultimately controlled in Luxembourg by the Said Trust.

I later met Wafiq Said and his partner, the managing director of Sifcorp, Dr Zaid Idilby, through Alan Curtis (a close associate of the Thatchers and a key man in the financing of British arms exports, operating from a suite at the Savoy Hotel in London) when putting together the finance for our acquisition of PRB.

Said has homes in Monaco, London (in Regents Park), Paris, Marbella and Riyadh, but takes his English connections especially seriously. He is a director of the Royal Shakespeare Company and a benefactor of Oxford University. It has been reported that in 1989 he was a guest with his wife at No. 10, at a dinner in aid of Thatcher's old Oxford college, Somerville, and was a regular visitor to No. 10 during the Thatcher years, on occasions taking Mark shooting or playing golf on Prince Bandar's estate in Oxfordshire.[45]

At the time of Al Yamamah, Said was acting as Saudi agent for British Aerospace, the main contractor. The commissions that he and Mark Thatcher are alleged to have administered are not in themselves illegal in Britain, though they would be in America and Saudi Arabia. That is one reason why Britain is such a good place to conduct arms business.

The memo was the first documentary 'evidence' to implicate Mark Thatcher in handling commissions on Al Yamamah and that the Tory Party was a beneficiary, and was taken seriously enough by Rooker for him to send it to Mark's mother, writing, 'I think it is in your interest, as Prime Minister, to be aware of the allegations which are being made about yourself, members of your family and your Party in the attached document.'

Margaret Thatcher's curt response was that she had put it in the hands of 'the appropriate authorities', and Rooker never heard anything more.

I was introduced to Mark Thatcher in the company of his

father, Denis, and an Arab business associate, at the Army Air
Corps show in Middle Wallop in 1988. It was only a brief meeting,
there was nothing particularly significant about it. Only later,
after my dealings with Alan Curtis and Wafiq Said brought me
into the circle known as the Savoy Mafia, would I begin to suspect
just how deeply involved Mark was through his 'front man'
Stephen Tipping.

I formed no particular impression on meeting Mark. We were
introduced by Richard Unwin, a leading force in the prime minister's Malaysian arms/Pergau Dam deal. Unwin kept saying that
if we wanted to get anywhere at Astra we must get Mark on
board – political influence, connections, etc.

Of course it was this aspect that encouraged all the financiers
and middlemen to put up with him. Mark offered them a direct
line to the Prime Minister, his mother, and he depended wholly on
her for his contacts and business. When she resigned, we are told,
he retired from the arms business. As assessments by the media
and his own associates suggest, his is not a personality that gives
any great confidence that he could 'facilitate' very much without
her. Sir Tim Bell, Mark's unofficial public relations man, represented him to journalist Russell Miller as 'rather brash, rude,
brutish in the way he behaves, maybe he boasts too much but he
is basically just an ordinary bloke . . . [not] the remotest bit interesting.'

However, it also has to be acknowledged that the Saudis and
other Middle Eastern businessmen like family involvement in
deals. Mark's role in his mother's work would have appealed to
them, while for Mark himself there may not always have been
clear benefits. There is a moment in the former Israeli Intelligence
officer Ari Ben-Menashe's book, *The Profits of War*, when he
describes a meeting with Mark Thatcher and Carlos Cardoen in
Cardoen's office in Santiago, that suggests a certain pathos lurking beneath his make-up, and one must question what it must
have been like to have a mother such as Margaret Thatcher,
although the circumstances of the meeting do little to warm us to
her son.

Ben-Menashe describes a trip to Cardoen to persuade him not to supply chemical weapons materials to the Iraqis:

I turned up at Cardoen's building as arranged and a secretary led me into his office where Carlos Cardoen was sitting behind his desk under the portraits of Pinochet and Saddam Hussein. There was somebody already there, a young man with his back turned towards me. He turned around, stood up, and stared at me.

'Mr Menashe,' Carlos Cardoen said, 'I'd like you to meet a friend of mine.'

The young man reached out his hand. I took it. Cardoen laughed.

'I don't believe you've met Mr Mark Thatcher,' he said. I recognised the British prime minister's son from photographs I had seen. His featureless gaze changed into a smile as he shook my hand. But I wasn't going to give him the pleasure of hearing me say that his face was familiar to me. In any case Cardoen hadn't finished his introductions.

'Mr Ben-Menashi works for the Israeli prime minister's office, and we've been talking business together,' he said.

Then, looking towards me, he added: 'Mr Thatcher is an associate and we also do business together.'

'Oh yes,' I said, 'What kind of business is that?'

'I'm just a private businessman,' said Thatcher.

'Do you have any connections with the British government?' I inquired. He seemed surprised by my question.

'Well, you know it's sometimes not very good to be related to a famous person,' he said.

I gathered he wanted to assume that I really knew who he was.

'I'm a private businessman. My mother has her job, and I have my own work.'[46]

The Jordan Package (1985) poses yet more question marks. Central to the mechanics of the initial £275m package was a management deal awarded to IMS, and variously valued at £5m and 5 per cent of total contracts to be placed with British manufacturers.

A defence industry report suggests that between £75m and £100m of funds processed for the Jordan Package, with ECGD backing, of course, by a group of banks led by Morgan Grenfell and supported by Schroeders, were never accounted for by actual contracts.

(Midland is said to have played a central role in the provision of commercial money, and it is interesting to note that before the management strategy with IMS and banking arrangements were implemented, but at the time they would have been worked out, Sir John Cuckney was both chairman of IMS, the controller contractor, and a director of Midland Bank, the principal commercial funder.)

The lingering question, however, is where did the unaccounted for money go?

Reference has earlier been made (p. 58) to the admission by ECGD that they erroneously dealt out £83m of public money to businesses, and that Robert Sheldon, chairman of the Public Accounts Committee, has admitted the total may be much more, though they can't be sure because the paperwork is missing. One cannot but be struck by the similarity in the size of the sum missing out of ECGD and the funds paid out on the Jordan Package but not accounted for in actual contracts.

These extraordinary payments by ECGD are supposed to have come to the attention of ECGD in 1992 when the organisation was computerised. Two officials have been reprimanded, but Mr Brian Willott, chief executive of ECGD, concluded in a statement to the *Independent* published on 25 January 1995, 'that this is the extent of the disciplinary action that is appropriate.'

In the arms trade, payments against non-existent contracts point to covert trade where the paperwork is necessarily, for the sake of secrecy, incomplete. By way of example, Tim Kelsey has pointed out in the *Independent* that in the export licensing paperwork for a contract drawn in 1987 by Allivane (the company then at the centre of the covert trade to Iraq) there are three anomalies which suggest 'evidence of either DTI incompetence or complicity' in the trade.

The contract was drawn by Allivane with Saudi Arabia for the supply of 155mm ammunition. The first oddity Mr Kelsey noted is that the licence allowed the export of 30,000 complete shells, whereas the Saudis had only ordered 15,000, 'as the DTI would have known from its own copy of the contract'. The second is that the licence is for complete shells, yet Allivane had undertaken only to produce two components for the shells – the fuses and propellant – and the order was in fact to be completed in Spain. Allivane did not have the capability to produce complete shells, and 'the DTI should have known and the MoD must have known'. The third and most telling anomaly is that when the DTI was asked to extend the licence by two months, Lawrence Byrne of Allivane wrote to Mr Macarthy at the Export Licensing Department saying, 'Our first consignment will be shipped 29 April 1988 and then two others in June and July/August. Yet, as Macarthy must have known from the contract, 'the legitimate Saudi contract was to be shipped in only two parts'.

What Mr Kelsey is diplomatically rehearsing here is the possibility that export licences may have been granted by the government to a company at the centre of the covert trade with Iraq for covert supplies outside the terms of any bona fide contract. It is a short passage from there to the idea that in the event of non-payment by the real end-user, taxpayers' money could be called upon through ECGD to settle for the full, legitimate and illicit parts of the project covered by the erroneous export licence for which no matching contract exists.

I have corresponded with Robert Sheldon to no avail on this matter, suggesting where an inquiry along these lines into the £83m+ missing from ECGD might lead, that the £83m would account for the missing millions from the Jordan contract.

In effect I was asking the chairman of the Public Accounts Committee to investigate the possible financing by ECGD of covert trade with Iraq with public money. Mr Sheldon refused my request, but of course his ability to mount such an inquiry would be rather limited by the 'unfortunate' absence of ECGD paperwork. (see p. 58). When I drew Mr Sheldon's attention to information I had received that Astra's name had been used to 'legitimise' the use of public funds to pay for another covert contract within the Jordan package (see p. 101), a propellant contract for which we did not even have a capability at the time, it made no difference to his attitude. No one, it seems, wants to handle this 'hot potato' of the ECGD's missing millions.

In the hunt for where the hidden perks for these massive ECGD sponsored arms deals ended up, journalists have been struck by the number of arms-related donors to Tory Party funds and the extraordinary amounts of money that were sloshing around various Tory fund bank accounts during the years marked, more than by anything else, by Mrs Thatcher's huge government-to-government arms deals. One of the most dogged investigations was undertaken by *Business Age* magazine and published, with impunity I might add, in February and May 1993.

Business Age discovered slush funds abroad at one time totalling almost £200m. Where were the donations coming from? How had the slush funds accumulated?

Even within the Party, questions had been asked about 'the black hole at the heart of Tory finances'. Two groups in particular, the Charter Movement and the Party Reform Steering Group, met with constant 'stone-walling' by the Party treasurer Lord McAlpine, the man whose company had sponsored the National Association for Freedom (NAFF) that helped Thatcher to power.

McAlpine was effective treasurer of the Conservative Party from 1975 to 1990. His first title was deputy treasurer. He resigned briefly in 1985 and then returned. He returned 'because,' as the magazine put it, 'he knew where the bodies were buried. No one else could do the job. Mark Thatcher in isolation has done nothing illegal. Nor has Wafiq Said. It is Margaret Thatcher and Lord McAlpine who stand accused of having wronged Britain and corrupted the political process . . . Lord McAlpine made Britain's party of government the creature of foreign rulers, foreign arms dealers, property speculators, and tax dodgers on a grand scale.'[47]

Donations to Party funds are channelled sometimes via British United Industrialists (BUI) into a series of 'river companies', so called because they were named after British rivers. One of them, Bourne Association Ltd, owns the lease on the Conservative Party offices at 32 Smith Square.

William Gosselin Trower set up the 'river companies' in 1949. Their registered office is at 6 New Square, Lincoln's Inn, which is the address of Trowers & Hamlins, whose role in Astra's story will be discussed in due course.

Business Age identified three slush funds, the most significant of which was managed by N.M. Rothschild from London. There is a certain irony, if that is all that it is, in an apparently Zionist bank working so closely with a party bent on an economic strategy dependent on arms sales to Arabs. Rothschilds were also in charge of the privatising of Royal Ordnance.

In 1988 a Rothschild-managed fund accounted for almost £200m of unaccounted-for donations. It was lodged in a Rothschild subsidiary on Grand Cayman island until media investigations, particularly by the *Sunday Times* in 1990, caused its removal to a Rothschild-managed account in Switzerland.

Meanwhile accounts of funds at home showed millions of pounds of unaccounted donations flowing through Party coffers – in 1992, £17.9m, and £71m all told between 1985 and 1993, the key years.

'Why arms dealers in particular should indirectly subsidise the Conservative Party is open to conjecture,' mused the magazine. They listed various arms-related donors, including 'Asil Nadir (£1.5million)', who has taken refuge in Cyprus from charges relating to Polly Peck brought by the Serious Fraud Office, and 'arms dealer' John Latsis, the Greek shipping and oil magnate, 'whose name has become a Greek byword for sharp practice'. He contributed £2m in 1991.

I can vouch for Asil Nadir's involvement in the arms trade. I have a letter on file from Panton Corbett of the merchant bank

Singer and Friedlander advising me as chairman of Astra in 1983 to go and see Asil Nadir because he was heavily involved with the Turkish government on arms supplies; if we wanted any new contracts, perhaps he could help us get them. One man who has been linked with Nadir is Lord Erskine of Rerrick. Lord Erskine was also involved with the Conservative Industrial Fund.

Among various donations from sources related to the 'arms-hungry' Chinese government, the single largest has come from Beijing's billionaire Li Ka Shing 'former representative on the board of the Hong Kong and Shanghai Bank, a member of the Chinese parliament, the People's Assembly, and the chief Western agent for Chinese state arms manufacturer Norinco'. Incidentally, the Chinese government had a 25 per cent stake via Li Ka Shing in the Hong Kong and Shanghai Bank – the bank that met no resistance from Thatcher's government when it acquired Midland, the British bank at the heart of the arms industry in the 1980s.

BCCI, the bank which laundered a vast amount of the dodgy arms money, was also a donor to the Party. Was there any donation which the Tory Party did not think suitable? Sir Brian Wyldbore-Smith, for twenty-two years director of the Conservative Board of Finance, told the *Sunday Times*: 'I don't think a cheque has ever been refused.'

Far Eastern countries, important as arms conduits to the Middle East, figure highly among donors to a Party which seems to find no conflict in combining fund-raising activities with British diplomatic missions. 'Party fund-raisers have been present on at least 16 different ministerial missions to Hong Kong, China and Taiwan' between 1988 and 1992. It is a short way from national to party to personal interests, and the phrase that comes most readily to mind is one used by Mark Thatcher when he travelled to Hong Kong in an international effort, after the party was over, to coerce beneficiaries of his mother's arms policy, among others, to donate money to the Thatcher Foundation. 'It's pay-up for mumsie time!' he was widely reported to have said.

*

Another aspect of these arms deals, which sits alongside the apparent nepotism of Mark Thatcher's case, was alluded to in February 1994 by the Labour MP Alan Williams when he pointed to what he termed the 'striking coincidence' that Thatcher's former foreign affairs adviser, Sir Charles Powell, and her public relations consultant, Sir Tim Bell, 'two of the most active supporters of her Malaysian arms/Pergau dam deal' are now involved with companies which have benefited substantially from it. Powell, who had been kept on in the Cabinet office for five months after Thatcher's resignation to put the mess into some sort of administrative order, is now non-executive director of Trafalgar House, lead contractor in Pergau and of course the Oman deal, where its subsidiary Cementation plays and played such a prominent part. In spite of his position, Powell was not called to give evidence at the Inquiry into Pergau.

Sir Tim is PR Consultant of Trafalgar House and of the Malaysian offshoot of GEC which is supplying the turbines at Pergau and is the recipient of a £235m arms contract from Malaysia in conjunction with British Aerospace.[48]

On 13 February 1994, the *Independent on Sunday* led with a story that taxpayers' money was being used, through the aid budget, to benefit a small number of companies with links to the government and the Conservative party:

> A handful of leading building and engineering companies . . . have been the main beneficiaries of Britain's industrial overseas aid programme . . . Directors of five companies sit on the little known Whitehall committees which form and direct overseas aid policy . . . The companies with an inside track on aid are led by Balfour Beatty, the joint contractor on the Pergau dam project in Malaysia. Its parent company, BICC, has since 1980 given £90,000 to Aims for Industry, British United Industrialists and the Economic League – all right-wing groups closely allied to the Tory party . . . The select group of companies also includes GEC, Amec, Biwater and Davy. Among them, these five have taken 42.5 per cent of the £1.37bn aid and trade

budget since 1978. During that period, GEC has given at least £100,000 to the Tory party.

The Pergau deal is riddled with all kinds of corruption which has been bandied about in the newspapers. We read in the *Sunday Times* (20.2.1994) that 'Wimpey, the British construction giant, was involved in negotiating "special payments" to politicians in Malaysia . . . Confidential documents show that an initial payment of $50,000 was approved for payment to a middle man, who was to pay it into nominated "account numbers in Switzerland" for a team of politicians in Malaysia which was helping Wimpey win the contract.' Allegations were also made in the House of Commons that other contractors paid £35m 'in "bribes and backhanders" to win the Pergau contract'. The Malaysian response was the banning of future public sector dealings with British companies until the *Sunday Times* apologised for the slur.[49]

Whatever anyone may think about the principle of using aid to sweeten arms deals – Michael Meacher MP, for example, deplored the 'ruthless hijacking' of the aid budget to conclude arms sales, while Alan Clark described it as a 'soft loan that went to support the construction of a dam from which civil engineering companies benefited' – the Pergau deal certainly cannot be said to come under the heading of charitable work on behalf of an impoverished Third World country.

The Malaysian government made millions out of it. One year after we agreed to give them the £234m for the hydro-electric dam at Pergau, they put the main beneficiary of the aid, its own Tenaga Nasional Berhad, up for sale. The share issue raised £700m. Those in Britain who knew the aid package was a trade-off for an arms deal, and thought they could justify it on economic grounds, might be surprised to learn that the British taxpayer had facilitated a killing for investors on the Stock Market.[50]

A study of aid-for-arms deals revealed that in addition to Pergau and the Indonesia Package (see p. 62), aid to Thailand increased 625 per cent from 1980 to 1992–3, and the country became the sixth largest importer of British arms in the same period. Aid to Ecuador increased 157 per cent and it became the fifth biggest importer. Figures given for Nigeria, Jordan and Oman were equally worrying – 'We believe there is strong evidence,' the investigation concluded, 'that there may well be a link between countries that are major buyers of equipment, and unexpected increases in British aid. Questions have to be asked.'[51]

The study is bound to raise the question as to when a 'soft loan' becomes a bribe. In early February 1994, *The Economist* contended that the £234m aid for the Pergau dam was linked by 'a mathematical formula' to the £1.3bn arms deal, which would contravene the Overseas Aid Acts. Aid-for-arms is but one example of the way the political interests of the country have been hijacked for the financial benefit of a few.

In 1986 the media covered the row between Margaret Thatcher and Michael Heseltine over Westland, the British helicopter firm, as though it was all about who should rescue an ailing British company. The American company Sikorsky, owned by United Technologies, was Thatcher's choice. Agusta, an Italian helicopter company, was pro-European Heseltine's choice.

In fact the row was really about Thatcher's Al Yamamah deal, and which company was to participate in the spoils. The argument culminated, in the year Al Yamamah I was signed, with Thatcher getting her own way and Michael Heseltine resigning as Secretary of State for Defence.

As I have mentioned, Astra was subsequently invited by Westland to tender for a contract to weaponise the one hundred Blackhawk helicopters to be built by Westland from technology supplied by Sikorsky for Al Yamamah. The customer's stipulation for the helicopters to be armed with American weapons was what brought us into the picture. They wanted the Hydra 70, a BEI 20mm rocket system, and the GECAL 50, a Gatling gun which we were building under licence from General Electric of USA at our BMARC plant in Grantham, plus the Hellfire anti-tank missile from Rockwell.

The argument between Thatcher and Heseltine had been

about who was going to provide the technology for the manufacturing of the helicopters for this and subsequent parts of Al
Yamamah. Thatcher's success in getting the deal for Sikorsky
seems, on the face of it, to have been just another example of the
way the US and UK worked together to beat Congressional limitations on arms supplies to the Middle East. The Americans were
not allowed to supply the helicopters direct, so Thatcher, who
had moved Sir John Cuckney into position as chairman of
Westland, arranged for the US company United Technologies/
Sikorsky to take a financial interest in the company, nominate
two directors, and license the British helicopter company technology to build them.

Undoubtedly this is what happened, and in sheer manufactur-.
ing terms it made sense. The Blackhawk was the better helicopter.
Agusta had manufactured under licence from Sikorsky too, but
Westland was getting the manufacturing; what was required was
the technology, which at source was Sikorsky's.

Leaving aside the dubious nature of the US/UK technology
transfer, and the fact that I discovered in December 1989 from the
Saudi Prince Mishari that the helicopter deal was not for Saudi at
all but for Iraq, there is another question mark over the deal.
Why was Thatcher and Heseltine's argument so intense?

Heseltine's position was touted as the pro-EEC answer to the
helicopter company's problems, although as we have seen it was
really about billions of pounds from Al Yamamah. If we accept the
EEC position, why did Heseltine resign? How did Agusta manage
to enlist Heseltine as such a champion of their interests, a champion so incredibly loyal that he was prepared to put his job as
Secretary of State for Defence on the line for a company in
another country, albeit part of the EEC? Equally, why was
Thatcher prepared to lose Heseltine's services rather than forgo
the US deal?

I offer three footnotes to the saga.

(i) Negotiations with Astra over weaponising the helicopters
     commenced just before the Iran–Iraq war finished, and this

particular contract never went forward. Not long after, Iraq tried to get Bell helicopters via Cardoen in Chile as a partial substitute for what they would have got via Saudi had the Westland deal gone through. The Bell helicopter deal was the one which Jonathan Moyle claimed was being equipped for Saddam Hussein with Helios, Britain's electronic guidance system for anti-tank missiles.

(ii) Evidence of bribery involving the Italian company Agusta was uncovered by Judge Veronique Ancia in Brussels when she began an inquiry into the murder of André Cools, the former government minister who had been investigating allegations of government corruption following our purchase of PRB. Later, the Socialist Deputy prime minister, Guy Coeme, Guy Spittaels, and Guy Mathot, the Walloon Interior Minister, resigned over allegations that Agusta paid bribes to secure a defence contract worth £2bn arranged in 1988.

(iii) In 1992 Thomas Dooley, a former Lieutenant-Colonel, sued Westland Group plc and Westland Helicopters Ltd, and his employers Sikorsky Aircraft and their owners United Technology Corporation, for $130m damages for wrongful demotion. He claimed that he had been demoted after threatening to reveal a conspiracy to bribe Princes Khalid bin Sultan and Fahad bin Sultan, sons of the Saudi defence minister Prince Sultan, in order to secure a Blackhawk helicopter deal and circumvent US export controls. As a result of my evidence to the American court in Washington in October 1992, Dooley achieved a satisfactory settlement. A consequence is that I have in my possession an internal company memo, field report notes taken between 18 and 27 April 1989, in Riyadh, written by an employee of United Technologies. Intelligence connections are implicit; the note shows real concern over, and I quote, 'Significant message traffic from UK and Wash DC *vis-à-vis* the commissions involved in AYII.'

'AYII' refers of course to Al Yamamah II. This memo concerns the Blackhawk helicopter deal in the Al Yamamah contract. The memo goes on: 'Rolls-Royce and BAe have moved approx. 4 bill US to a Saudi to delay the engine decision . . . Note: This 4 bill [sic] US was mentioned in connection with M. Thatcher's son . . . "A son of the king" is also concerned about the credibility factor for the kingdom and the alleged payoffs.'

An extract from the memo has since been shown by Dispatches on British television in a programme about Mark Thatcher. It is an extraordinary fact that whenever I show it to journalists, they never quite grasp its significance. They pick up eagerly on Mark Thatcher, of course, yet more evidence that he has been involved in commissions. What interests me is the sheer size of this payment – 4 billion dollars! I couldn't believe it at first, but it is quite clear and the figure is mentioned twice. Now, there is no company in this country, and certainly not Rolls-Royce or British Aerospace, who can put up that sort of cash to secure a deal. Such a payment can only have come from one place – the government; it was your money and mine, and it even worried the Saudis receiving it.

CHAPTER FOUR

THE CABAL

In understanding these major Thatcher-inspired arms deals it is essential to appreciate that they all involved the same companies and individuals.

Powerful and secretive, the group which dictated the whole covert policy drew its membership less from among elected politicians, than civil servants, particularly the Cabinet Office, and from Intelligence circles, industry and the City, the very forces which brought Mrs Thatcher to power. Some elected politicians are nonetheless allied to the group, where their political position or some area of mutual interest – the City, the Middle East – suggest it would prove beneficial.

Jonathan Aitken was someone who fitted into the latter category, not a member of the inner sanctum exactly, though he very much wanted to be, but one whose contacts in the Middle East later earned him an important position as Minister for Defence Procurement in the MoD at a difficult time, when the covert deals were emerging and the government under pressure needed certain key positions to be filled with those who were not 'wet behind the ears' about policy towards the Middle East.

Our registered office was in Aitken's constituency from 1981 to 1988. In the autumn of 1988, we were having discussions with him about what help he could give us to make doubly sure of our winning the opportunity to weaponise the Westland Blackhawk helicopters for the Saudis – part, you will recall, of Thatcher's Al Yamamah deal.

Aitken attended a number of meetings when the deal was discussed, and told us that he could be very helpful in relation to

Saudi Arabia in particular because of his long-standing connec-
tions with the Saudi royal family, and suggested that I fly over to
Geneva where he would introduce me to Princes Khalid and
Bandar, Wafiq Said and Sheik Al-Athel.

Aitken's offices in Upper Grosvenor Street in Mayfair were
really quite lavish, and when I commented on it, he said they
weren't his own personal offices, but those of Al-Bilad, a company
that I understood to be involved in arranging trade with the
Middle East, Saudi Arabia in particular.

When I took the trouble to have a search done on the company,
I found that Aitken was a co-director of Al-Bilad UK with the
Saudi Sheik Fahad Al-Athel, and Aitken had told me that Sheik Al-
Athel was particularly influential with the Saudi royal family in
connection with military contracts like the helicopter deal.

Wafiq Said was the government 'golden boy' at this time, having the position of link man with British Aerospace (BAe) and the
British government in the Al Yamamah project. Said is really the
linchpin in the whole Al Yamamah saga, not merely as some sort
of go-between, but as an adviser to the Saudi royal family, the
source of Saudi finance. Aitken enjoyed both a personal and a
business relationship with the man, and a close relationship with
the Saudi royal family going back many years. There is no doubt
from my investigation that the Al Yamamah deal was originally a
main conduit for Iraq arms supplies.

Said controlled, through his company Sifcorp and another
company, based I believe in Geneva, approx. 30 per cent of Aitken
Hume, a public company of which Aitken was then chairman.
Said had come to the rescue when Aitken and his cousins had got
involved disastrously with TV AM. They had hired Anna Ford,
Angela Rippon, Peter Jay and Michael Parkinson and so on, and
got into financial difficulties, too dire for the family bank, Aitken
Hume, to resolve alone. Aitken never disclosed the Saudi interest to
anybody. Eventually he was rumbled and had to resign from TV
AM, which created a lot of embarrassment and adverse publicity.

Later, in April 1992, Dr Zaid Idilby (an old friend of Said's
from Syria and the director of Sifcorp I dealt with there) became

chairman of Aitken Hume through Sifcorp's 30 per cent stake, following Aitken's relinquishing of the chair when he was appointed Minister for Defence Procurement. Until approximately January 1992 Aitken Hume and Sifcorp shared the Sifcorp address at Old Park Lane. It was in fact Aitken Hume's West End office.

Wafiq Said and the Saudi sheik Fahad Al-Athel were in fact about as close as you could get to the Saudi royal family, and Aitken assured me that Sheik Al-Athel would be the person to push the weaponisation of the helicopter on our behalf. He advised that we shouldn't leave it to Westland and Sikorsky to get the work and subcontract it to Astra, but should establish ourselves independently with the royal family to ensure that Astra got the deal. The way to do that, he advised, and to see if we could pick up some of the many other projects that were coming out of Saudi at the time, would be to join him at the Geneva Hilton and meet them.

It was September 1988 and I stayed in fact at the Hotel Bergues, which lies on the edge of the lake, a few hundred yards nearer the centre of the town than the Hilton. I spent two days there and didn't meet anyone. Aitken kept saying, 'I'm afraid they are too busy', when I turned up for lunch, which I eventually had with Aitken and his wife – 'They're tied up.' I went off and filled in time, took a boat trip round the lake and so on, only to hear once more that the time was not right. It was an extraordinary way to carry on, and I eventually decided to pack up and go back to London.

All this time Aitken had been pressing me to invite him to become a director on the Astra main board, but after the débâcle in Geneva we agreed only that he could come on to the board of our subsidiary, BMARC, which he duly did in September 1988. It is interesting that prior to our purchase of BMARC, Aitken wished to be only our MP, not even a consultant. His coming onto the BMARC board was never to our advantage. I deputed him to seek contracts in Saudi Arabia, but he achieved nothing; we didn't even get a whiff of a contract. Yet Aitken's involvement with the arms trade has always intrigued me, as however ineffectual he

may have been for Astra, there is no doubt that he was close to the
nerve centre of what was going on.

One of the minutes from BMARC board meetings recently
released, in fact minute 3.8 of a meeting held on 2 November
1988, reads: 'Mr Aitken proposed that a presentation should be
arranged to be made in Saudi Arabia during January 1989, products to be as selected by BMARC . . . Consideration given to
question – which countries are financially assisted with their
defence budgets by Saudi Arabia? . . . The agent acting for Mr
Aitken, [who] pulled off the Vosper contract, is ambitious and is
working hard at establishing relationships.'

The agent for the Vosper contract – for three minesweepers
built by Southampton shipbuilders Vosper Thorneycroft as part of
Al Yamamah – was Sheik Al-Athel, Aitken's co-director at Al-Bilad
UK.

Again, Aitken Hume supplied a non-executive director, Stewart
Twentyman-Graham (a former general manager at Midland
Bank), to Sheffield Forgemasters, one of the two British companies
that built the tubes of Gerald Bull's Supergun. Aitken Hume were
also financial advisers to Walter Somers, the other Supergun manufacturer. The other connection of Aitken with Supergun was of
course Astra, whose subsidiary PRB was the Supergun propellant
manufacturer – an extraordinary coincidence. Such a close
involvement with the companies in the Iraqi Supergun affair by
the man who was later to be made Minister for Defence
Procurement for the government would seem an extraordinary
situation, unless, after the party was over, it was advisable from
the government's point of view to keep knowledge in as few hands
as possible.

Whether Margaret Thatcher was herself at the real centre of
power as the leader of this inner group cannot be said for certain.
However, she was more concerned for the group's freedom to act
than any other prime minister in history.

Junior ministers such as Alan Clark and William Waldegrave
appear more as 'fall guys' in its strategy, as their squabbling like
public schoolboys in the commonroom obviously showed, as they

tried under questioning at the Scott Inquiry to pass each other the buck on a policy which had been given them to rubber stamp.

When, on the other hand, we listened to Sir Robin Butler (Cabinet Secretary) attempting at the same Inquiry actually to redefine human concepts of truth in his defence, and Thatcher presenting the, for her, extraordinary persona of pussycat, alarm bells should have started ringing in the minds of the public, and did in the minds of some newspaper editors, who demanded that Scott turn his investigations towards the most accessible body of the cabal – the businessmen and financiers in the City.

Scott's response was that 'if businessmen are in a position to assist with evidence about relevant matters, their evidence is being, and will be, obtained', but the key players were not called to give evidence and, as the *Guardian* pointed out, 'Written statements and replies to questionnaires are scarcely sufficient. Only cross-examination at public hearings of leading businessmen engaged in the arms trade . . . will reveal the truth.'[1]

I detailed what I regarded to be a proper inquiry to Robert Sheldon MP, chairman of the Public Accounts Committee, in a letter on 25 November 1994: 'it would have to include . . . all the records of IMS, Royal Ordnance . . . and other companies involved with the Propellant and Arms cartels. It would also be necessary to look at the secret and detailed records of ECGD and the records of the government Intelligence agencies like MI5, MI6, GCHQ, as well as those of the MoD, DTI, FCO and the various arms export control committees and bodies. In addition the detailed and secret records of Midland Bank and its arms department, MITS, Morgan Grenfell and other bankers involved.'

Scott's failure to investigate the City/political connection was always bound to lead to a charge of inadequacy, as Michael Meacher MP wrote in a letter to the *Guardian* in June 1994: 'Only cross-examination at public hearings of . . . Sir John Cuckney, Sir James Blyth, Mr Stephan Adolph Kock, Sir Colin Chandler, Sir Peter Levene, and representatives of the Midland Bank International Trading Finance Department – will reveal the truth of what arms were traded and when, how the deals were set up, what was the role of the intelligence services, what commissions were paid and to whom, and which politicians and civil servants authorised this trading.'

The Connection between the Cabal and the City

The cabal needs the City to finance its deals and launder its funds. BCCI, the London-based Bank of Credit and Commerce International, which was given its more appropriate appellation, 'Bank of Crooks and Criminals International', by CIA Chief Robert Gates, was exposed after its crash in 1991 as a laundering operation for the British and Middle Eastern intelligence services and others. BCCI Cayman Island accounts were used by MI6 to fund arms sales to Iraq, and the bank backed BNL loans to Iraq, masquerading as 'agricultural credits', at the unheard of rate of 0.5%.[2]

The passage of officers from British Intelligence to the City is a common enough occurrence and, as we have seen in the case of Sir John Cuckney (ex-MI5) and the crash of Liverpool Docks, where there were political overtones involved, such men are especially welcome. When Thatcher militarised the economy of Britain, they – and Cuckney in particular – came into their own. Once in a City position, these men maintain their Intelligence connections. That is the purpose. Ideally, like Cuckney again, they build up political connections. It is in this mix of City, Intelligence and politics that is constituted the profile of the cabal.

The Connection between Intelligence and the City

Firms like Kleinwort Benson, where George Kennedy Young worked after retiring as deputy head of MI6, and Morgan Grenfell have had their Intelligence associations for years, as have Hambros, Schroeders, Rothschilds and Barings. While I was at Hill Samuel, two former private secretaries to Churchill were employed – Jock Colville and Sir Philip de Zuluetta. Peter Middleton, chief executive of Lloyds of London, came out of the Foreign Office and MI6, and has worked for the International Division of Midland Bank. His career development is not wholly typical, however; he started off as a Roman Catholic monk.[3]

I have discussed the purpose of the Midland Bank Group International Trade Services (MITS). Midland Bank was a veritable junction box of the UK establishment's arms dealings during the Iran–Iraq war – it handed over £1bn worth of credits from the mid-'80s on, and it has a history of connections with the Intelligence services that goes back a long time. Under the chairmanship of former Cabinet Secretary Lord Armstrong, who had been wartime head of MI5, Sir John Cuckney was hired and MITS was the product of the mix. The bank's overseas representatives were frequently also spies. Among them in Armstrong's time was a man called Dennis Skinner, who had no banking experience but had undertaken front-line undercover work for MI6 in Moscow, while working for ICL. In 1983, Skinner tumbled through the fifth floor window of his flat and fell to his death on Leninsky Prospekt. He had discovered a KGB 'mole' in the British embassy, but his fears for his own safety had been put down to paranoia and excessive drinking. After his death, not a trace of alcohol was found in his blood. In fact, Skinner had been sufficiently in command of himself to have given up both drink and cigarettes some while before.[4]

It is a convention born out of an obvious requirement for security that agents of this sort 'don't exist'. Few at the bank, if anyone other than Armstrong, had known of Skinner's existence, and no doubt Skinner when alive would have denied knowing Armstrong. This is a relationship between Intelligence operative and City boss that I came to know particularly well in the case of one of our own directors at Astra, recommended to us by Midland from MITS, while Sir John Cuckney was a director of the bank. All that remained after Skinner's body had been removed was a note found in the drawer of his desk, which confirmed that he was an employee of Midland Bank.

The Relationship between Intelligence and Politics

Stephen Dorril tells us that when, in July 1961, Cabinet Secretary
Norman Brook failed to pass to the Prime Minister information
about War Minister John Profumo's affair with Christine Keeler (a
friend of KGB officer Eugene Ivanov), 'Harold Wilson stumbled on
a crucial secret, namely the fact that the Cabinet Office, not the
Prime Minister's office, had overall control of the security service
and, crucially, the overall flow of information': putting the real
power into the hands of permanent rather than elected government.[5]

Intelligence about arms comes from intercepted communications, MI6 agents and informers, embassy officials, and arms
dealers. Robin Robison, former administrative officer for the Joint
Intelligence Committee (JIC) responsible for disseminating that
information, has put on record that GCHQ arms-deal information
goes via JIC to the Bank of England, the DTI, FCO, MoD and
ECGD, but is rarely passed into the parliamentary arena.
Robison's job was to sift through transcripts of bugged telephone
calls and other intercepted material for inclusion in JIC's 'Red
Book' before its distribution.[6]

'Although the Director-General [MI5] has a right to direct
access to the Prime Minister, he does not lightly go over the heads
of permanent under-secretaries for fear of creating future problems,' writes one former intelligence officer. Ex-Deputy Chief of
MI6, George Kennedy Young, admitted that, when it comes to
keeping the Prime Minister informed, the Cabinet Secretary may
conveniently fail to find an 'opportune moment' to pass the baton
of power from permanent to elected government.[7]

Dorril and Ramsay quote another security source saying that
the Home Secretary 'hasn't got a clue what is going on. If he
comes around, you lock away any sensitive files and set up a display file specially for him to look at – a spoof file on some
imaginary subversive with lots of exciting material in it. He's not
going to know any better.'[8]

Lurking behind the argument for the non-accountability of

the Intelligence services Dorril seems to detect a pseudo-patriotic appeal to the monarchy. 'Tinkerbell', the services' phone-tapping service operated with British Telecom, is regularly justified as an exercise of Royal Prerogative. Again, every week the Queen receives JIC reports while our own ministers remain relatively in the dark. We are told that Her Majesty makes useful comments on these, and it may be that her comments are more useful than those that might be forthcoming from ministers, but I believe that many ordinary people, brainwashed by the tabloids into thinking that the purpose of the Royal Family is to offer entertainment along the lines of soap opera, would be surprised to learn about this system of disbursement of information vital to government, and they might, on reflection, consider that its continuance a) benefited most the security services bent on safeguarding their independence through non-accountability, b) is out of kilter with a democratic constitution, and/or c) that it is open to abuse, which, as I will explain, in the case of intelligence information about covert arms sales during Iran–Iraq war, it most definitely was.[9]

It was a main plank of Margaret Thatcher's 'defence' at the Scott Inquiry that she didn't receive information; that she was unaware of intelligence reports that British machinery was being used to build up Iraq's indigenous arms industry.

In actual fact, just as she kept in touch with government departmental decisions, so she made it her business, even before becoming Prime Minister, to be wholly informed by the Intelligence services so that she could maintain a hand in its operation.

If most prime ministers take up office without much or indeed any knowledge of the security services, in Thatcher's case she was briefed by people associated with Brian Crozier's Institute for the Study of Conflict even as leader of the Opposition during Jim Callaghan's government. Maurice Oldfield, head of MI6, and Dickie Franks, Oldfield's successor, both of whom were involved with the Pinay Circle, with its unique blend of political and security service personnel, also kept her closely informed.

Not only was she uniquely accustomed to moving in such well-informed intelligence circles when she came to Downing Street, after she arrived she became the first Prime Minister to insist that she sit in on the highly secret Joint Intelligence Committee meetings. Far from being ill-informed she did her utmost while in office to harness the effective power of intelligence to her purpose – even to the point of insisting on a direct line between MI5 and her office.[10]

In *Smear*, Dorril and Ramsay tell the story of how Harold Wilson was dogged by the activities of Intelligence to disrupt his government. But the services were bound to the political purposes of Mrs Thatcher's Tory government from the start. In the 1984 miners' strike, under the cloak of 'national security', GCHQ and the US National Security Agency were used to trace the movement of National Union of Miners' funds and eventually, as has recently been confirmed on television, Intelligence mounted a concerted effort to smear Arthur Scargill, president of the NUM, which secured victory for Thatcher but which was based on the utterly false charges of the diversion of Soviet funds to the NUM, support from Libya, and actual embezzlement.

These revelations bring meaning to a statement by David Hart, who was a friend of William Casey, former director of the CIA, and who, as official adviser to National Coal Board chairman Sir Ian MacGregor, became part of Thatcher's inner circle and in close contact in particular with Sir Percy Cradock, chair of JIC – 'Thatcher's told me so much,' Hart said, 'I could blow her out of the water in five minutes.' Ironically, Hart was the son of my managing director, Boy Hart, while I was a director of Ansbacher.[11]

Like so many of those of the faithful who knew too much and were employed to maintain 'continuity' in departments sensitive to criticism, David Hart was subsequently employed as assistant to the Secretary of State for Defence, Malcolm Rifkind, who was similarly rewarded for his loyalty as Secretary of State for Scotland (see p. 101).

In November 1989 William Waldegrave published a Whitehall

guide called 'Central Intelligence Machinery', which identified Sir Robin Butler as the official with ultimate responsibility for 'intelligence and security matters overall'. As Douglas Hurd admitted to the Foreign Affairs Committee the Cabinet Office, or Cabinet Intelligence Unit, collates intelligence from MI6, MI5, GCHQ, etc. for the JIC. In the context of the Scott Inquiry, as Cabinet Secretary and Head of the Home Civil Service, Sir Robin stood at the crossroads where public interest and the accountability of 'permanent government' meet, and he did not fare well.[12]

Scott told him that he was dismayed that vital documents seemed to be being withheld by Butler's office. Later Butler sought sanctuary in the diplomatic merits of half-truth – half an answer could be accurate and was sometimes necessary, and he gave Scott an example: the Government statement that 'negotiations were not being undertaken with the IRA', was both accurate and not false (the government was in fact negotiating with Sinn Fein). 'This was an answer which was true but not complete,' he said, and maintained, more curiously still, that 'it was not designed to mislead.' Why else the statement had been made remains a mystery.

The whole truth, it appears, is a luxury the Cabinet Secretary cannot afford. He can deal only in its negative values, that is 'what is not false'. He must operate in a world cut off from the absolute moral root of law because – and this is his point – truth is deemed not to be in the public interest.

In this, Sir Robin was of course following the example of his predecessor, Lord Armstrong, who admitted at the 'Spycatcher' trial to having been 'economical with the truth'. The relationship between 'truth' and 'the public interest' is really what my book is about.

Drawing a comparison between attitudes in 1994 (the time of the Scott Inquiry) and 1963 (the time of the Profumo scandal), the commentator Hugo Young saw one big difference, that by 1994 corruption had spread from Parliament into the civil service, that is into 'permanent government'. 'In 1963 . . . Sir Norman Brook, cabinet secretary and head of the civil service, presided over men of loft and rigour, far removed from the degradations of Westminster . . . Brook's modern heir, Sir Robin Butler, personified a different world.'[13]

If so, the democratic process itself is under dire threat, for what does it matter whom the public elects to office if 'permanent government' is in charge and rotten to the core?

David Cornwell, who writes as John le Carré, with direct experience of the workings of the security services, has mentioned the 'natural intimacy between the secret services and the Conservative Party.' If so, and Tony Blair has not changed his party at root, he too may have a difficult ride. Were Labour to win the next election, 'the secret services would be cuddling up with the Conservative Party in exile day and night.'

In the light of recent media coverage and the appearance in Tony Blair's entourage of Alan Judd, perhaps one can detect the process of assessment already in action.

In April 1989 the *Daily Telegraph* described the novelist Alan Judd as 'formerly of the Foreign Office where his duties were not incompatible with those of a spy.' '"Judd",' states the December 1994 issue of *Lobster*, the journal which studies the security and Intelligence services, less circumspectly, 'is a serving MI6 officer called Alan Edwin Petty . . . A graduate of Oxford University, he joined MI6 in 1975.

1975	Second (later First) Secretary, FCO
1980	Consul, Johannesburg
1980–	FCO
1988	On leave to write biography of Ford Madox Ford
1990–	First Secretary, FCO'

ISC Ferranti provides a fair working model of the power exercised by the cabal in Britain in the 1980s, and the in-built security net for those who play to its tune.

In 1987 Ferranti, Britain's third largest defence contractor at the time, purchased for £450m Jim Guerin's ISC, which British Intelligence was aware had been side-stepping US arms exports controls by means of its London base and fronting a covert CIA operation on behalf of South Africa and Iraq from 1984, when all such sales to South Africa were outlawed until 1991. No merger of this kind could have gone through without the sanction of the military and Intelligence establishments, and the Ferranti directors have avowed that it did have their support.

In September 1989 ISC Ferranti collapsed with the loss of 30,000 jobs (80,000, including sub-contractors).

Three ISC contracts current before the 1987 Ferranti deal went through were cited as the underlying reason for the company's collapse, all of them for a precision guided-missile system known as PGM, developed in South Africa by Armscor and capable of carrying a missile with a nuclear or chemical warhead. Armscor was able to furnish Guerin with competitively priced components for manufacturing PGM because it was already in production itself thanks to a blueprint 'acquired' from America for the Rockwell AGB 130. This is now a matter under investigation in America.

The ISC contracts were drawn with Pakistan, China and the United Arab Emirates (UAE). The UAE contract was for a particularly sophisticated PGM system capable of carrying a nuclear or chemical warhead. Fifteen hundred of these PGMs were licensed by the British government for delivery to the UAE, which, in the words of Michael Meacher MP, left 'this small Arab country with a supply greater than that held by NATO. Since the UAE could have no strategic need for such a huge reserve, and since the order was placed when the Iran–Iraq war was still at its height, it is believed that the ultimate destination was Iraq.' There is no reason to doubt that the Foreign Office would have reached the same conclusion before granting the licence.

The contract with Pakistan was a personal deal with the President, General Zia, and died with him when Zia's plane was blown up in 1989. As regards the China contract, since the Iranians were already buying Silkworm anti-ship missiles from the Chinese, it is likely that this too was bound for Iran. All three contracts were illegal.

Now, when Derek Alun-Jones bought ISC in 1987, Ferranti was in trouble. It had failed to compete with various MoD orders and was attracted to ISC specifically because it had these enormous orders and presumably the ability to get more. Was Ferranti aware of the true nature of these ISC contracts? Certainly all the background information on ISC's sanction-busting trade with South Africa became available to the company when it bought ISC, if indeed it wasn't known already. Leaving aside these three contracts, in the light of ISC's dodgy reputation in the past, such an important company as Ferranti could only have gone ahead with the acquisition reassured by the government's support.

As for Guerin, in order to facilitate these and other major orders with Iran or Iraq, he wanted the clout with government elements of the cabal, which Ferranti undoubtedly had as a key establishment defence manufacturer. For business reasons, Guerin wanted an 'in' with the establishment.

So it was a cosy and potentially a profitable situation. In 1987 it seemed it could not fail. Guerin had read Britain's defence industry absolutely right. He was not to know that it was about to change radically. When it did, and the clean-up began, Derek Alun-Jones called up the resources available to him as part of the establishment and blew the whistle on Guerin, who, back in America, had to face trial.

Meanwhile in the UK, there was no inquiry, no inquest into the collapse of Britain's third largest defence manufacturer, no inquest into the loss of 30,000 jobs, no questions about why the British Government had supported Ferranti's purchase of ISC in the first place, and no question about the government export licences for the PGM system with a nuclear or bacteriological capability which were for Iraq. On the contrary, what happened was quite extraordinary. In a letter to the Prime Minister, John Major, Michael Meacher wrote that for six weeks before Alun-Jones blew the whistle on Guerin, Robert Shireman, ISC Ferranti's financial director, 'removed all ISC's secret records from London to the US. Neither the police nor the Serious Fraud Squad Office nor UK Customs made any attempt to stop him or to interview any ISC staff . . . I want to know why the ISC HQ in West London was not immediately sealed; why documents were removed, unimpeded, to the US; and why there was no official inquiry and no report to Parliament on the complete destruction of the country's third largest defence contractor.'

In the US they promised Guerin an easy sentence if he co-operated fully, but there was never a chance of it because he was the British and American governments' scapegoat. Jim Guerin got fifteen years – long enough to ensure that no one would be interested in his story any more.

The case of ISC Ferranti has all sorts of interesting parallels with Astra, which will become clear in the second part of this book, but the one big difference is that in Ferranti's case, the chairman was never made a victim of Thatcher's strategy of damage limitation. They homed in instead on the one who was outside the inner circle. The difference is that as part of the estab-lishment, as head of one of Britain's leading defence companies, Alun-Jones had the government's support for more than mere contracts. He was part of the elite, one of the untouchables, unlike Paul Henderson of Matrix or the Grecians at Ordtech, or Peter Mitchell at Walter Somers, or indeed myself at Astra. Alun-Jones was safe.

At Astra we operated at a different end of the industry. We were not part of the establishment, indeed we were, as an inde-pendent, treading on existing monopolies, disturbing cosy relationships which went back over years. I have tried wherever possible in this book to bring to bear independent witnesses; people like Michael Meacher, reports by other authors and inde-pendent journalists, and evidence quoted from the various inquiries into the trade with Iraq, precisely because I want to avoid the easy criticism that I am just whingeing about my own treatment at the hands of the cabal. There was a time at Astra, which I will describe, when I could have thrown my lot in with them. But I didn't. Not because of any high moral purpose but, I suspect, because I have rather an awkward streak in me and if someone comes along and says, 'Accept this', or 'Don't question that', I find it very hard to comply even if it is in my immediate interests financially.

There may be still among some sections of the public a feeling of what is the point in investigating the arms-to-Iraq scandal? It is idealistic to expect politics not to be dirty; there must be secrecy if government is to achieve anything in the world in which we live. But few of those same people would sacrifice democracy to such a principle, and that is precisely what has happened and is happening.

Implicit in the policy of the cabal is a conviction that Parliament is an out-of-date process for managing the country's affairs. Its voice, heard in Whitehall, bent the ears of even junior ministers in Mrs Thatcher's government. Alan Clark admitted at the Scott Inquiry that there is 'an understandable reluctance in Whitehall to stir up Parliament . . . The House of Commons is a very volatile place. They are a bit of a nuisance.'[14]

At Astra I saw the real consequences (to freedom, to justice and to democracy) of the exercise of such a power in its clandestine dealings both during and after the Iran–Iraq war, when the cabal sought to absolve itself from prosecution by developing a witch-hunt of independent companies it had encouraged and used.

On the face of, it the witch-hunt was unsuccessful; it resulted in the ultimately failed prosecutions of directors of Matrix Churchill, Ordtec, Euromac and Atlantic Commercial, and the abortive attempt to convict the Astra directors of fraud. What it appears to have confirmed is that British law, as presently constituted, abhors the very idea of undemocratic rule.

So what is all the fuss about? Why not leave it there? Why not sit back and say, the law is our protector, it doesn't matter what the cabal of permanent government, the City and the Intelligence services get up to, we'll be all right in the end. It's a canny system! The law won out; the cabal, the inner sanctum, failed.

But did it? Remember, the only point of the witch-hunt was to protect those in the inner sanctum. They would not waste energy on revenge. They failed to bury us, but their aim was only to

divert attention from themselves, which they did – Scott interviewed virtually none of them. The point, the reason why – in the
public interest – we cannot leave it at that, is that the cabal is still
operating, controlling and manipulating.

Already it has its feelers out into the media, which, however
tarnished, is still the last protector of our freedoms before the law.
Spooks in Fleet Street, how the cabal uses Intelligence to exert its
power over the media, is only one other example of its misuse of
power, as recent press coverage shows.

On 16 December 1994 *Private Eye* led with the story that the
television journalist and newscaster Jon Snow was approached in
January 1976 by a Mr D. Stilbury to meet him at room 055 at the
Old War Office for a meeting. Stilbury's letter began: 'I think it
just possible that you might be able to assist me with some confidential work I have in hand.' At the meeting, Stilbury promised
Snow to match his salary at LBC (£3,600) if he would provide
information about the political activities of his journalistic colleagues. The money would be paid directly into Snow's bank
account and there would be 'no problem' with the Inland
Revenue. He was further assured that the security services had no
political allegiances – 'We are as loyal to Tony Benn as we are to
Callaghan.' Snow did not accept the commission and he was told
never to contact the SIS/SS again. What one wonders is how
many of Snow's colleagues have proved more susceptible to such
an approach. 'The probability is,' concluded *Private Eye*, 'that
every main newspaper office and every main television station
employs at least one highly paid agent of the SS whose chief job
is to spy on his/her colleagues', and suggested that the recent revelation in the press that Richard Gott had made a couple of trips
twenty years ago paid for by the KGB, which MI6 had monitored
and approached Gott about in 1989 and to all intents and purposes 'cleared' him of, had suddenly emerged in the *Spectator* only
because Gott's paper, the *Guardian*, had been hounding Jonathan
Aitken, 'who has very close links with the intelligence services'.

I have been involved with a number of journalists in research-
ing this story. At any one time there might be as many as half a

dozen following up this or that line of inquiry and we keep constantly in touch by telephone. It is to our mutual benefit, except that the relationship, which has now been going on for nearly five years, has frequently been marked by sudden changes of policy by newspaper editors or the unexplained removal of a journalist from the case or even from the paper (sometimes to a more exalted position on another where the arms-to-Iraq inquiry is not part of the brief).

Aware that newspapers must of course follow the editorial policy of the day and that journalists have lives to lead which, unlike mine, do not, whether I like it or not, revolve around this subject twenty-four hours a day, it never really surprised me until I was amazed to receive, from one of my other sources, a list of journalists with affiliations to MI5, on which were posted some of my own contacts in the press, indeed some who had at the beginning made something of a name for themselves on the back of the arms-to-Iraq affair.

The truth is that there is no flag to march behind any more. The public image is that the arms business is beyond the pale, but I found most business corrupt to some extent. There is much more national politics in the arms business and of course that leads to a greater degree of duplicity and crookedness. In government-related business, there is a greater acceptance of duplicity dressed up as the national interest. There is a degree of hypocrisy in the arms trade which doesn't exist elsewhere, certainly, but it is largely government-inspired.

What is needed is a bill of rights like they have in America, where people are not governed by the whims of ministers able to manipulate acts of Parliament and doctor reports and give work to their friends in the City. We want a totally open system of government, as far as it can be achieved. In the cases which have come to court, the government has perverted the course of justice.

A system of government is required where the law is divorced from government interest (which in theory it is supposed to be but in practice isn't), open government where select committees can examine people properly without any inhibitions, a system where 'national interest' is no longer uncontested as a defence against open government.

For example, the Public Accounts Committee produced a report on Mrs Thatcher's Al Yamamah deal which has been suppressed by the Auditor-General, Sir John Bourn, on the grounds of national security/national interest, and also on the grounds of damaging British industry, because if the true facts were revealed, the companies would lose business. But this is also to hide massive corruption charges, some of the worst to hit this country. I don't think that can be tolerated. Members of the Public Accounts Committee were 'furious at not being trusted to see even an edited version of the report'.[15]

Also, the report was suppressed by a man, Bourn, who was Deputy Under-Secretary for Defence Procurement in the MoD at the very time of the negotiation of Al Yamamah and other Thatcher defence deals. It really won't do.

They will say, 'Oh, he wasn't involved directly in the negotiations of Al Yamamah,' but not only was he there at the time, his active interest in and acquaintance with defence survived his appointment on 4 January 1988 as Comptroller and Auditor-General. In the summer of the same year he flew in by helicopter at the invitation of his friend, Stephan Kock, a non-executive director of Astra, to visit BMARC at our expense. On other occasions, again following his appointment, Bourn met with and advised both Chris Gumbley and me on government defence policy. How can such a man be put into an impartial position of judgement, the essence of the role of Auditor-General, on a case involving allegations of corruption in government defence?

There has to be a much much greater degree of openness in government. The only time you need total secrecy is when you are actually in a state of war with another country. A number of the clandestine conventions of government in this country are rooted in the need for secrecy during wartime and have never been removed, and of course these are very useful tools for a corrupt government and civil service. If the Bourn Report came out, it wouldn't undermine the nation, it would only undermine the government. There is this confusion of interests.

If you are in the senior echelons of the civil service, the City and Intelligence, you are above the law, you are all powerful. If anybody gets out of line – it doesn't matter what walk of life they are in – you wheel out a government department to bash them – it could be the Inland Revenue, the Customs and Excise, Social Security, whatever.

An aspect of government which should be altered to resist this attitude is the movement of Treasury/Intelligence personnel (sometimes via the Foreign Office) into key positions such as chairman of H.M. Customs and Excise or the Inland Revenue. Sir Brian Unwin, as head of H.M. Customs during the Supergun affair, is a case in point.

It is quite clear, if you read the transcripts of the Scott Inquiry, so far as it relates to people like Geoffrey Howe, Sir Stephen Egerton, David Gore-Booth of the Foreign Office and the rest of them, you will see that this attitude comes out very clearly: 'Rules are for the obedience of fools and the guidance of wise men' and clearly don't apply to the likes of them. 'We are on a totally different stratum, old boy. We are the elite. We can call up the resources of the establishment, whether it is the judiciary or the police or the Customs or the Inland Revenue and we'll slam anybody on the head whom we don't like or who doesn't conform to our view of society. And that applies even to your elected representatives. We'll deal with them the same way if need be.'

CHAPTER FIVE

ASTRA UK, 1986–7: INFILTRATION BY THE CABAL

Towards the end of 1985 I was approached by Roy Tucker, a friend of mine. Roy was a director of Channel Trust and Jizoa, which together held 11 per cent of Astra, following conversion of a loan into shares after a private placing of the company in August 1985. I had first met him before taking on Astra when advising the Rawlings family, the pioneers of Mateus Rosé. He said he had been watching our progress and suggested that I meet Roy Ricks (see p. 85), who had a company called MFA International. When I asked what business Ricks was in, he told me, 'Security systems – airfield, military bases, prison security etc. – he goes to the Middle East a lot, he's terribly well connected. He goes to Abu Dhabi, Dubai, you name it. He seems to know everybody out there, and he's put security systems into prisons and military bases and airfields. I think he would be a great asset to your company. If meeting him does nothing else, it'll give you tremendous contacts in the Middle East.'

Ricks was significant in the story of Astra because he was one of the first of a whole succession of people with connections to Intelligence and in the Middle East – from businessmen to bankers, fixers to agents, civil servants to politicians – who engineered, approved, were involved in or simply overlooked illegal deals with Iran and Iraq, and who came to swarm round our company from all sides (American, British and Belgian), as we pursued our policy of expansion through profitable acquisition.

We did not acquire MFA as such, but took Ricks on as a consultant and supported MFA's bank position by guaranteeing its overdraft, taking an option to buy the company by the subscription of shares, a strategy devised by our lawyers and accountants. We had high hopes for MFA's new computer-based security system, System 6000, and felt that its work in security systems would give Astra an electronics capability possibly of great value. At the time we were interested in electronics expertise for fuse manufacture, and were also keen to take advantage of Roy Ricks' contacts in the Middle East.

Tucker was right about Ricks' contacts. They ranged from British Intelligence – from Sir Brian Tovey, former Head of GCHQ, the top British Intelligence establishment near Cheltenham – to the Middle East, and to the Syrian Waddi Anees Mansour, who had a hot line to Iraq. Ricks went on to become a key figure in the build-up of the Iraqi procurement network. He was responsible for £40m worth of British contracts with Mansour and the Iraqis, and helped set up the Iraqi procurement network. Since the Iraqi business finished, he has set up a series of companies with Sir Brian Tovey; an electronics company since sold for around half a million and another, IES, whose shares on the Stock Exchange have reached £6 each. It was reported recently that 'in December 1993 [IES] was worth just over a million pounds. Now it's worth £9.5m. The value of Ricks's stake is up from £300,000 to more than £3m.' The Foreign Office, which runs Tovey's old hunting-ground, GCHQ, is, incidentally, one of IES's customers.[1]

That Ricks is now well 'in' was confirmed for me when I saw his name on a membership proposal on the board at the Naval and Military Club. His proposer was Sir Brian Tovey. I couldn't believe it when I saw it.

Things have gone well for Roy Ricks since his forced departure from Astra in 1986–7, an event which is still shrouded in some mystery. It was such a strange decision and, in the context of

Intelligence-related subterfuge that was going on inside and outside our company at the time, it is worth consideration.

The facts are as follows. A man called Bill McNaught came on
to our staff in 1986. He had approached us at the Farnborough Air
Show and said he would like to join us. I thought it odd, as we
could only offer him a job looking after MFA, and McNaught had
been twenty-five years with Westland Helicopters and had a good
position. However, as Bill McNaught was Chris Gumbley's
brother-in-law and we needed someone with engineering experience whom we could trust, I agreed.

Almost as soon as he arrived, McNaught was telling Gumbley
that Ricks was not doing a good job and that his company (MFA)
was going to cause us a lot of problems. I was away in America,
and when I returned I heard that Ricks had left the company.

McNaught had somehow got hold of tape-recorded telephone
calls of an apparently incriminating nature. It sounded a load of
balderdash to me. I certainly wouldn't have agreed to Ricks's
departure had I got to hear about it, and found it very strange that
I had not been consulted. I had had high hopes that Ricks's contacts would open up lucrative markets for Astra in the Middle East.

The very method of his departure, the tapped telephone calls
and the honey-trap style pressure which forced him out, smacked
of an Intelligence operation, not the kind of thing Chris Gumbley,
John Anderson, Jim Miller, Martin Guest or I could have dreamed
up.

In considering what lay behind these events, there are various
facts which emerge as relevant.

1   Ricks has never been touched, even though he was involved
      right up to his neck in Iraqi procurement. The MoD police or
      Customs have never prosecuted him or chased him.

2   Ricks's associate, Waddi Mansour, had been contacted by an
      Iraqi official, Kassim Abbass, to set up its procurement net-
      work for Iraq's growing indigenous arms industry before
      Ricks came to us.

3   Again without our knowing it, after having facilitated Ricks's
       departure, McNaught began negotiating with the man he
       had got rid of over a massive fuse contract for Iraq. The sub-
       stance of the discussions was the Iraqi requirement for fuses
       and 155mm shells.

The McNaught–Ricks deal finally came to a head about
September 1988. I remember it well. I was in the office in Linen
Hall late on a Thursday evening, and Chris Gumbley came
through from our small boardroom where he had been having a
meeting with McNaught. He said, 'Bill wants to take on this contract with Iraq. I have told him that's fine, but everything we do
has to be 100 per cent approved by the MoD and the Department
of Defense in America. I think you'll agree that's the right attitude.
I've told him that if he thinks he's such a smart-arse, he can go
round to the MoD himself and get me the clearances, and if they
say it's all right, then we'll do it.'

I agreed with that, our hard-and-fast rule being not to get
involved with anything without MoD or DoD approval, which is of
course not the same as saying none of our goods would find their
way to Iran or Iraq. What perplexed me was how McNaught could
be negotiating with Ricks after what had happened. After saying
he was no good, he then produced a contract worth around £37m
with him, far larger than any other contract then offered to the
company.

In the end, as it happened, the Iraqis opted instead for a deal
with Cardoen, valued at £37.5m, to construct and equip an entire
fuse/artillery line. Matrix Churchill, as sub-contractor, provided
the necessary machine tools for £12m and the government provided the necessary export licences. The factory was up and
running by the middle of 1990. Matrix, of course, was later
destroyed over it.

(Similar contracts were also awarded by the Iraqis via Bull's
SRC, in which we did become involved.)

There are various observations worth making on this turn of
events.

1   It is certain that at the time Ricks left us he was well into discussions with Mansour about a major involvement with the Iraqis, which he could not have organised from his position with Astra.

2   Astra was considered as a vehicle for this, and very likely a decision taken later, that while Astra had certain advantages, on the grounds of security and Astra's involvement with Iraq via Allivane, it might be better to keep further involvements separate and take the Cardoen/Matrix Churchill route instead.

3   There is no doubt that, deliberately or otherwise, McNaught found Ricks an easy and profitable way out from under the Astra umbrella at the right time for Ricks to benefit from the Iraqi procurement opportunity.

4   How has Ricks managed to lead such a charmed life since the Iraqi business? Clearly he must have been working for, or under the protection of, someone on the British side involved in developing the pro-Iraqi policy in Thatcher's arms strategy.

5   A key acquisition in Iraq's procurement strategy for an indigenous arms industry was their purchase of machine-tool manufacturer Matrix Churchill from TI Group. Who was a director of TI Group at the time? The same man who was chairman of Westland Helicopters when Bill McNaught came to us – Sir John Cuckney, ex-MI5, ex-chairman of IMS, which traded with Iran and Iraq for HMG and, from 1987, chairman of Astra's main shareholder, 3i.

The McNaught–Ricks affair is one clear indicator in Astra's history that the impetus behind the arms industry was a group operating with or through all sorts of companies, both with and without the knowledge and acquiescence of their managements.

Much later I was to discover, and not from any of the parties involved, that our own lawyers, Baileys, Shaw & Gillett, who had advised us on the strategy of the relationship between Ricks's company and Astra, were acting for Ricks and the Iraqis and that the registered office of TDG, the Iraqi procurement HQ, was at their address – also the correspondence address of Kadhum and Habobi, both senior members of Iraqi Intelligence.

The story doesn't end there. When in 1988 we bought BMARC, the armaments and ammunition manufacturer, McNaught moved across from MFA to look after the new acquisition. No sooner was he ensconced in this position than he was talking to his old chum Admiral Treacher back at Westland. What did they come up with? Major cabal business, the deal for arming Blackhawk helicopters, part of Thatcher's Al Yamamah, bound for Saudi but really going to Iraq.

When the weaponising deal failed to go forward, the cabal persisted with one aspect of this potentially lucrative deal with Iraq which, you will recall, involved the GECAL 50, which we were building under licence from General Electric of USA at our BMARC plant in Grantham. In August 1995 I received information from Glynn Kay, who worked for Gerald Bull's SRC in China and Iraq, that the drawings for the GECAL 50 were being worked on without my knowledge or Astra's consent by Yugoslav draughtsmen in Bull's office in Baghdad after the Westland Astra weaponising deal was put on hold. Astra had exclusive worldwide marketing and manufacturing rights in GECAL 50 outside America. The drawings can only have come to SRC from BMARC.

Does it not begin to look as though Cuckney had something of a central role in the cabal's business? We will look at this further. In the meantime it is worth noting that McNaught's placement in Astra was at least as advantageous to the cabal as to us.

One further thought about Westland at this time: Admiral Treacher was a founder director of Jim Guerin's ISC, the company we were trading with through Accudyne in America on fuses bound for Iraq.

*

In mid-1986 another man appeared on the scene, well known to the ex-Brocks personnel at Astra.

Two of the agents who had dealt with Brocks when the company became involved in the defence industry were Tengku Safi, a Malaysian connected by family to one of the leading royal families of Malaysia and to the Sultan of Brunei, and one Richard John Rainey Unwin. Unwin, who acted across the board for other pyrotechnic companies and had connections with Royal Ordnance, also had good contacts in Malaysia, having done his military service there, but dealt widely with Third World countries in Africa (Nigeria, Kenya, Zimbabwe, Zambia, etc.), the Middle East (Jordan, Iraq, Oman, Abu Dhabi, Dubai, Kuwait, Saudi, Iran, etc.) and the Far East, particularly Brunei, Malaysia and Thailand.

All of a sudden Unwin began pestering me to buy his company, which seemed to me at best not vital to Astra's progress. He was dealing, in particular, in large and 'do-it-yourself' firework displays, smoke-grenades, stun grenades and thunder-flashes, and a range of pyrotechnics, including an infantry training simulated artillery fire of all calibres. He had been in the arms trade for a long time and enjoyed a lavish lifestyle with offices in Mayfair, in Park Lane, and latterly in Charles Street, near Berkeley Square. His managing director was John Sellens who, at Thorn EMI, had sold the Cymbeline artillery-locating system to the Iraqis.

For us it was a time of great expansion, and around June–July 1986 we found ourselves in need of a bigger bank facility. We were with Barclays in St Albans, which at that time ranked as a City branch – they had a very good manager and there was quite a good relationship, but the overdraft required to fund our stock, as ever bigger military orders came in, was pushing our requirements up towards the four or five million mark. Barclays could not accommodate us. At the same time, Richard Unwin was knocking at our door, forever calling me up to invite me out for lunch.

I told him we had a lot of other business going on. We had had an over-the-counter issue through Hichens Harrison in 1985, when we raised £750,000, and we were working towards a full quotation on the Stock Exchange. I couldn't be bothered with Unwin. But in order to ingratiate himself, he said, 'I know a very good chap, a man called Kock at the Midland Bank.' He told me that this Kock had helped him out tremendously, that he understood all the military side of the arms business – 'You won't have the problem with these idiot bankers,' Unwin said. 'I had a tremendous cash flow problem with an order for Nigeria, and Kock bailed me out . . . Why don't you go and see Midland?'

I recalled hearing the name once before, but in fact didn't go and meet this Mr Kock. Instead I made an appointment with Unwin's bank manager, a Mr Robson, who was at this funny branch in Queen Victoria Street, SW1. (The other senior manager, whom I had met before, was Philip Barnett, who later was retired. Barnett was a very capable banker and very perceptive, which, in the context of what we were to discover about this branch, may not have been the most valued quality in a senior manager.) The branch was on a second or third floor and there was no banking hall as such; all the clearing was done through the Central Hall Westminster branch, up near the House of Commons.

We had dealt with Midland before and had found them pretty hopeless, but when we arrived to meet Robson we knew at once that we had got the right place. They were very accommodating. 'Come to us,' they said, 'and we will give you the facility you need.' This was Thatcher's Britain and apparently I had been led to the deepest well, the very source. The branch turned out to be the place where IMS, the Iranian procurement network, Allivane, and the Iraqi procurement companies banked – the whole lot of them! 'You want six million, seven million?' Mr Robson said. 'No problem.'

So we moved to Midland.

By this time (August 1986) we had obtained a full Stock Exchange listing and were in good financial shape, and it was suggested by our new bankers that we look again at Unwin.

Coincidentally, there arose a possibility of our winning a contract to fill mortar bombs for the MoD, but we couldn't service it at our own site in Richborough, Kent, because of a lack of suitable storage facilities. To store mortar bombs you have to meet certain safety distances in the storage schedule. Back in 1984 Unwin had acquired a former Paines Wessex munitions site near Dartford. He had done this because someone had taken exception to his membership of the Defence Manufacturers Association, which obviously requires of its members that they own a manufacturing site, which Unwin did not. Desperate not to be excluded, he had rushed out to find a factory to buy, and come up with the Paines Wessex site, which had previously been owned by Vickers and was situated in a remote area of the Thames estuary. It met the storage conditions of the mortar-bomb contract perfectly.

Remembering this, and prompted by Midland, I did contact Unwin and looked again at his company, which I was not surprised to see had been making quite horrendous losses, but was about to make – because of certain overseas contracts – quite reasonable profits. We finally took it on board that October, paying him about £600,000 in shares and cash, and giving him a consultancy contract for three years at £75,000 a year.

Prior to the deal, Unwin had gone off to live as a tax exile in Guernsey. It wasn't to be a permanent de-camp; in fact he now has a home in Ramsden, near Burford in Oxfordshire, and an antiques business. But he used the Guernsey move to promote his friend Kock to me once again. He started to say that as he was going to end up with rather a large number of shares in our company, he would like a representative on the board.

I told him: 'Absolute rubbish! You're very lucky that we have taken you over,' and refused his request to put one of his friends on the board. 'I might have considered you,' I said, 'but I am not going to consider any old joker.'

Unwin replied, 'Well, the chap that I am going to recommend is more than any old joker, he is this chap Kock.'

Now I remembered the first occasion that I had heard the name. It had been in October or November 1985, in the course of discussions over MFA, at a meeting with Peter Weaver at the Maidstone branch of Midland, where Roy Ricks banked. Weaver had been the first to tell me about MITS, too, the secret defence department of Midland. Stephan Adolph Kock, who was one of their special arms consultants, was, said Weaver on that occasion, 'a man with influence and contacts at the highest level, including Mrs Thatcher'.

This first suggestion by Midland that Kock might be useful to us occurred at about the same time as we committed to the Aba Chemical deal in Canada, which you will recall marked the first resolution of the overtures made to us there by the US defence establishment via Roger Harding of the British embassy and Dick White.

At the time we completed the deal with Unwin, we were taking financial advice from the corporate side of Hong Kong Bank Ltd (a subsidiary of the Hong Kong and Shanghai Bank), which was really the old Anthony Gibbs firm. A fellow subsidiary was the broker, James Capel. They told us that the Stock Exchange requirement for a fully listed company was to have at least two non-executive directors. We had inherited Edward Album from a deal with a company called Francis Sumner Holdings PLC in our pursuit of a Stock Exchange listing. This will be covered in due course. But now, it appeared, we needed one other. So, as it turned out, Unwin's friend Kock suddenly became a serious proposition and I decided to ask Midland in more detail what they thought of him.

Midland agreed to send me some information and back came a brochure which contained a short biography of the man. That sounded fine. 'But I want a reference,' I said. So Robson signed a reference, and then I received a letter from Head Office also recommending him.

Apart from being a little uneasy that there didn't seem to be a proper *curriculum vitae* available, with information about nationality, where Kock had gone to school and so on, I felt that if the Midland was content, he must be OK, and of course Unwin said he was a friend – 'my best friend!' So, in October 1986, I rang up this Stephan Adolph Kock and told him that he had been recommended by the Midland and Unwin as a non-executive director on the Astra board. Would he like to consider joining?

'Well,' he said, 'it is very good of you to ask me,' and concluded that he would let me know shortly.

He spoke with a relaxed, bluff and hearty tone, but like some other immigrants to the English boardroom from Eastern Europe, who believe that they have mastered the cultured English manner, his performance on that first occasion went a little too far. Nevertheless, I had no serious second thoughts. I had consulted all the people I should have consulted, who were in agreement that it would be politic to have a representative of the bank on our board, particularly one who was an arms expert.

When I met him, I believe at the 'In and Out', the Naval and Military club in Piccadilly, he had a perfect picture of the company in every conceivable way. I assumed naturally that this had come to him via Unwin. I remember being quite irritated at one stage because he made some comment about his only being prepared to join a company which was wholly reputable (the irony of this will become clear, and is almost too bitter to take even at this distance in time).

'For goodness' sake,' I had laughed, dispersing my irritation, 'you have been helping out Unwin's company, how can you possibly doubt us?'

Unwin had been an agent, an arms facilitator like Mark Thatcher, and then had spread his wings a bit with the Kent site. He had been in at the 'glamorous' end of the industry, all fast money, big commissions and so on, and this man Kock, Unwin's friend, was playing for the moral high ground. It was a bit ridiculous.

It pinpoints something about Kock which marks him down in even the most objective appraisal of the man. He played these grand strategies, employed all sorts of ingenious tactics, but because he was trading so transparently on the gullibility of all around him, these tactics appeared almost patronising.

I asked him which major companies he had been connected with, and he mentioned Biddle Holdings and Shell Oil, which had been on the Midland brochure, and bluffed his way through, saying he had been connected with so many. One of his great expressions, I remember, was 'Africa is my parish.' He reckoned all Africa was his. I knew he had connections with Rhodesia and South Africa, and later I discovered that he was connected with Zambia, when at one of the military shows a whole delegation of Zambians suddenly descended on him, and one man in particular came forward and said, 'My father will be so glad that I have seen you.' Kenya was also important; and he had knowledge of Zaire and Nigeria. But he never told me that he spoke Arabic, although according to the *Observer* he was an Arabic-speaker, which was why he had been used as a bagman (besides other things) on Thatcher's Middle East contracts.

Kock is the sort of person who, if he goes out of his way to be pleasant, most people would not question, but would go along with the performance. John Anderson was the first explicitly to question his credibility. I remember him saying that he had a feeling there was something not right about him from the start. 'If you ask Kock what he has done before a certain date,' he said to me, 'you never got an answer – "I've done quite a lot of things in my time, ho ho!"'

It did cross my mind that he might be connected with Intelligence, but I have to counter that with the view of our lawyers, Baileys, Shaw & Gillett, and of our accountants, Stoy Hayward, who were wholly taken in and used to laugh and think he was a drunken old buffer; Laurence Kingswood of Baileys collapsed in hysterics every time he had to enter his middle name in a prospectus. To these people, at the start, Stephan Adolph Kock was something of an object of fun.

Kock has been described by Dr Mark Phythian of the Political Sciences department of Wolverhampton University, who has done a great deal of research into the activities of Intelligence operatives in the defence establishment in the 1980s, as 'one of the more mysterious figures to emerge from "Iraqgate" and the often shadowy world of arms packages and financing.'

Apparently Kock was born in May 1927 in Czechoslovakia. The Midland Bank brochure claims that he served with the Royal Air Force, then worked in civil aviation, and 'subsequently he carried out specialised duties for the British government in various parts of the world, including as Political Secretary to the Rhodesian Prime Minister in the early sixties during the period of constitutional change. He had further military service abroad in the intelligence corps as an infantry officer. He also saw service for some years in the SAS regiment.'

There is in fact no trace of his ever having belonged to the RAF. Research by Phythian and Tim Laxton, who worked on Astra's affairs for accountants Stoy Hayward and, following his experience of Astra's manipulation and victimisation, dedicated himself to frontline journalistic investigation into government corruption in the arms industry, points to Kock's emigrating, in 1944, to Southern Rhodesia, where fourteen years later (until December 1962) he did indeed serve as Political Secretary to the Rhodesian Prime Minister Sir Edgar Whitehead.

During his Rhodesian period, Kock picked up, among much else that determined his future, one particular contact that would stand him in good stead. Walter Monckton, 1st Viscount Monckton of Brenchley, one of Churchill's Cabinet and then chairman of Midland Bank, headed the Advisory Commission that undertook a review of the Rhodesian Constitution. Walter's son Gilbert, a former major-general, the 2nd Viscount Brenchley, would be one of Kock's patrons when Kock came to Britain in 1967. Kock's house bordered Monckton's estate near Maidstone in Kent.

It appears more likely that Kock's alleged earlier experience in the RAF was in fact in the Rhodesian Air Force, and if one is to believe Kock's own assertion to the 1991 DTI Select Committee Inquiry into Exports to Iraq, that he served as substantive captain and rose to major in the SAS 'in Rhodesia just before UDI'. It is more than likely that the SAS service he saw was in 'C' Squadron, formed by 'Mad Mike' Calvert at that time from a pool of 1,000 Rhodesian ex-SOE and SAS volunteers for action against the communists in the jungles of Malaya. Alternatively, he was an Intelligence liaison man who used the SAS.

'Following his retirement from the army', the Midland brochure continues, Kock 'was for a period International Director for a major international Dutch mining and manufacturing group and subsequently again as International Director for the Shell Oil Company . . .'

But this is not strictly true either. As he was forced to admit to the DTI Select Committee, he was in fact a director of a metals mining company called Billiton, a Shell subsidiary known to provide 'retirement' posts for Intelligence officers. Kock was far from retired, however, for according to information he supplied for an internal Astra newsletter, at the very same time he 'carried out special assignments for the Foreign Office.'

Various people are on record as to Kock's role in Intelligence. The CIA/State Department referred to him as SIS (MI6). Gerald Bull has said that he was a member of MI5 – 'He's a Yarpie – a South African. He works for the Midland Bank arms department, but he's also part of MI5 like Cuckney.' When I mentioned this to Lt.-Col. Colin Mitchell, former MP, late of the Argylls and now with Halo Trust, a charitable company involved in clearing mines from territories like Cambodia, Iraq, Afghanistan, Somalia, Ethiopia and Mozambique, he told me, 'No, he was MI6.'

In an unguarded moment Richard Unwin told me that Kock, in his more active days, had been head of Group 13. The Foreign Office is said to draw Group 13 operatives from the SAS as well as from private security firms. Its duties involve 'service to the nation' of a kind given only to the most ruthlessly experienced SAS officers. Kock certainly still moved in such circles when he was working for Astra, and was close to former SAS personnel and men active in the private security business, including Major Peter Hamilton, a former Military Intelligence man who has admitted having 'spent much of his life in the Security and Intelligence world', and was linked to the 'highest echelons of British Intelligence'. Hamilton's firm, Zeus Security Consultants, provided services to the government, as did Defence Systems Ltd, the firm of another of Kock's friends, SAS Major Alastair Morrison MC. Viscount Monckton, who acted as one of Kock's patrons in 1967, was a director of Morrison's company, and Morrison was an associate, too, of Jonathan Aitken both before and at the time that Aitken was a director of Astra's BMARC.[2]

During the DTI Select Committee Inquiry, in the final report of which Kock's evidence played a curiously insignificant part, our mysterious non-executive director denied ever being a member of MI5 or MI6, or an officer in MI6, but no one reading his evidence would be left in any doubt that he had these connections:

'If I find anything which I consider to be contrary to the interests of this country,' Kock said to Mr Stan Crowther MP, ever confident of his interpretation of our country's interests, 'I will report.'

'The question is, how do we report it?' pressed Crowther. 'How do we get in touch with them [the security services]? You certainly know how to get in touch with them all the time, do you not?'

'I know how to get in touch with some of them, yes,' was as far as Kock would go.

As Kock's crucial involvement in the arms-to-Iraq scandal began to fall clear, further attempts were made, this time in Parliament, to uncover information about the man. In April 1993, Allan Rogers MP asked the House 'what the official duties of Mr Stephen Adolphus Kock [*sic*] have been since 1980'.

The apparently definitive answer, 'None,' will do little to disperse the suspicions of the curious historian, however, for the date in question, '1980', has been entered in Hansard as '1990', although it was perfectly clear in the original question.

Other questions followed in February 1994 (MPs Menzies Campbell and Sir David Steel), and on 1 July 1994 Michael Meacher asked, 'for what reason Stephan Adolph Kock has Special Branch protection; and what other names he uses or has been known by.' Four days later the answer came, 'It is not in the public interest to disclose whether any person has received official protection or not. There is no Ministerial responsibility for names by which Mr Kock is known or has been known.'

Then, on 24 May, Meacher tried once more, digging deeper into his past, asking to know, 'what duties Stephan Adolphus Kock has performed for a. the Prime Minister, b. the Ministry of Defence, c. the Foreign and Commonwealth Office, d. the

Department of Trade and Industry, and e. any other Department between 1964 and 1979; and in which countries overseas each of these duties were carried out.'

Meacher was rewarded with an answer that at least seemed to verify that Kock enjoyed a protected status: 'Mr Kock performed no *official* [my italics] duties for any Government Department during the period 1964–79. It remains the Government's policy not to comment on the contacts which an individual may or may not have had with the security [MI5] and intelligence [MI6] agencies.'

But whether or not he is or was a member or an officer in MI6 or MI5 or was ever involved with Group 13, he was by his own admission 'a military intelligence officer in Rhodesia' with 'access to private information of a nature that might endanger the security of the state' and the 'capability to convey [such] information', whatever precisely that means in terms of job description.

The close connection between the SAS, MI6, industry/the City and politics will be seen to have formed the route by which Kock found his way to Astra in 1986.

Kock was active in these areas when British policy towards southern Africa was no less duplicitous over sanctions and apartheid and the pressing need to trade, than it became in the 1980s towards Iraq, over sanctions on arms and the desire to take advantage of the enormous economic opportunities offered by war in the Middle East.

When, in 1965, during Harold Wilson's government, Southern Rhodesia issued its Unilateral Declaration of Independence (UDI), civil servants in the Cabinet Office drew up sanctions with so many loopholes that subsidiaries of British oil companies were effectively encouraged to continue to supply.

The situation provided Kock with a perfect training ground for success in the British defence industry in the 1980s. With official government policy short-cut to economic expediency, the situation in both cases favoured the rise of clandestine operatives who, in the unlikely event that they were called upon to do so, could, with establishment backing, justify their activities with an appeal to patriotism and/or realism.

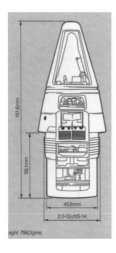

Proximity fuse produced by Accudyne, a subsidiary of Astra Holdings plc

Highly advanced Oerlikon 25mm KBB cannon, used in the Sea Zenith gun and produced by BMARC, another subsidiary of Astra

BMARC's explosives production at Faldingworth

[POPPERFOTO/REUTER]

Sir John (now Lord) Cuckney: chairman of International Military Services 1974-85; director of Midland Bank 1978-88

Sir James (now Lord) Blyth: Head of Defence Sales, MoD, 1981-85

[TOPHAM PICTUREPOINT]

Sir Peter Levene: Chief of Defence Procurement, MoD, 1985-91

Sir Colin Chandler: Head of Defence Export Services, MoD, 1985-89

Mark Thatcher

Wafiq Said

[MIRROR SYNDICATION INTERNATIONAL]

POPPERFOTO/REUTER]

The Gulf War, 1990-91

[POPPERFOTO/REUTE

[POPPERFOTO/REUTER]

Saddam Hussein

A box of mortar bombs found in an Iraqi gun position during the Gulf War. 'MOD' stands for Ministry of Defence, 'RO' for Royal Ordnance, 'L/C' for letter of credit and '86' for 1986. In 1986, Royal Ordnance was wholly owned by the Ministry of Defence. The photograph was taken by my son, Christian *(left)*, while he was serving in the Gulf War.

Margaret Thatcher

[POPPERFOTO/REUTER]

Geoffrey Howe

Jonathan Aitken

[MIRROR SYNDICATION INTERNATIONAL]

Michael Heseltine

Ian Clark

Lord Trefgarne

William Waldegrave

Archie Hamilton

[FINANCIAL TIMES PICTURES]

Stephan Kock, who became a director of Astra in 1986, giving evidence to the Trade and Industry Select Committee

Friday 16 April 1993

(Answered by the Prime Minister on Thursday 22 April)

UNSTARRED   Mr Allan Rogers: To ask the Prime Minister, what the official
No. .ɔ̣7   duties of Mr Stephen Adolphus Kock have been since 1980.

THE PRIME MINISTER

None.

Mr. Stephen Kock

Mr. Rogers: To ask the Prime Minister what the officia duties of Mr. Stephen Adolphus Kock have been sinc 1990.

The Prime Minister: None.

An interesting discrepancy between the tabled version *(top)* and the *Hansard* reco of a question put to the Prime Minister regarding Stephan Kock. In May 1994, whe replying to a question from Michael Meacher, the Prime Minister elaborated on h response: 'Mr Kock performed no official duties for any Government Departme during the period 1964–79. It remains the Government's policy not to comment c the contacts which an individual may or may not have had with the security ar intelligence agencies.'

Kock proved himself in Rhodesia, and in 1969, as was the case with others who helped Britain's covert foreign policy at this time, he was rewarded with British citizenship. Once in Britain, he set about cementing his contacts in political and business and Intelligence circles here.

By 1973 he had a position as non-executive director of Biddle Holdings and the former chairman, Frank Biddle, recalls his boasting that he had dined out with Margaret Thatcher. By the time he joined Astra, and Thatcher had come to power, Kock was available to co-ordinate the major arms deals that underwrote her economic policy.

In 1978, when Kock gave evidence to the Bingham Inquiry into sanction-busting in Rhodesia, he described himself as National Accounts Adviser to British Petroleum. Later, through his friendship with a man called Bernard Wheeler, he could put this experience to good use.

Having served in the Special Operations Executive (SOE) during the Second World War, Bernard Wheeler is, like Kock, a member of the Special Forces Club, indeed a former secretary. The SOE trained resistance groups in the Second World War and engaged in sabotage, assassination and general mayhem; thereafter, its government-sponsored assassination duties passed to MI6, who out of pique or envy had betrayed SOE agents during the war.

We know that Wheeler and Kock operated through a company called Onedin Developments (Devon) Ltd until it was struck off the Register of Companies for failing to file accounts in 1978. There is evidence of mutual back-scratching before then. Kock's appointment as a non-executive director of Biddle Holdings in 1973 was, according to Frank Biddle, a pre-condition imposed by Biddle's merchant bank, County Bank Limited, for the flotation of the company. 'Coincidentally', Wheeler was a partner in Mann Judd & Co., the reporting accountants of Biddle Holdings, at the time of the flotation.

In 1980 Mann Judd merged with Touche Ross, where Kock's eldest son, Egmont Stephanus, served his articles as a trainee accountant and is now partner, and where Mark Thatcher was a trainee accountant.

Wheeler and Kock were close. Indeed, Kock is godfather to one of Wheeler's daughters. Wheeler left Touche Ross in 1985 and became involved in the Conservative Industrial Fund with Lord Erskine of Rerrick (see p. 114). For a period of three or four years he worked from the former headquarters of the Economic League, in Vine Court, Fleet Street, and as a council member of British United Industrialists, which, as we have seen, is a front company for donations to Tory party funds laundered through the 'river' companies.

'BUI,' confirmed the January 1994 edition of *Parliamentary Affairs*, 'provided an effective front for the companies that wished to make donations to the Conservative Party secretly. By 1989 [by which time Wheeler had left], BUI was no longer an important component in fund-raising, principally because its main activities were so widely known . . .'

The registered office of the 'river companies' which processed these funds is at 6 New Square, Lincoln's Inn, the address of Trowers & Hamlins, the company which Kock would employ secretly, without the knowledge of the Astra board, from 1989 following his attempt to unseat me as chairman, to advise him on strategy that culminated in my dismissal and the break-up of the company. I would discover what had happened from board minutes of meetings which Kock conducted only after we, the founding directors, had left.

William Gosselin Trower set up the 'river companies' in 1949 at Churchill's request. His son, Anthony Gosselin Trower, a former senior partner at Trowers & Hamlins and a director of Bourne Association, another of the river companies, was, during the Second World War, a member of the SAS and an Intelligence officer.

Among Kock's associates is former SAS Major David Walker who, in the 1970s, with former SAS Colonel Jim Johnson, a wealthy stockbroker, co-founded Keeny Meeny Services (KMS), a name taken from a phrase coined in Kenya during the Mau Mau campaign, meaning 'undercover operations'. KMS flourished at a time when the government first co-opted private security operations to undertake political activities of a sensitive and dangerous kind. In 1974 Walker and Johnson won a contract to train and equip the special forces of the Sultan of Oman, whose coup to remove his father and take power four years earlier had been organised by SAS operatives under the command of Brigadier Tim Langdon.

Langdon was in Margaret Thatcher's entourage when she signed the controversial Oman 'university' deal in 1981. Trowers & Hamlins has maintained an office in the Sultanate of Oman since 1977. Walker was reported to have been 'on first-name terms' with Thatcher during her term in office. Kock, who boasted also of his special entrée to No. 10, was, in addition, a close colleague of Dare Newell, another former recruit to Calvert's 'C' Squadron and seen side by side with Kock at SAS regimental dinners and at the Special Forces Club in London. From 1973 to 1985, Dare Newell was reputed to have run SAS Group Intelligence when it was a clearing-house for MI6 mercenary operations in Oman.[3]

I hope you can begin to understand something of the milieu in which Kock moved. I give it to you as essential background to understanding the story of the cabal's covert abuse of Astra, which follows.

Kock's contacts in the political echelons of defence were no less extraordinary. Following his move in 1987 from Kent, his often weekly trips to London from a hideaway in Scotland at West Barravullin, near Ardfern in Argyllshire, where I believe he still lives, included meetings at the Foreign Office and the Cabinet Office where he was an adviser to the Joint Intelligence Committee. His links with JIC have been independently corroborated by Robin Robison, formerly on its administrative staff. You will recall that JIC controls the activities of the security and Intelligence services in Britain.

There were top-level connections also with the DESO. Major-General Christopher Last of DESO was the first to alert me to

Kock's activities abroad. 'Wherever we're selling arms,' he said, 'your Kock usually pops up from nowhere.'

At the MoD he was well in with Sir John Bourn, Colin Chandler, and Peter Levene and Brigadier Peter Landrey on the Procurement Executive, as well as with industrialists like Lygo of British Aerospace, and Clive Hunting of Hunting Engineering.

It seemed to us at Astra that Kock knew everyone who was anyone in the arms business. Indeed, at the time he joined us towards the end of 1986, his connections appear to have raised him on to a virtually untouchable plane. Years later I bumped into Peter Shore in the changing rooms of the Roehampton Club and asked him why Kock had not been interviewed for the Foreign Affairs Committee investigation into the Pergau Dam/Malaysian arms deal affair, of which Shore was acting chairman. How could such an investigation proceed without interviewing the man who had orchestrated the whole thing, a man who had admitted on television that he was involved? What I actually said to Shore was, 'Why has the main witness not been interviewed?' Shore, assuming that I meant Thatcher, began to reply – 'It is her prerogative as Prime Minister . . .' When I interrupted, telling him I meant Kock, Shore's telling response (to what must have seemed something of a fast ball, as he changed from swimming trunks into boxer shorts) was, 'But that is another level of government altogether.'

Kock's connections put him in an extraordinary position of power, as unsupported by Astra shareholders as is the power of permanent government by national ballot. In his own words, they put him 'in command' of our company. 'I am in command,' he told Campbell Dunford, formerly of Midland Bank whom I had hired as a consultant in 1989, and who wanted Kock to back him in an effort to become a member of the Astra board. 'There is no question about that. I am in command because of all the various people who have taken an interest in Astra.'

This is part of a telephone conversation, taped by Dunford, which I have in my possession and to which I will return.

*

At the time that Kock joined the special defence unit at Midland Bank, Sir John Cuckney, its creator, was still a director. To get a job in the unit you had to have good contacts in the international arms business and in the Intelligence business and be able at the same time to hold your own in diplomatic and political circles. You had to be a tactician, charming, single-minded, conspiratorial, at once urbane and totally ruthless, and above all, loyal to JIC and the Cabinet Office.

Sir John Cuckney was born in 1925 in India. His father was an Air Vice-Marshal. Cuckney is where, in the more dramatic part of Astra's journey – from 1986 on – all roads lead. Cuckney was chairman of IMS (1974 to 1985) and, from 1978 to 1988, director of Midland Bank, commercial funder of the British arms trade during the Iran–Iraq war. He was chairman of Westland when the US defence transfer requirement with United Technologies/ Sikorsky was effected for Al Yamamah; he was deputy chairman of TI Group when, in 1987, it sold Matrix Churchill to the Iraqi procurement company, TDG; and he was chairman of 3i, Astra's main institutional shareholder, when Astra was 'sold out' to the interests of the cabal. Sir John Cuckney thus presided over five of the companies involved in major controversial aspects of the arms-to-Iraq/Iran story.

Between 1978 and 1988, while he was non-executive director of Midland and for much of the same time chairman of IMS, he really cemented the Intelligence service links with the bank and in particular between Intelligence, Midland and British defence. Yet he was never called by Scott to bear witness at the Inquiry. As a result, as the *Independent* put it, 'the underlying culture out of which Matrix Churchill and the Scott Inquiry grew looks likely to remain unexamined.'

How significant a role he played in Astra's story will probably never be known for sure, but he was in charge at Midland when the bank recommended Kock to Astra in 1986 and in charge at Westland when McNaught came to us and later when we were offered the Al Yamamah/Westland helicopter weaponising deal. He elected to become more personally involved as the new

Chairman of 3i Group plc, Astra's main shareholder, when we began to move, through our acquisition of BMARC and then PRB, into the heartland of government-inspired and approved covert arms deals with Iran and Iraq.

Kock was by then already at work on Thatcher's £1bn Malaysian/Pergau Dam arms deal. Its 1988 signing was, as the *Financial Times* revealed publicly for the first time in July 1991, 'preceded by a team from Midland's defence department led by Mr Stephan Kock, together with Ministry of Defence and other officials and a small delegation from Britain's Special Air Services.'

On 28 January 1994, hounded by Channel 4 News, Kock himself admitted that he had indeed been 'involved with the Malaysian Dam project'.

At Astra it was an open secret that Kock and Richard Unwin were orchestrating the whole deal. It irked me particularly that Unwin's heavy involvement meant that he was able to do little for us despite being paid £75,000 p.a. as a consultant. At various stages Kock and Unwin were able to whistle up Laings as the prime contractor, then Trafalgar House, and finally British Aerospace. Martin Laing was a schoolfriend of Unwin, and Unwin was also close to Trafalgar House and BAe, where he retained an office, and, like Kock, had served in the armed forces in Malaysia.

Kock was in regular contact with Unwin between 1986 and 1990 on this and other deals, meeting frequently at the Special Forces Club among other places, and in 1990 and 1991 Unwin 'commuted' to Malaysia with Dick Evans of BAe, sometimes weekly. Unwin and Kock made a fine duo, but there was no doubt about who was in the driving seat. Kock talked constantly about his meetings with Thatcher and his ability to contact her at any time, and boasted that he was personally organising the deal and would see that Astra would get 'one or two crumbs off the table', as he put it.

We never did, but in my opinion none of Kock's boasting was hot air. He was a man whose background had largely been as a field operative and I believe that as he became older he wanted desperately to transfer his covert experience to the arena of the company boardroom, but found it hard to remain in the shadows when he felt superior to 'pipsqueak' MPs and industrialists. That, I am sure, is why he took a delight in boasting about his Malaysian arms connections.

Invariably the boasts were backed up by our experience later, as happened indeed in the case of his involvement with the Malaysian arms/Pergau deal.

I recall in particular one occasion in July 1988, when Gumbley, Kock and I attended a meeting with Nigel Rudd, chairman of Williams Holdings, at Midland Bank's Cannon Street offices. When Rudd left, Richard Unwin and various Malaysian military personnel trooped into the office. They included Harry Adnam and General Jacob, also representatives of the Malaysian High Commission. Adnam, Unwin and Jacob clearly deferred to Kock, who started talking about the Malaysian arms deal quite openly, mentioning some very sensitive matters. He said they were having problems with Malaysian prime minister Mahathir's bagman, who was an Indian or an Indian Malay, or a Malay of Indian extraction. Certain parties at the UK end, who were named, were getting too greedy, and had complicated matters by doing private deals with this bagman.

In 1987, Kock and Unwin organised a Malaysian evening at the Porchester Hall, a supper and 'knees-up' for the Malaysian High Commission. Both Gumbley and I were invited, although, unlike Kock and Unwin, we did not of course sit at the VIP table. Then, in 1989, Gumbley and I and our wives were invited to a weekend 'beano' at Laing's country house in Hertfordshire, which involved an elaborate dinner and mannequin parade with pyrotechnics for charity, and lunch on the Sunday. The guest-list included the Malaysian High Commissioner and Deputy Commissioner as well as other Malaysian personnel.

Kock was operating ostensibly on behalf of Midland's defence department, and it is unthinkable that this was without Cuckney's knowledge or the approval of Cuckney's associate and Kock's immediate boss, Comte Hervé de Carmoy, who we will meet again.

It is extraordinary that neither Kock, Unwin, de Carmoy, nor Cuckney was called to witness in the Foreign Affairs Committee investigation into the deal; nor was my evidence about Kock (or that of Tim Laxton) ever published. There seems to be a wall of silence in front of these men. In protest I wrote to Helen Irwin, Clerk of the Committee, as follows: 'It is very surprising that the evidence from TRW Laxton and myself re Stephan Adolph Kock and Richard John Rainey Unwin was not published. I also find it amazing that neither [Kock nor Unwin] was interviewed . . . as without these two figures there would have been no deal . . .'

It seems to me just as revealing that, in line with the rule of Intelligence operatives never to admit whom they work for, it was a determined feature of Kock's evidence to the DTI Select Committee on Exports to Iraq that he went out of his way to deny knowing Cuckney well, referring to him, laughably (perhaps Freud might have said, guiltily), by using my name – 'I have not known Sir Gerald Cuckney [sic] that well.' In the same body of evidence he agreed with Dr Keith Hampson that he was 'deeply involved' with all Astra's major shareholders – 'all these powerful players' – which of course included Cuckney in particular, as chairman of 3i.

Kock knew not only Cuckney well at Midland, but also of course his own immediate boss at the bank, Comte Hervé de Carmoy, the man who later engineered for SGB/Gechem the sale of PRB to Astra, which caused us so many problems. De Carmoy was director and chief executive of the Bank's Global Banking Sector until 1988, a main board director and a friend of Cuckney's.

Cuckney, de Carmoy and Kock in a descending hierarchy at the Bank, whatever 'seniority' they enjoyed in other capacities, made a formidable team. Midland must have wondered what had hit them when they all cleared out of a department which had sustained losses of up to £100m, put down to 'funny practices'. I wonder how patriotic those who remained to clear up the mess felt.[4]

I believe that Cuckney through Midland wrote out the ticket on which Kock hitched a ride on Astra, their interest in us signalling the same 'fated interest' which had been shown in us by the British Embassy, the US Defense Department and related intelligence personnel in the United States back in 1983.

In 1986–7, the trans-Atlantic lines buzzing with Astra's US acquisition of Walters/Accudyne, events began to move into overdrive in Britain too.

CHAPTER SIX

THE ENTREPRENEURIAL FALLACY OF THATCHER'S BRITAIN

In August 1985, in order to fund our expansion, I had arranged through stockbrokers Hichens Harrison (where Dennis Bailey, a contact of mine, was a partner) an issue of Ordinary shares worth £750,000. Hichens Harrison would continue to act for Astra until March 1990. The issue was not a Stock Exchange listing as such; it was a 'matched bargain' basis of trading (as S532 under the then Stock Exchange regulations), which meant that brokers could deal in our shares provided they could match up a buyer and seller. It was not a full listing or even a listing on the USM, where a broker can buy your stock whether they have a purchaser or not. As a result of this move we had taken on board about a hundred shareholders. We were still not very big. We showed about £340,000 profit then, and as we went into 1986 with our Canadian operation all set to go, I realised that if we really wanted to make progress we had to have a full listing. And since we didn't have enough of a track record to do that, I began to cast around for a public company to reverse into.

It seemed to me crucial to move now, as the whole defence industry was talking of competition and in particular of the break-up of the government-owned Royal Ordnance ammunition monopoly. Thatcher herself talked regularly of privatisation and competition, and the MoD procurement guru, Peter Levene, spoke of the advantages that competition would make to our armed forces. I felt that we should move into a position to take advantage while there was a window of opportunity.

As it happened I had been talking to the Hong Kong Bank during 1985 on behalf of the Norton Telecommunications Group. Nothing in fact had materialised for Norton, but the bank had seemed keen to get involved with Astra. When, now, I told them of my plans for Astra, a proposal was made to effect a full Stock Exchange listing by a reverse takeover of Francis Sumner Holdings PLC.

Francis Sumner Holdings was a full publicly-listed company with really no trading income at all. They had £1.5m in cash and 4,000 shareholders, but the only trading activity was via interests in John Grey, a little textile company in the Burnley area, which made lining material for nuclear/biological warfare suits, wellington boots, and via another company in which they had a shareholding in Whitehaven, Cumbria, which made service uniforms and other clothes. Otherwise there was no trading operation. It did look to be the ideal shell vehicle for Astra to move into.

When the textile industry had dived, Max Maimann, the Sumner chairman, had hived off the better part of the company into a separate company, Harton, leaving a few odds and ends in Sumner. The original Sumner shareholders had become shareholders in Harton too, which had achieved a full listing, and as time went on, virtually all that was left in Sumner was cash and two investments. When we came along and said what we wanted to do, Maimann, who had 30 per cent of the Sumner shares and 30 per cent of Harton, saw it as a good move. At the time he needed cash to subscribe a Harton rights issue. He and his managing director were supposed to have stayed on the board, but when, following the deal, the Sumner shares rose sharply, Maimann departed with his managing director, Colin Astin, at once, giving the extraordinary reason that he had been threatened by the IRA for becoming involved with a defence company. We

never saw them again. In fact they didn't even turn up at the
meeting ratifying the deal. All that they left behind was a non-
executive director, one Edward Album.

The deal with Sumner was completed in August 1986, and by
the time the really big business started to come through in
America we were already an attractive vehicle, with a full London
listing. We began cautiously to re-consider our whole strategy at
home, a strategy which, when fully realised in March 1989, had
taken us from net assets of £1.5m and an annual turnover of
£6.2m to net assets of £54m, an annual turnover of £96m and
profits before tax of £9.5m.

With every reason in 1985 to expect that with the new spirit of
competition there was a good chance of securing small arms contracts from the MoD, we began by looking around for a company
with suitable plant. We discussed the purchase of plant for small-
arms ammunition production from Fritz Werner in Germany,
which would have been tailor-made for the job. We also looked at
the Witton factory in Birmingham, and on more than one occasion
made an offer to purchase Eley Kynoch from IMI, which could
have readily been adapted to small-arms (as well as larger calibre)
ammunition manufacture – they were already producing .22, .50
and shotgun cartridges – though in the end our final offer of
£19m was rejected. We also considered buying Sterling
Armaments, the only UK-based small-arms manufacturing company apart from Royal Ordnance.

In all, we spent a great deal of time and money considering
how we could position ourselves to benefit from the government's
stated intention to open up the UK arms market to competition.
Then, late in 1985, the government unaccountably pulled the
rug on small-arms ammunition production by granting Radway
Green and Enfield, Royal Ordnance facilities, a five-year monopoly as suppliers to the MoD.

Understandably, this experience found us extremely sceptical
when, in 1987, there was once more continuing and unrelenting
pressure by the MoD for Astra to tender as a competitor to RO.

The background to this was that the government had made

various attempts at distancing themselves from their armaments company. First there was a disastrous attempt to float Royal Ordnance on the Stock Exchange. Then there was talk about selling off one or two of the RO plants, but when we made approaches to buy individual plants like Glascoed, Radway Green, and Enfield, all of them were rejected.

Finally, the government announced their intention to sell the company in its entirety through N.M. Rothschild (a surprising choice of advisers for the sale of the main government-controlled UK armaments company in view of Rothschild's Zionist sympathies and RO's Arab customers). It was mooted by our bankers that Astra might be used for a management buy-out of RO. Our resident non-executive director, Kock, was keen on the idea.

Astra was to have been the vehicle; Hong Kong Bank and Midland would provide the funds. But again we were to be disappointed. To begin with, we experienced considerable difficulty in obtaining prospectus documents from Rothschild. Only after political intervention from our MP, Jonathan Aitken, and two consultants inherited from Richard Unwin, Gerald Howarth MP (who became Mrs Thatcher's PPS) and Sir Anthony Kershaw MP, were they provided – on a Friday evening, and we were supposed to have a bid prepared by the following Tuesday. British Aerospace (for whom it subsequently transpired Howarth was also a consultant) and the other bidders, which included GKN and Trafalgar House, had had the documents for more than two months.

Clearly it would have been foolhardy to get involved under such ludicrous conditions. With Astra out of the way, and the various stooge bidders allegedly ruled out owing to plans to denude RO of some of its plant assets, in April 1987 Royal Ordnance was sold by the government to British Aerospace, with whom it had maintained essential ties since that company's privatisation. BAe was the safest option available.

Of course I hadn't realised that the sale of Royal Ordnance was always going to be a difficult business for the government because of the company's dealings with Allivane, the arms and propellant cartels, etc. There could only ever be lip-service to competition. RO was so locked into clandestine operations as a government department that when it was privatised it had to remain tied to government. Thatcher's play to the political gallery was unrealisable.

Nevertheless the MoD continued to encourage us to tender. In particular, John Bourn, then a senior MoD civil servant responsible for the sale of RO and procurement, encouraged us through Kock to acquire the necessary plant to get into the UK ammunition market in competition to the newly privatised company.

Despite our scepticism, we decided to consider the only other feasible alternative to Eley Kynoch, which was British Manufacture and Research Company (BMARC).

BMARC had its beginnings in a joint venture between Hispano Suiza with the Ministry of Supply in 1938, in anticipation of war. BMARC had been the first cannon-manufacturing facility. I had first encountered the company during my days at Peat Marwick Mitchell, and knew that Hispano Suiza had, in 1971, been acquired by Oerlikon Buhrle of Zurich, which had a prime position in medium-calibre weapons and ammunition with tremendous international sales. To Oerlikon, the United Kingdom was a cheap base for manufacture, owing to low labour costs compared with Switzerland and a low-base exchange rate. It also favoured the UK as one of the easiest countries to obtain export licences for arms sales, provided the necessary procedures and formalities were followed.

As a result Oerlikon had entered into a substantial capital expenditure programme on BMARC's behalf, at its Lincolnshire sites at Grantham, where its 390,000 square feet of factory was mechanised to a very high standard, and at the 800-acre Faldingworth site, a former wartime Lancaster bomber base, which had been upgraded into a nuclear bomb storage facility for nearby Scampton before becoming Oerlikon's filling and high explosive facility, with 255,000 square feet of factory, office and storage buildings.

We approached Oerlikon with utmost secrecy, routeing our

enquiry through Peat Marwick Mitchell, its former auditors, rather than through our own bankers or accountants. A preliminary meeting was arranged during the 1987 Paris Air Show with Michael Funk, head of the armaments division, later to become chief executive of the Group.

Funk asked for time to consider our proposals, which was understandable. At the time, Oerlikon was in negotiation with BAe for the purchase of the whole Group. Time passed, and Oerlikon did nothing to encourage our approach. We made a final attempt to speed things up in August, but progress was slow, which brought us to September 1987 and the Naval Equipment Exhibition at Whale Island, Portsmouth.

Suddenly on our stand appeared Peter Levene, the UK government's Head of Defence Procurement, appointed by Thatcher and Heseltine. He said, 'We have been watching you chaps with great interest. What we desperately need is someone to compete with RO because the army, navy and Royal Air Force are fed up with them. They are very expensive, very slow on delivery, and their quality is not all that good [all of which was well known in the business]. If you are prepared to quote on the hard-core ammunition area you should be able to get at least 40 per cent of the MoD market which is running at more than £500m a year.'

He then laid out the full annual UK market potential as per defence estimates – £500m for land services, £1.5bn for the air force, and £750m to £950m for the navy. Although the navy and air force figures included mainly expensive weapon systems supplied by the usual monopolist gang of contractors, a reasonable amount, together with the entire land services budget, concerned ammunition and filling work.

Levene repeated that if we were to put in tenders for the hard-core ammunition contracts (which meant everything from mortar ammunition to 76mm armoured car rounds, 105mm artillery and tank rounds, 120mm tank rounds, 155mm artillery and 4.5inch naval), we would get at least 40 per cent of the contracts as long as we could show we had the plant to service them and our prices were competitive.

I said that it all sounded fine but we had spent enormous energy and resources trying to do just that since 1985 and had always been thwarted by government volte-face. I mentioned the small-arms ammunition monopoly agreement with RO's Enfield and Radway Green in particular. Indeed I made it crystal clear to Levene that we had become familiar with dealing with politicians and we didn't intend to go over the whole gamut again. We were well set up in America now, our future was in America, and I didn't want anything to do with Britain or Europe unless there was a very genuine desire and intention to let us compete.

It was something of a showdown. But I was fed up with government inconsistency that read like sleight of hand, and was determined, once and for all, to get the position straight. Chris Gumbley repeated the message at greater length. Levene sat on our stand for about two hours, and he harangued Gumbley and me, and promised that this time it would be different provided we furnished ourselves with the requisite plant. He emphasised this, and revealed that he was aware of our approach to Oerlikon. He suggested we renew our efforts to acquire BMARC, pointing out that they were exhibiting at the Fair, a fact of which we were well aware, having caught sight of one or two faces looking apprehensively our way down the main aisle. Subsequently, there was a mass of correspondence with Levene and his assistant Stephen French, in which they reiterated their intention to let us compete. On the basis of this, great pressure was put on Oerlikon to get on with the deal.

It is important to realise that Astra would not have looked at BMARC had we not been assured by the MoD that we would be allowed to compete in the UK market, that the ammunition manufacturing monopoly in Britain was over. The sheer cost of a deal with Oerlikon for BMARC plant was prohibitive without an opportunity to participate in fair and above-board tenders for the UK arms market.

We were confident that provided there was tendering, we would be assured of a large slice of the UK market, because the only opposition was Royal Ordnance, which had a reputation throughout the trade as complacent, inefficient and spoon-fed. But a solid home base was the *sine qua non* of any deal with BMARC. We simply did not need its basic manufacturing capability in the medium calibre area for exports only, and it was on the basis of Levene's assurances that we proceeded with the deal.

After the Portsmouth Exhibition, doors miraculously opened to us. Suddenly Oerlikon agreed to begin serious negotiations, and for the first time we began to feel that there was genuine interest from the MoD in what we would be able to offer in collaboration with BMARC. We calculated that with the BMARC facility our tenders for the MoD's hard-core ammunition requirement would come in well below RO's, and though time and again we emphasised to the MoD the very big investment that Astra would have to make in order to acquire the facility, Levene and his assistants, Stephen French and Brigadier Peter Landrey (later an executive with Valentec Dayron), consistently reassured us of their commitment to Astra after the deal went through.

That apart, as we looked more closely at what BMARC had to offer in terms of plant, it became clear that BMARC was a high-quality investment on grounds of assets alone. It would have cost Astra half a billion pounds to build up their plant from scratch. Faldingworth comprised 800 acres with very modern storage facilities, and the engineering set-up at Grantham alone would have cost a sum well beyond our capital-raising abilities.

When we sat down to negotiations it emerged that Oerlikon had considerable cash problems. It had developed the ADATS missile (anti-tank, -aircraft, -ship) at a cost of $1bn. This weapon was of excellent quality, but quality alone had not been enough to sell it in the heavily political, main US market. Even a partnership with Martin Marietta did not deliver what was expected.

It was clear to me that we might get all of BMARC for £33m plus an inter-company debt (owed by BMARC to Oerlikon) of £30m. Had it not been for the urgency of MoD tendering, we might have achieved an even better deal. At any rate, negotiations proceeded smoothly and quietly and finalisation was set for the end of October.

Meanwhile, these negotiations focused our minds too on the wider benefit of BMARC to Astra's whole strategy of arms manufacture. We saw that if we had BMARC in the UK alongside our base in America, it would be possible greatly to enhance the transfer of technology from one Astra company to another, from one country to another, on a reciprocal basis, increasing our potential to steal a march on our rivals and to service more ambitious contracts. When, in September 1987, the BMARC deal began to mature, I acted on a further opportunity offered to us in America that would increase our flexibility in this regard.

Kilgore Corporation based in Toone, Tennessee, was one of the original pyrotechnics companies in the USA, making everything from toy pistol caps to the most sophisticated anti-missile decoys for the US navy and air-force, to which it was a major supplier. We acquired the company from Allegheny International for $3.8m.

Let me illustrate by two examples how, after the BMARC and Kilgore deals went through, this strategy worked to Astra's advantage.

One was a contract from the UK (that had nothing to do with the hard-core ammunition market promised us by Levene); the other came from America.

The first was the UK Seagnat contract, worth £7m, for a defence system of great complexity. In a missile attack, a ship has basically three lines of defence. The first is an anti-missile missile (like Sea Wolf), which can attack missiles a long way out. Seagnat fell into the category of second line of defence. It is a system which throws up a whole lot of pyrotechnics and chaff in the pattern of a ship next to the target ship, creating an image of the target ship but next to it, and then another, and another, a succession of images receding, which deceives the enemy's radar or heat-seeking missile into believing that the target ship is moving in a direction and occupying positions which in fact it is not. You will have seen those fireworks that explode like bombs; the Seagnat rockets work in a similar way, each new image forming and drawing the missile further away from the target ship as the last image dies.

It is quite expensive, as you might imagine. But the point is that

Astra would not have won the Seagnat contract had it not had the specialist skills at Kilgore. Our American base, in this case Kilgore, had put a totally new product into BMARC. Kilgore proved itself useful in other ways, too. At Toone it had the space to fill the Walters larger calibre ammunition and fuses contracts, but more crucially it would be the means by which Astra secured the Phalanx order from the US government, a contract worth $20m, which in a complementary example depended upon BMARC's ammunition-filling technology.

The Phalanx (or Goalkeeper or Vulcan) system is the third line of defence possible against missile attack at sea. It is a close-quarter defence system, a Gatling gun with a rate of fire of about 4,000 to 8,000 rounds a minute. However, its efficiency against Exocet-type missile attack, its prime capability, resides in the nature of its ammunition. The warhead in an Exocet is in the tail and can be destroyed head-on only if it is hit with something hard enough and powerful enough to punch right through the nose and length of the missile to the armour-plated warhead in the tail. Kilgore won the $20m order from the US government principally because of BMARC's expertise in making ammunition with depleted uranium or tungsten, uranium being the heaviest metal you can get. This was used in the arrow-shaped armour-piercing tank rounds in the Gulf War.

At the heart of the advantage that BMARC offered Astra was the 'political' ability to manufacture across countries, exploiting their different embargoes.

So the BMARC deal promised (and would deliver to Astra) enormous potential, although whatever big successes we achieved with the company these would not obviate the basic day-to-day requirement of hard-core ammunition contracts from the MoD.

Then, right on the eve of signing, the Stock Exchange collapsed – Black Monday, 19 October 1987.

Encouraged by Stephan Kock, we had earlier appointed Samuel Montagu, the Midland subsidiary, in place of our own merchant bankers, James Capel/Hong Kong Bank. There was no particular reason at this stage for me to have any suspicions about

Kock. I did not disagree with the appointment of Montagu in place of Capel, nor did I disagree with Montagu's subsequent appointment of the broker, Savory Miln, in place of our own, Hichens Harrison. The sales pitch from Midland was that we were getting more muscle.

With hindsight I should have considered the position more carefully. The Midland and Stephan Kock were both, in their different ways, agents of the government, the former as a principal fundraiser for government arms deals to Iran and Iraq, the latter as the principal government fixer for these deals and a lot else besides. Their involvement with Astra was never to be to the benefit of the company.

But the logic of Kock's advice had its own brand of infallibility. The Midland was the only bank with a specialist arms division, so I had every reason to believe that at Montagu we would be dealing with people who knew what they were talking about. Again, at Capel's, Astra's business had been handled by a very capable but then relatively junior executive, David Hickey, whereas at Montagu we were promised two main board directors. Again, Montagu, while having a similar power of underwriting as Capel, combined under one roof the banking syndications and transactions that the BMARC deal would require.

As it turned out, even the immediate benefits were non-existent. On Black Monday, Montagu and Savory Miln were thrown into total chaos. So taken up were they with their own problems, following the collapse of the Market, that neither seemed able to advise Astra how to proceed with the Oerlikon deal. Also, David Hind, the Montagu director closest to our account, was despatched to Hong Kong to deal with Hong Kong Bank's initial well-publicised investment in Midland.

There were additional problems. Other companies had heard of our initiative concerning BMARC via leaks from the MoD. Hunting, a company with which Kock had especially close ties, had made an approach through Warburgs to Oerlikon, and I heard that British Aerospace had also learned from the MoD that we were in negotiation for BMARC.

Leaving aside this appalling breach of confidence, at the time what concerned me was beating off this interest, and, additionally, outwitting the hostile manoeuvrings of BMARC's UK-based deputy MD, one Major-General Isles who, as Werner Leuch, the Swiss managing director of BMARC prior to its takeover by Astra, informed me, was not keen on the sale. What was clear was that if we were to falter at all at this stage, BAe or Hunting or some other company might step in. So there was a lot of pressure on us, and I took matters into my own hands.

I flew to Zurich with Chris Gumbley and Jim Miller, our finance director, and made an agreement with Michael Funk to stabilise the whole situation. We put down £3m for a licence with Oerlikon, whereby Astra would have the right to manufacture on their Faldingworth site for five years, and took an option for a nominal sum of £1 to buy the shares, and to complete the acquisition of BMARC by 30 April 1988, when I hoped the Stock Exchange would have overcome its problems. As I saw it, Oerlikon couldn't lose. It got £3m cash whatever happened, and for £1 Astra had bought the time necessary to re-group and sort out the whole deal, while also retaining plant sufficient to tender for the promised MoD ammunition contracts.

In spite of their ludicrous fees, the City had been unable to see us over a crisis precipitated by the City and other financial markets. In the end it was the initiative of the Astra team, of Gumbley, Miller, and James, and Funk of Oerlikon, which saved the day.

This agreement was signed on Sunday 13 December 1987 at the Savoy Hotel, and the arrangements were announced in the press the following day, an event which sparked the first approach to us by the American investment broker, Paine Webber. It was the first of many approaches by them on the basis that they could arrange a leveraged buy-out of BMARC with bank finance.

Our contact at Paine Webber was one Brian Havill, head of their corporate finance department. He was a nice enough guy, but my immediate reaction to Paine Webber was not a good one, although later they were to play a big part in Astra. It is hard to put a finger on precisely what bothered me, but my first thought on entering their fancy offices in the new Broadgate development behind Liverpool Street was to recall a remark by my erstwhile client John Rawlings (the promoters of Mateus Rosé in the UK) when I had wheeled in the busy young men of Stoy Hayward (by now Astra's own accountants) to solve his business problems. 'It reminds me of *The Sting*!' he had said, and I knew exactly what he meant – all smart young men in waistcoats. At Paine Webber, there were smart offices, self-important receptionists, all the kit – intercoms, faxes, telexes, perpetual luncheoning, the smell of coffee and cooking in the air, plush carpets, fancy furniture, people running around pseudo-busy.

When you have been in the City and sat up all night checking through prospectuses and avoided the mistake of leaving the printer to do the corrections; when you know what it is like getting down to the detail and sat through all the meetings with lawyers, when you have understood the grind that goes into acquisitions and loan stock issues and all the considerations, the depth in detail, you are less than encouraged to find these smart young men jetting around Europe – Switzerland, Germany, France, back and forth across the Atlantic – as if they are going down to Clapham, when they don't always grasp how the London Stock Exchange works. 'Mr Havill's away on business', 'Mr Havill's flying here', – I actually made the remark, 'How does Mr Havill have time to write a letter?' When all this is going on, you know there is something wrong, and you ask yourself where the money is coming from.

Havill had previously been with Thomas Tilling in the US. The Tilling Group, with industrial stakes in many subsidiaries all over the world, was taken over by BTR after a very bitter battle. It was run with a lot of ex-military people on board, again from fancy offices, this time in Curzon Street. The chairman, now dead, Sir Patrick Meaney, was one of the key figures in the Parlour, the industrial end of the 'cognoscenti', linked with Intelligence and the City and the political. In November 1989, when Meaney was chairman of the Rank Organisation, I was invited (November 1989) to a Parlour dinner in the Royal Garden Hotel with Sir John

Nott, Cecil Parkinson, Sir David Plastow, Patrick Sheehey and the rest.

Now, who would be in the American office of Tilling? Again, it was military, political, government. This was Havill's springboard to Paine Webber. Havill's boss was John Lehman, a managing director of Paine Webber and particularly their defence side. A former member of the American National Security Council, Lehman was a friend of Henry Kissinger, and a member of Kissinger Associates. As US navy secretary under Reagan (he resigned in the wake of the Ollie North affair), Lehman had presided over the biggest build-up in US naval power as part of US policy to break the Soviets through competitive military spending. Interestingly, he was also very closely connected with Westland, where Cuckney, of course, was chairman. When United Technologies/Sikorsky took a 7 per cent stake in Westland, Lehman was one of two directors they appointed to the board, thus completing another circle of associations in the development of the cabal's 'interest' in Astra. (The other director was Thomas G Pannoll, former chairman and chief executive of Martin Marietta.) Lehman was also a consultant to VSEL (Vickers Shipbuilding and Engineering) in Barrow, the submarine builder, through his close ties with General Dynamics (all the technology for the nuclear submarine Trident programme comes from General Dynamics). Lehman's own book makes clear his Intelligence connections, and I discovered too that he was a close friend of Lord Chalfont. Chalfont is himself Intelligence connected, listing among his credits 'various . . . intelligence appointments'; he became Defence Spokesman under Wilson, worked as defence correspondent of *The Times*, and was a Minister of State at the Foreign Office before taking his present position as chairman of VSEL (where Lehman was a consultant).

Brian Havill pushed us close to Lehman, and I remember one occasion in particular that I felt gave me a pretty good insight into the level of operations. Lehman had invited me to a skiing weekend out at Beaver Creek, Colorado, where ex-military people employed by Paine Webber were mixing with men from various defence companies, and Al Haig was billed as star of the show.

Haig was supposed to fly in to address us. In the event, he couldn't get in because of the snow.

Havill himself let out a telling remark one day. He told me that the very day of the disaster at Lockerbie he had been in Frankfurt with two Americans, CIA/DIA men, who were killed in the plane. At least five US agents were on that plane, and recovery operations were held up for security reasons. Lockerbie, it is said, occurred in the wake of an Intelligence operation that had gone horribly wrong. American government agencies created the channels without which the bomb could never have been put on the plane and then blamed PanAm for the disaster. The CIA/Drug Enforcement Agency (DEA) were facilitating drug operations from Lebanon in order to trap those who were involved Stateside. Channels were set up for the Lebanese to get drugs into America in a controlled manner, so that the CIA/DEA could trace where they ended up. Unfortunately Iranians and Syrians infiltrated the distribution network and used the safe channels to put the bomb on board. That is why five agents (from the Defence Intelligence Agency (DIA) and CIA and the DEA) were on board when the plane blew up. The book by Lester K. Coleman, a former DIA agent, *Trail of the Octopus*, spells out some of the realities of the affair.

Anyway, at the beginning I didn't feel that Paine Webber would do us any favours at Astra, and much later I would be proved right. But the reason that I vetoed their involvement in the first place was the high level of gearing that their scenario for a leveraged buy-out of BMARC implied. I told them so. I made it quite clear. Yet they continued ringing us up, pressing us, saying that if there was anything at all they could do to help, to let them know. In fact, they continued to do unsolicited work for us for three months.

In my efforts to organise the finance for the purchase of BMARC we arranged trips to the plants for institutions and bankers, all of whom were amazed at the size and scope and sophistication of the operation. I remained optimistic even though the attitude at Montagu was still unenthusiastic. No senior member of their staff had even bothered to take up our invitation to visit BMARC until, in January 1988, David Hind returned to the UK for two weeks and I persuaded him to look over the operation. He too was greatly impressed. You couldn't fail to be. But what came back from that meeting was not at all what it seemed.

Montagu agreed to get on with co-ordinating and arranging the finance for the takeover, which was fine. At last, it seemed, we could begin making progress on the end-deal. But then their proposals came through, and I was less than happy.

They proposed financing the deal with redeemable Convertible Preference shares. But when they produced a written proposal at the eleventh hour, the terms were much less favourable than had been originally suggested. Thirty-three million pounds worth of Convertible Preferred Ordinary shares were to be issued by Montagu and we were to take on a £35m syndicated loan. Now it was immediately clear to me, as I looked at this deal, what it meant for Astra. We already had a substantial number of Ordinary shareholders, but however loyal they might be, because of the yield and conversion terms, the Preference shares would have seemed far more attractive as an investment than their Ordinary shares, which in the Stock Market crash had see-sawed between £0.80 and £0.10. In effect many would have switched to the Preference shares, and the Ordinary shares would have been further depressed. Also, since Montagu was offering the Preference shares to their own clients, Montagu would effectively control them, and the banking arrangements would push the position even more in Montagu's direction. So, you can imagine, I was very uneasy about it, and when I spoke to Dennis Bailey, our co-broker at Hichens Harrison, he expressed grave disapproval of what Montagu were up to.

He pointed out that, even overlooking the power that the deal would give Montagu, the capital structure would leave the company absurdly geared with £10m worth of Ordinary shares, £33m of Preferred Ordinary shares, and a loan of £30m to pay off the inter-company debt between Oerlikon and BMARC. And when the Ordinary shareholders switched into Convertible Preferred or sold their Ordinary shares, as he agreed they were bound to do, this would have the effect of seriously depressing the value of the Ordinary shares.

Bailey begged me to allow him to map out a straightforward equity issue. I told him that Montagu had advised us that this was impossible in the market conditions that prevailed after the collapse on the Stock Exchange. Bailey insisted that this was not the case for a deal such as this, and in the end I agreed he should look into it. I made it clear that a firm proposal was essential.

Late on Friday 25 March, while I was at a meeting with Oerlikon's lawyers, Allen and Overy, Bailey called to say that he had managed to arrange the underwriting of a £33m Ordinary share issue with the Prudential, 3i, and Clerical and Medical.

Contrary to all that Montagu had told us, Bailey had come up with a sound plan to deliver the deal by an issue of Ordinary shares.

Immediately I rang Ian Mackintosh, head of the Montagu corporate side, but all save a junior employee had already gone home for the weekend. I left a message for Mackintosh requesting a meeting on the Saturday or Sunday, explaining the situation and asking him to return my call at the offices of Allen and Overy, where I waited fruitlessly until 9pm. I then went round to Dennis Bailey's office with our lawyers from Baileys, Shaw & Gillett, Laurence Kingswood and Kim Nicholson. Bailey confirmed the deal. Returning home by midnight I found that Mackintosh had left a message to call, requesting no calls after 10pm (a well-ordered life for some!).

On the Saturday morning I rang Mackintosh at home and told him our news. Instead of agreeing to look into the proposal, which was clearly a better scenario for Astra, he said that I must make up my mind whether I was with Bailey or with Montagu, and that I must do so that very morning within one hour. I took this calmly, soliciting his agreement that the £30m loan package with his banking colleagues that Ernie Cole, a director of Montagu, had masterminded, would be unaffected whatever we decided to do. Mackintosh stressed the existence of Chinese walls and total independence.

When I discussed the situation with our directors and the unanimous verdict was to go with Bailey, I rang Mackintosh and told him of our decision. He was horrified and in spite of his undertaking, immediately withdrew the banking package.

I was baffled and extremely perplexed at the prospect of having arranged an equity issue with no banking back-up. There was no reason I could see for Mackintosh's reaction. Montagu were retained by Astra as advisers for the good of the company, the equity issue was clearly more beneficial for the company than the Convertible Preference share issue, there was nothing to prevent him working together with Bailey, and Mackintosh knew that Montagu would be paid anyway. Yet his response – if not overtly obstructionist – left us hopelessly at sea.

Owing to time pressure and the deadline for exercising the option with Oerlikon, and with BAe and Hunting still in the wings, I turned in the only direction I could have turned, to Paine Webber. I rang the Paine Webber offices immediately on that Saturday, and luckily there was someone there to give me Brian Havill's home number. I said I wanted a meeting the next day, the Sunday, and asked him to bring in his banking people. He said he would get a team over from the US. That is what happened. The meeting was held in the Meridien Hotel in Piccadilly and later at our lawyers' office, Baileys, Shaw & Gillett, in Berners Street. In April, after ten days' continuous work, the deal with Oerlikon was at last signed up. The consideration involved £31m-plus of equity and a multi-currency loan facility of £50m (sterling, US dollars and Swiss francs) negotiated with Bank of Boston for the Oerlikon BMARC inter-company debt, and extra finance for testing and setting-up purposes on future contracts with the Ministry of Defence.

During this ten-day period rumours abounded in the market to make the issue more difficult and then the lawyers for the underwriters (Norton Rose, who were incidentally retained by Midland Bank) pulled out, followed by their replacements, Simmons and Simmons, who acted for us for only one week before retiring from the fray. Montagu's final salvo was a threat to issue Astra with a writ for £450,000 worth of fees, an absurd amount for the work they had done, and the manner in which their business had been conducted, which at best had caused serious problems, and at worst could have sabotaged the value of the company whose interests they were retained to represent.

Underlying the deal with Oerlikon, which was ratified the following month, May 1988, was a manufacturing and licensing agreement for BMARC to continue to manufacture Oerlikon's equipment. So, in addition to owning BMARC, Astra became Oerlikon's principal manufacturer. We were making all their ammunition right up to 35mm cannon. This was a fairly complex aspect of the overall agreement. While on the one hand it allowed us to make all their ammunition and guns, which of course we supplied directly to them, there were places where we could sell and ship their equipment direct and other places where we had to go through them. In addition, it was agreed that there would be flexibility if it was to our mutual advantage.

Upon completion of the deal most of the Swiss employees left quickly. Chris Gumbley and I appointed Bill McNaught as managing director of BMARC in place of the Swiss Werner Leuch; retained the services of Major-General Donald Isles, a former director of weapons at the MoD and director of munitions at the British Embassy in Washington, as McNaught's deputy; Lieutenant-Colonel Avery as Isles's assistant; and one Bob Jolly as senior management at BMARC. I did this in spite of the antics of Isles and half a dozen other staff prior to the purchase. Just as we were about to sign the deal, new terms were introduced to change the prevailing statutes of the company's pension fund in a way that would benefit its senior members, Isles included.

With hindsight it was a key error of judgement on my part to retain these people, but at the time I suppose I preferred a moderate policy in favour of continuity, and Stephan Kock was vociferous in Isles's support, citing his closeness to the MoD as being of crucial value to the company. This view was expressed by others outside the company. The logic was that Isles knew BMARC's business intimately and was very experienced in the arms business, and, despite the incident with Roy Ricks, I had some confidence in McNaught (who was Gumbley's brother-in-law, after all) that he would be able to keep a close eye on BMARC's sites at Grantham and Faldingworth on our behalf and run the show to the advantage of the entire Group.

The opposite happened. Major-General Isles began at once to dominate McNaught and to meet secretly with Kock, who became his ally on the Astra and BMARC boards. I would later bitterly regret not retaining Werner Leuch as MD of BMARC. An experienced and capable engineer, who knew how to run an engineering shop, Leuch's plain antipathy towards Isles should have served me with a warning.

It was May 1988, eight months after the Portsmouth Exhibition when Peter Levene had urged us to buy BMARC and compete for MoD contracts with Royal Ordnance, and three months only before the end of the Iran–Iraq war. The calendar is crucial to an understanding of what then transpired.

During my chairmanship of Astra (June 1981 until 2 March 1990), we made three major acquisitions in three totally different countries – the Walters Group in America in April 1987, BMARC in England in May 1988, and in September 1989, Poudreries Réunies de Belgique (PRB) in Belgium. All three of these companies turned out to be dealing in contracts destined eventually for Iraq, Iran, etc., and general covert business with the full knowledge of government and/or the Intelligence services. The extent of illegal or covert dealings beyond Astra can only be guessed at, but official UK arms manufacture figures show annual consumption running at around £500m a year for land services, while the British army budget ran only to about £250m. Where was the other £250m going? And these are only the admitted figures. As I have shown, there is reason to believe that nearer £1bn of arms was going to Iran and Iraq per annum from the UK alone, and that figure does not take into account Thatcher's arms deals.

But now, in May 1988, three months only before the end of the war in which, as in all wars, there had been a complete information clampdown, politicians were becoming aware that when the seven-year war came to an end the post mortem would begin. There would be an inevitable relaxation of control, information would begin to filter through about who had been making money out of it. People would begin to talk.

It is not easy to close down a trade that has become so lucrative. There are many vested interests. Businesses have made investments and have expensively tooled up for the supply. Contracts and licence agreements extend over long periods, they are not bound to peace treaties and the like. There is no easy way to turn off the tap. At the same time, the economy was now dependent on the arms industry. While most industry outside the arms area had been reduced, Britain had moved to No. 2 behind the United States in the arms sales table. There was, therefore, an urgent need to keep arms sales at the highest level even after the end of the Iran–Iraq war. Too much employment, too much of the economy, was dependent on it. Added to this, the kickbacks and commissions had become something of a habit.

What does such a government do faced with such a dilemma? The answer is that at first it begins to keep its cards closer to its chest when conducting its business, it deals only with those companies over which it has power. Then it looks for ways to rid itself of potential embarrassment by 'sanitising' those companies outside its immediate control with which it has been involved in illicit deals.

At Astra we had a unique, if grim, opportunity to watch this strategy unfold.

The first step of the strategy was clear almost as soon as the ink was dry on the contract for BMARC. At once we lobbied hard to compete openly and fairly with Royal Ordnance. It was time to take Peter Levene at his word. Rather oddly, Kock began to advise me not to push so hard. 'Never push your enemy into a corner,' he told me. 'Always give him room to extricate himself with honour.' I would have reason to remember this in our own personal dealings, but I failed to see the logic of not upsetting such a feather-bedded giant as RO.

I thought little about Kock's opposition until one night at dinner at the White Hart Hotel in Lincoln, when he delivered an extraordinary performance on this subject of competition with RO. So fervently was he against our competing with RO that had I then been more keenly aware of his knowledge of the inner workings of government strategy, I might have concluded that Kock had a foot in both camps. As it was, our finance director, Jim Miller, to his credit, accused Kock of sounding like an agent for British Aerospace (RO's new owners)! He was not too far from the truth.

Besides Kock's extraordinary attitude, we had to contend with a hostile reaction from BAe and RO the harder we lobbied the MoD. At the time I put it down to old habits, the fact that they still felt they were the favoured government party.

Both these companies, as I have said, were formerly state owned, funded by the taxpayer. They had been privatised in the spirit of competition that characterised Prime Minister Margaret Thatcher's free market. That at least was the theory. In practice, neither BAe nor RO could be properly privatised, neither was as independent of the government as might appear.

It has been admitted, though it is not commonly known, that the sale of Royal Ordnance to British Aerospace involved incentives which were, all told, in excess of those attached by the government to the Leyland deal with BAe (about which, you may recall, there was so much fuss). The incentives were in various forms: cash funds allocated to cover pollution at RO's Waltham Abbey site; the vesting in RO of the MoD's intellectual property rights (the MoD 'know-how' on weapons and ammunition) for only £1 (these rights were arguably worth billions, see below); settling a price of £90m on RO's physical assets (against the enormous development potential of its Waltham Abbey, Enfield and Bishopton sites); and finally, the government actually paid BAe subsidies for the manufacture of the 105mm light gun and a huge sum on the Alarm missile.

The fattening of the lamb was so blatant that when I asked Nigel Ridd of Williams Holdings why he had not bid for RO, he said that it would have made him feel like one of those bank robbers in a Western who always go too far.

It is worth looking in particular at this business of 'intellectual property rights' in that it sheds light on the continuing dependence of RO on the government following privatisation. These rights are the technology of arms manufacture and ensconced, physically, in data packs. The development of RO's data packs had been paid for by the taxpayer and were probably worth in the region of £2bn, yet the government sold them for £1. The point is that it is not possible to manufacture British specified equipment without them. Any company commissioned by the government to manufacture arms for the forces has to get these packs from RO. While RO are obliged to let manufacturers have the packs for UK contracts drawn with the MoD, there is no such obligation for export, and in practice RO made difficulties – delayed deliveries, etc. – even when they were to participate in a deal as a subcontractor. These data packs were the key element in the RO privatisation, yet they were handed to BAe on a plate.

There were of course various strategies behind the sale of RO by the government. There was Thatcher's denationalisation, her free market principle of competition; there was the need to make Royal Ordnance more efficient than it was when run by civil servants; but there was also the political necessity of distancing RO from the government in line with its official policy of an arms embargo to the Middle East. For this reason, too, BAe was the only company RO could have been sold to for security reasons, because if it had fallen into the hands of an 'outsider', what secrets might have been released?

The government wanted rid of Royal Ordnance, but could not afford to let it slip away completely. It was this contradictory muddle that led to the circus of a sale. BAe had to win because BAe was still, ideologically, government-sponsored, and the government couldn't afford the possibility of an outside company discovering any dubious contracts among RO's files. Hence the sweeteners. Hence, too, I believed, the uproar in May 1988 when

Astra began pushing harder for MoD business and pitching in with prices that were way below what RO's unwieldy set-up could manage.

Failing to appreciate the true nature of the situation, we continued lobbying in the expectation that contracts would be forthcoming. One in fact was. We won a 76mm practice ammunition order from the MoD worth £1m, but it served only to underline our position in the scheme of things. We had great difficulty in prising the necessary data packs from RO, and when we did get them we discovered that we had to go back to RO for certain material components which were impossible to obtain more cheaply elsewhere. They had the whole business tied up.

The crunch came in late May or early June when Brian Peet, an assistant in Levene's procurement department at the MoD, expressed amazement that we were continuing to lobby so hard. As far as he knew, the government had signed an agreement under BAe pressure which gave RO a monopoly for the next five years on 80 per cent of government business plus an ability to compete for the other 20 per cent. Peet described it as The Explosive and Propellant Agreement (EPREP), a contract shrouded to this day in great secrecy.

I couldn't believe it at first. We had had such a lecture from Levene and others that I couldn't believe that they would behave so hypocritically. I rang up Levene immediately and made sure Chris Gumbley was present in the office. I asked what on earth was going on. I said, 'You've been telling us that we can tender for this hard-core ammunition and I have just been told that the government has signed an agreement with BAe giving them a five-year monopoly. We have given you good prices, done everything you asked of us.' I became very annoyed: 'You tell us on the one hand to buy BMARC because you want competition and then we find the bloody PM and Trefgarne have made this secret agreement!' [Lord Trefgarne was Arms Procurement Minister at the time, Levene's boss.]

Levene replied, 'You don't know what you are talking about. I am in charge. I know what's going on; you're talking rubbish!'

I said that we had been told about it by Brian Peet 'in your own department', and Levene went very quiet.

To this day I am unsure whether Levene himself knew about EPREP. Our conversation took place on a Wednesday or Thursday evening. I was told that on the following Saturday morning he called in sixteen to twenty of his staff and read them the riot act. I would like to believe that he genuinely didn't know what was going on, that back in September 1987 he was still an outsider brought into the MoD from industry and that the well-rooted officers of permanent government only brought him into the 'know' slowly. But by May 1988? Surely, if one of his assistants was aware of the secret contract with RO, he too would have known about it.

I am less unsure that Kock had known about EPREP. Leaving aside the occasions when he advised us not to press the MoD to allow us to compete for orders with RO, he seemed to have an inside line on such matters, as was shown by his story to me of how in 1986 he had been in the next office to the Defence Minister Michael Heseltine when the latter was having a furious row with Fred Clark, then chief executive of RO, about the privatisation of the company. Why had Kock been there? What special position permitted Kock that kind of access?

The details of the EPREP agreement remain secret, in spite of the fact that BAe is a company quoted on the London Stock Exchange where disclosure of information is normal. It is understood that the details of it are governed by the Official Secrets Act.

For the truth behind EPREP and the reasons why such a restrictive measure was drawn up at this crucial point towards the end of the Iran–Iraq war, one needs not only to point to RO's involvement in covert business, but also to look deeper into the government's relationship with BMARC and the role it played in covert arms strategy in the 1980s.

One of the first changes we made at BMARC was to bring control of sales under Chris Gumbley at Astra. Before taking over the company we had been told that while BMARC were efficient in manufacturing, they were no good in the sales department and had very much relied on their previous owners, Oerlikon, for this. They had in fact set up their own sales unit under Isles and Avery, but it had suffered from the lieutenant-colonel's attitude towards their Middle East customers in particular, which had proved less than conducive to sales. In short, the unit had not been very successful. However, the new policy was hotly resisted by both Avery and Isles because it disrupted the close relationship they had with the MoD, which, as I have said, grew out of BMARC's evolution from a joint venture with the government Ministry of Supply in 1938, and which Isles and Avery (who had worked with Isles at the MoD) had originally been moved into the company to protect and nurture.

When we began to look closely at their contracts, we saw just why such protection was needed. Immediately apparent were a number of arrangements carried out with the support of the MoD which involved BMARC in the Iran–Iraq war. I discovered that Iranian gun crews had been trained at Faldingworth by special arrangement with the government. After 1984/5, the emphasis had been on Iraqi gun crews masquerading as Saudis, etc. I found various contracts drawn with IMS via the MoD and destined for Jordan; nothing going to Jordan at this time was above board. I discovered that at its Grantham plant BMARC had manufactured Skyguard, the twin-barrel 35mm anti-aircraft guns which Saddam Hussein installed around Baghdad, and continued to make the principal parts of Skyguard under licence for its old parent, Oerlikon, in Switzerland.

Skyguard was a particularly lucrative deal for Oerlikon, as one of the features of the rapid-fire system is that the barrels tend to wear out quickly when overlong bursts are fired. Oerlikon had a company in Italy dedicated to 'nitriding' (hardening) Skyguard barrels, and Casalee, the company that fixed the Skyguard deal for Oerlikon with Iran and Iraq, built a significant part of its enormous wealth on this fact.

Casalee, I discovered, was the agent for many of Oerlikon's sales; in particular there was a BMARC project called LISI, an order to supply medium-calibre armaments – ammunition,

weapons and tooling – to Charter Industries of Singapore, a
recognised conduit for Iran. The project had been initiated under
General Isles for Oerlikon.

The presence of Casalee was itself a pointer to the depth of
BMARC's involvement with government-backed covert trade.
Casalee I now know to have been a very important company in
the context of covert arms dealing by both the US and UK governments. It was set up in Rhodesia during UDI and was run by
Rhodesians and South Africans to sell tobacco leaf in exchange for
weapons and simply as a cover for arms sales. Officially there
were sanctions against Rhodesia, of course, but the reality was
that the South African regime was virtually the sole Western supplier of chrome metal and other strategic minerals, and for
defence and economic reasons this was not a market either MI6 or
the CIA could leave to the Russians. Equally important, Rhodesia
was close to other key mineral-producers like Zambia and the former Belgian Congo. There were also the communist-inspired
problems in the former Portuguese colonies of Angola and
Mozambique, and for all these reasons, as I have explained, the
stability and friendship of key African states was important to
Western governments, which looked after their interests with
covert tactics that favoured South Africa in particular in its rise
(ironically under official arms sanctions) to becoming one of the
world's most important centres for arms manufacture and distribution.

Casalee played a principal role in this and became closely
bound up with both British and American intelligence services.

The covert political culture of Africa, which we have seen provided Jim Guerin through Fuchs Electronics with a main supply
line to Iraq (and which we were involved with through
Walters/Accudyne), was also of course the seeding ground for the
likes of Stephan Kock and Bernard Wheeler, with their links to
British United Industrialists and Tory Party funds. But at the very
heart of the covert arms business in South Africa is the state-
owned arms company, Armscor.

Armscor is the company that in the 1970s operated, over a

period of six years, in league with the CIA and Jim Guerin's ISC. An estimated $15m worth of arms were involved in the traffic each year. Armscor is also the company that supplied Guerin with the PGM missile system for the conventional and nuclear weapon contracts that brought Ferranti to its knees. In 1977, it was Armscor that bought 20 per cent of SRC in order to ensure its survival and to acquire Bull's valuable patents and licences. It is also the company that operated with the CIA and Gerald Bull's SRC-I and landed Bull himself in prison in 1980.

Finally, Armscor is the company that in the 1970s and 1980s was exporting massive quantities of arms to Iraq, facilitating Cardoen's exports to Iraq from Chile, and dealing (even as late as this year, 1994) with one of the British companies that turns up again and again in the big deals – Trafalgar House, a major donor to Tory Party funds.

In November 1994 Trafalgar House was the subject of a letter from Michael Meacher MP to the Prime Minister, in which he wrote: 'Trafalgar House . . . was the major supplier to Armscor of 155mm shells which the South African company sold to Iraq between 1980 and 1990. No doubt Lord Justice Scott will deal with this, but I want you to tell me what steps were taken in the UK to find out what else [Trafalgar's associate company] Blockberg Engineering was making for the apartheid regime, and let me know whether this included components for the South African A-bomb.'

Ironically, British and American sanctions on South Africa over apartheid, which should have thwarted the trade, provided the ideal environment for covert arms deal to proliferate. 'Sanctions meant making money,' said Mike Pelham, former manager of Casalee. 'When you are breaking sanctions, people are likely to keep quiet about it . . . the publicity is very little.'[1]

I find it very interesting that nothing ever happened over apartheid in South Africa until the Iron Curtain collapsed. It happened almost immediately afterwards, and of course Mandela was pushed to the fore. Sanctions, far from crippling South Africa and Rhodesia, had provided the context in which money could be made. And this, rather than any posturing about apartheid, is what drove our policy towards Africa. UK and US Intelligence services thrived in the covert context, just as no doubt MI5 and MI6 thrived in Ireland and will thrive as long as it remains a covert context.

Now that sanctions have been lifted and the removal of apartheid is on the official agenda, will we see a big change? How serious the politicians are, remains to be seen. When you get down to it, what do you hear now about South Africa, other than trade? Who is actually running South Africa now? There is a mixed elected government, but who is actually running the country? The answer, I fear, is, the same people as before.

What of the future? What industry is going to provide all the benefits to the 'new' South Africa? I'm afraid it must be Armscor. That is why John Major went there in the autumn of 1994. He went 'armed with sportsmen', but what he discussed was the export of South African munitions and Bull designed artillery, what we will buy from them and what they will buy from us, from GEC, frigates from Yarrow and so on. Because the reality is that nothing has changed.

Casalee was set up after UDI in Rhodesia (November 1965). It was named after the two daughters, Caron and Sarah, and the wife, Lee, of one John Bredenkamp, a former captain of the Rhodesian rugby team and former Rhodesian SAS officer, who later ran the finances of the Zimbabwe national army. Today, Bredenkamp lives in Hurst in Berkshire and is one of the richest men in Britain, his wealth estimated recently by Mike Pelham as 'in excess of £200m cash, and that excludes fixed assets'.

Before he sold out, Casalee had bases all over the world, including America, Luxembourg and, of course Brussels, with its special understanding with the Intelligence services of Britain. In 1991, the Group employed 1,400 people and declared sales of £500m. Casalee made its vast wealth acting as middleman (introducing supplier to purchaser) to all the major players in the arms industry with the blessing of both US and British Intelligence. According to the Belgian Public Prosecutor, Casalee was in fact largely connected and controlled by MI5, the British security service with Intelligence responsibilities in former colonies.

In acquiring BMARC, we had acquired not just LISI and a history of involvement with both Iran and Iraq, but close and regular contact with a company at the very heart of illicit arms trafficking sponsored by the UK and US governments. I believe this was one reason why Major-General Isles had been nervous about our acquiring the company. The fresh-faced team at Astra was hardly in the same league. The last requirement was for ambitious nosey parkers who might actually find out and meddle in what was going on. This was one reason for the early apprehension in BMARC about Astra, its new owners, and the source of the friction to come. So concerned were the powers to ensure an uninterrupted and secure flow of illicit business that it was seen fit to place one of Casalee's own key executives, Robert Jolly, on the payroll of BMARC just two months before we completed the purchase of the company.

Jolly has an interesting background. In 1977 Bredenkamp had been arrested for breaching trading restrictions by smuggling planes and helicopters into Rhodesia. Plane-spotters had photographed an aircraft in a shed in Belgium. As was recently revealed by *Dispatches* on Channel 4 Television, Robert Jolly (Special Branch, Rhodesia) had been the arresting officer. When, as White law in Rhodesia collapsed, Bredenkamp was allowed to flee to South Africa, Jolly had subsequently come to work for him. Our Robert Jolly, it is safe to say, was no ordinary Astra employee.

Secrecy and security was paramount in Casalee, a company which represented the interests of the most powerful governments in the Western world. So close was Bredenkamp with the apartheid government in South Africa, with its crucial contacts in British and US Intelligence, that in 1986 he had been allowed to appoint the managing director of Armscor to spearhead a drive into Europe just as the British government was getting its own arms-to-Iraq business into top gear. I suggest that the appointment of Armscor's Jacobus Coetze, who now lives near Bredenkamp in Berkshire, was a significant pointer to the official

sponsorship of Casalee by both British and South African governments.

In February of the same year, a Casalee deal to deliver nine million anti-personnel mines manufactured by Valsella in Italy to
Baghdad, again via Singapore, came to a successful conclusion. As
usual, Baghdad had asked BNL to open letters of credit, on this
occasion for $150m. It is an interesting and unprecedented feature
of the eventual collapse and investigation of BNL that many agencies, including the Customs service, refused point blank to hand
over hundreds of documents which the investigating committee
had subpoenaed. *Dispatches* reported that 'the Committee is currently being denied information from the White House, the state
department, the Treasury Department, the CIA, the National
Security Agency, and the Department of Defense . . . [rekindling]
longstanding suspicions on both sides of the Atlantic that there
was a hidden hand behind Casalee and its bank.'

It was a feature of Casalee deals that the company was paid
commissions by the manufacturer, out of which further commissions were paid to 'officials' who had facilitated the deals, often in
cash. Bob Jolly told me that he used to have to transport huge
quantities of cash personally. While Letters of Credit existed for
manufacturers and purchasers, there was little paperwork, little
evidence of transactions naming Casalee, and presumably none
naming the officials receiving commissions.

It is interesting what became of Jolly. He slipped away from
BMARC in spring 1990 as soon as the decision was taken to run
Astra down, and subsequently went to work for Heckler and Koch,
whose managing director was prosecuted for covert deals with
Royal Ordnance. In fact, Heckler and Koch is now owned by RO,
itself still so close to the British government that it employs MoD
police at its sites.

Stephan Kock meanwhile was positioning his pieces to secure
his own power base and some sort of autonomy for BMARC
within Astra, and began to effect control over it through his own
appointments to protect its special status within the covert arms
business.

After the BMARC acquisition, he insisted that we keep General Isles because of his connections with the MoD, from which of course contracts like LISI stemmed, and a matter of months after he joined Astra he turned his attention to promoting the position in the company of another man, John Sellens.

Sellens had come to us as managing director of Kock's friend Richard Unwin's company, which you will recall we acquired in October 1986. Previously, Sellens was involved directly with government trade to Iraq when, at Thorn EMI, he spearheaded the sale of the Cymbeline artillery-locating system to Saddam Hussein.

I liked Sellens and got on well with him personally. His past record meant that, if not exactly one of the 'cognoscenti', he was certainly more in tune with covert government arms policy than the rest of us at Astra. But, after being a bit wary of the founder directors initially, he did his best for the company, split as it became by false loyalties. Indeed, ultimately it would prove to be to Sellens' detriment that he showed us loyalty.

At the time that Kock started on his antics regarding Sellens, I was out in America working on the complex contractual details of the Walters/Accudyne deal with Bob Martin and Bill Simon of the US lawyers Leva, Hawes, Mason and Martin, and Dick White and Walters' Chicago-based lawyers, Jenner and Block, one of the most forward commercial firms on company matters in the US.

The whole business proved very onerous – Walters' lawyers quibbled over every last word in the contract – and there was a time constraint, so I was under quite a lot of pressure both from our lawyers in America, and at the same time from Laurence Kingswood of our British lawyers, Baileys, Shaw & Gillett, who were working on the requisite documents for the Stock Exchange.

I was working every day co-ordinating the whole operation, Saturday, Sunday included, sometimes two or three nights on the trot – we used to have a break or two and I'd go back to the hotel and take a bath before going back again, and on it would go.

It was quite late one Sunday evening, 8 or 9 o'clock, so 2 or 3 o'clock in the morning in the UK, when the phone rang. It was

Kock, tired and emotional, saying, 'I want to know about John Sellens; that idiot Gumbley is not dealing with his salary properly. I feel I should take a hand in it.'

It was the last matter I wanted to become entangled with. 'Look,' I said, 'I'm extremely busy, under a lot of pressure, so I'll talk to you about it when I get back. I don't want to be interrupted with all this now. Talk to Gumbley about it.'

Through the evening Kock rang back two or three times about Sellens' pay and Gumbley's hopeless inability to sort out the problem. Each time I repeated that I would see to it on my return. Finally, Kock insisted that I tell him where he could contact Gumbley that very night, and to get him off my back I did tell him that Gumbley was staying over in London at the Tara Hotel in Kensington, 'but don't bother him about it and don't ring me again,' I said. 'I'll deal with it when I get back.'

I learned later from our finance director Jim Miller that Kock had raised Gumbley from his bed in the middle of the night and subjected him to the most ridiculous pressure over Sellens. Gumbley had apparently been on the point of resigning. I dare say Kock would not have shed any tears if he had.

Sales were to be a main bone of contention at the outset with BMARC, when we moved the responsibility from Isles and Avery to under Gumbley's wing. Of course the post of sales director, in the proliferation of covert government business, was key and required someone in the know.

When I returned to London and spoke to Chris Gumbley and Jim Miller about it all, the only suspicion I had was whether perhaps Kock and Unwin had promised Sellens a rake-off from the sale of Unwin's company to Astra, and sought rather to reward him through his salary. I would not be aware until some time after we acquired BMARC of the deeply covert nature of government dealings through its satellite companies.

What I did see for sure for the first time was that, on the basis of the way he had handled himself, this man Kock might be a source of trouble for Astra. I said to the others that as far as I was concerned we could get rid of him. But Gumbley felt that on balance we should keep him. Kock's connections, particularly with the Midland Bank, seemed too important to lose. In the end we agreed to see how things matured.

Later, we did in fact give Kock what he wanted and appointed Sellens as sales director with appropriate salary, though he never had a place on the main Astra board. Just how difficult a path Sellens trod, being party to inside information about covert MoD work going through BMARC, was shown at the Naval Equipment Exhibition at Portsmouth in 1989, when we were making a presentation of new orders.

Sellens was chatting with the journalist Jane Renton of the *Observer*, who has since exposed a great deal of the government's illicit trade with the Middle East and was subjected to such pressure from Lord Trefgarne at the MoD over her investigation of the EPREP agreement that, as Melvyn Marckus, her boss on the *Observer*, told me, she had to be put up in a hotel for her own safety.

On the occasion of the Portsmouth exhibition, when we were announcing our forward programme of contracts, Sellens whispered to Jane Renton something to the effect that 'these clowns don't know half the projects that are going through this company.' Jane asked him why he hadn't told me or Chris Gumbley about it, and said something about corporate responsibility. The conversation petered out, but Jane came up to me afterwards and repeated what had been said.

After the incident with Gumbley over Sellens, Kock appeared to lie low for a while, moving between the MoD, FCO, Downing Street, Midland, Astra and BMARC from his base at the Special Forces Club, and commuting up to his new home in Scotland to sail his boat, a heavy sea-going, ex-fishing vessel. Meanwhile I became wholly involved in other matters.

Following the discovery of EPREP, we saw our immediate priority as finding a way to replace the hoped-for revenue from the MoD. With our UK/USA operation going well, and with early talk of the EEC 'free market' in mind, Europe seemed a good way to develop.

Peter Levene had talked to the industry of the desirability of UK defence mergers with Europe, France in particular. Under EEC arrangements, European defence companies were supposed to be in a position to tender for UK defence contracts by 1992.

A European company would provide Astra with an efficient and competitive way of working within NATO, where common standards and systems are required, as was the case, for example, with the European fighter, the Tornado, and Jaguar fighters, and the tripartite agreement between Germany, Italy and the UK on 155mm guns and ammunition.

In June–July 1988 and with impeccable if not to say well-informed timing, Paine Webber approached me with a possible way to effect this. Poudreries Réunies de Belgique (PRB) was up for sale and we were the first to hear.

Chasing this, the third of my three big acquisitions for Astra, took up much of my time, and I left BMARC very much to Bill McNaught, deploying new Astra personnel on a day-to-day basis in an attempt to balance the effect of the influence Isles and Avery now exerted over the managing director.

Kock, who made it his business to be close to BMARC from the start, now began to form his power base down at BMARC's Grantham offices. Unaware of his purpose, I am afraid I had encouraged this. When he first moved up to his Scottish hideaway, Kock would breeze in and out of our office in Linen Hall and, being a non-executive director and having no official office of his own there, would try and push into mine, making use of my secretary whenever he could, especially when I was away.

Eventually I had to say that this couldn't continue, and we reached an agreement that he should come in only when there was a meeting. So it was that he took to going up to Grantham and using the secretarial and other office facilities, phone, fax, etc., of his buddy Major-General Isles.

My encouragement of Kock's more regular association with the BMARC contingent and my leaving them too much to themselves did not turn out to have been a wise move, but you will appreciate that by then we were a large company with between

2,000 and 3,000 employees and it would have been hopelessly inefficient for me, Chris Gumbley or the group finance director Jim Miller to spend time looking over the shoulders of people, all of whom had the background and experience on paper to enable them to run the business to the benefit of the Group.

My priority, as I saw it, was to pursue this PRB acquisition, which I regarded as a sound riposte to the duplicity of EPREP and our best means to strike back at RO through a company with superior commercial technology and larger markets.

Even while this was going on, however, my attention was drawn increasingly to something not quite right at the Lincolnshire plants.

On one occasion, in 1988–9, BMARC was asked to quote for supplying 35mm ammunition to the Cyprus government, which seemed to me an excellent opportunity. The deal was the work of a salesman called Graham Willett who had come to us from Royal Ordnance. He had worked under one Lionel Jones, whom later we came to know particularly well and would be an invaluable source of information on the EPREP agreement among other matters. Willett knew the political set-up in Cyprus and was close to ministers in the left-wing government and other people there, because he had dealt with them at RO. But frequently RO had had to buy in from Oerlikon or BMARC, or BMARC via Oerlikon in the servicing of these Cyprus contracts, because of the ammunition calibre involved. Naturally when Willett joined us it was an immediate strategy of his to bring these deals direct to BMARC and miss RO out.

Major-General Isles, however, when he heard about this, summoned Willett into his office and dressed him down as if he were some private in the Duke of Wellington's. Willett, who would have none of it, went to see Gumbley, which was the point at which I was drawn into the matter.

In conversation with me, Isles became concerned to a degree that seemed to me totally out of context with the importance of the contract. I found that odd enough, but his explanation was even more inexplicable. He claimed that supplying Cyprus direct with this calibre ammunition would cut across our licensing agreement with Oerlikon. True, under Astra/BMARC's licensing agreement with Oerlikon, 35mm was to be manufactured by us and sold by Oerlikon. However, we had agreed with Michael Funk to consult closely over just this kind of deal and, in this particular case, had already cleared the matter with Oerlikon at a dinner at which Isles himself had been present.

I put it to him plainly, with Chris Gumbley, that we should proceed with the contract. But in spite of my instructions, Isles arranged with his erstwhile employers, Oerlikon, for them to look after the supply part of the contract, BMARC retaining only the manufacture of the ammunition.

Only later did enquiries, such as those into Casalee by the media, and by Swedish Customs into Scandinavian Commodities, one of the co-ordinating companies (like Allivane) of the arms and propellant cartel, reveal that Cyprus was a regular false end-user for Iraq.

Where there is covert supply there are fat commissions payable en route. My insisting that we handle the 35mm ammunition contract with Cyprus had threatened to upset the supply and commission arrangements of the arms network which took arms and ammunition via Cyprus to Iraq. There is a memo dated 4 January 1989 from McNaught to Isles which shows that the route this contract took was Singapore–Cyprus–Iraq. As with LISI, Singapore was the critical MI6 springboard for illicit contracts to the war zone. Unwittingly, I had touched a raw nerve in Isles, and the whole business was an indication of our and BMARC's wholly divergent paths.

I want to make quite clear what these divergent paths meant at this time. If you were to ask me if I wanted to join the arms and propellant cartel that BMARC and so many of the establishment companies were involved with at this time, then I would repeat what I said about Walters/Accudyne's work in this field in America. I was happy that we were making money. I was concerned about the repercussions, but it was the US government, the DoD, which was guiding the trade in the direction it went.

In the UK the situation was the same in that the MoD was in control of what was going on, and I believe that at the time Kock first came on the Astra board, right up to the time we made our bid for BMARC (1986 to 1987–8), the arms cabal were disposed to welcome us into the fold. Kock's work for us, his redirecting our financial and broking services through 'safe' Midland-connected channels, Montagu and Savory Miln, in line with government form, was part of the policy of Astra's 'recruitment'. I believe also that the purchase during this period of 200,000 shares in Astra in the name of Valerie Harkess, former mistress of Trade Minister Alan Clark, marked out pretty clearly how the government viewed the potential of BMARC in the covert context in 1987–88.

These were the earliest significant signs of what amounted in the end to a takeover of Astra by the cabal.

Even at the start I did not read these signs opportunistically. Our rule at all times was to ask the DoD or MoD, and provided they were agreeable that a particular contract was in order, we would take on the work. Because of the kind of man I am, determined I admit, but also fiercely loyal to the company and the people with whom I had set out to build Astra back in 1981, and wholly averse to falling in line with the plans of the spongers who swarmed all over us, I resisted the encroachment and drove those who were engaged in it underground, so that there ensued a bitter struggle with the same forces that had wooed us. There was never a 'holier-than-thou' decision by me not to participate in BMARC's business with the arms cartel back in 1987 – I never saw it as an option. What I did see, however, and it became increasingly clear to me, was that our control of Astra was in danger of slipping away.

Every month we, the Astra board, looked at the BMARC production figures, and around the same time as Isles became hysterical over the Cyprus contract – at the end of 1988 and into 1989 – I became concerned that BMARC's profit margins on contracts seemed very thin on the volume of business.

When I put it to McNaught at a BMARC board meeting at Grantham, the consensus was that they had to get to a certain throughput figure to reach breakeven point. Basically, they were saying that they needed more contracts to raise turnover if they were to realise the profit margins we required.

But when Gumbley's team then produced the contracts, they complained that they couldn't handle the extra load. This went on for a number of months, and none of it was making any sense. I suggested to Gumbley that McNaught should be replaced as managing director if he couldn't make the show work to its potential. Gumbley, however, was all for letting Bill get on with it.

I had agreed to put McNaught into BMARC because I had hoped that the family connection between the two of them would work to cement a good working relationship between Astra and BMARC and strengthen loyalty to the holding company. It was a mistake, for it served instead to encourage Gumbley to soft-pedal on McNaught and give him the benefit of the doubt.

I do not, however, wish to claim to have always been right. On the contrary, Chris Gumbley had gone to the root of the problem at the outset. He had wanted to sack Isles, and because of the MoD connection I had shared Kock's view to keep him.

Chris then put in a man called Frank Percival to keep an eye on production at Grantham. Frank was a man I could trust, an engineer and consultant who had been brought on to the Brocks payroll when Arthur Reed's management had fallen out with the family. He put him in to improve the efficiency of production cost-wise, and Frank soon came back to us with what he saw as the problem. It appeared to him that production was consuming far too large a quantity of materials for the project output.

I became so concerned that even while I was involved in the complexities of the PRB deal I started getting up at 5 and 6 o'clock in the morning and going down to look at what was actually going on in the factory.

On one occasion I chose to look in at the production line which was machining fuses, and was struck at once by the huge amount of wastage in the bins. You might expect two or three rejects, but here were buckets full of nose-cones. I took it up with the foreman, saying that we seemed to be creating an inordinate amount of wastage for the level of work I knew to be going through. He replied, 'We're getting some of these made by your chum.' I asked him what he meant, and he said, 'We're getting some of the cones made by your Mr Barchard.'

Barchard ran a small engineering firm which did sub-contracting work for Royal Ordnance. I had asked him to come in as a consultant and see whether we could tackle the problem with the production figures by organising or running the plant more efficiently in some way.

This was not the act of someone trying to make trouble, it was organised in a proper way with the management of BMARC for the good of the company. Barchard had had a look round and suggested some improvements in the way the production line was laid out and that we should install more wholly-automated machines which process themselves, alter tools and so on. While he was there, he had agreed to take on a sub-contract for them, which was nothing to do with me. Yet this foreman's assumption was that he was 'my chum', that Barchard's nose-cones had come part-machined and that because the originals were not good enough there was a higher than usual reject rate.

I was not satisfied; it seemed too pat, too weighted an excuse. I told him I would be coming back to it.

When later that day I took it up at a BMARC board meeting I got no more satisfactory an explanation, though significantly it was nothing to do with Barchard. I was told that there was a high reject rate because of the precision nature of the fuse and that when you are making large numbers you do get a high reject rate. This is simply not true. They also told me that the bins were emptied at the end of the week and that at certain times they would be bound to be full or overflowing. This, I discovered by making frequent trips to the same part of the factory, was not true either.

I became increasingly suspicious and wrote a string of memoranda to McNaught and suggested that he might do well to consult with Isles, who, as BMARC's deputy managing director before the takeover, had direct experience of the workings of the plant. The more suspicious I became, the more pressure I exerted, and the more marked became the latent hostility to Astra from BMARC.

This obviously concerned me greatly, as it did the other original members of the Astra board. There had always been a difference in attitude between the Astra people and those at BMARC, a difference which I had read as a difference between the big company ethos (BMARC having been a part of a large corporation, Oerlikon, monopolistic in its field) and that of the relatively small aggressive independent, Astra, outsiders in terms of the domestic defence establishment.

I could take this on board, even a certain amount of resentment on their part. I could live with that. What bothered me was that they had now become surly and uncommunicative.

I discussed the situation with Miller and Gumbley. But we agreed that while it was an unsatisfactory situation in company terms, we should continue to find out what was actually going wrong at the subsidiary. We agreed to investigate further and sort out what we regarded as the assailable day-to-day problems and find a solution to them as soon as we could.

One of the people I spoke to in the course of these investigations was Dr Roy Kelly, one of RO's senior technical people we had put in to manage the BMARC site at Faldingworth. Kelly was the one who first alerted me to BMARC's Iraq-bound Ordtec contract. He let slip in the course of conversation that BMARC was involved in a project to supply Gerald Bull's SRC with booster pellets for his Supergun propellant. I was amazed, having heard nothing about the contract or the Supergun. The contract, so secretive that even Kelly could tell me little more, was drawn by BMARC in early 1989 with B & J Industries, a Sleaford company now defunct. There was no mention of Ordtec or SRC.

When I gave evidence in 1991 to the House of Commons Trade and Industry Select Committee Inquiry into Exports to Iraq I reiterated Kelly's story. It was still all that I knew about it. But since then I have discovered that while it is true that the contract flowed from one drawn between Ordtec and SRC (Geneva), and was going via Jordan to Iraq, the pellets were in fact for fuses for shells for Bull's 210mm self-propelled gun, not the Supergun. It was the Iraq-bound contract over which the Ordtec executives were prosecuted by the government. No one at BMARC was ever touched, although documents supplied to the Select Committee make clear the involvement of Isles, Kock, Avery and McNaught. So close were they with the MoD that Avery was all set to be their main prosecution witness until the government's gagging orders (the PIICs) led to the Ordtec defendants' lawyer advising his clients to plead guilty and do a deal with the prosecution.

The fuses BMARC were boostering were coming from Rexon in New Jersey (in all probability from Accudyne originally). The instructions to Avery were to remove labels to prevent tracing.

When I resigned in April 1990 it was the time of the arrests of various Forgemasters, Walter Somers, and SRC executives over the Supergun project, the assassination of Gerald Bull, the seizure at Heathrow of the Euromac 'nuclear' capacitors, the murder in Santiago of Jonathan Moyle and the seizure by Customs of the steel barrels for the Supergun. Suddenly, it seemed that no one was safe whatever the closeness of their working relationship with government, and Isles, Avery and McNaught began running around like crazy covering their tracks as best they could. The Ordtec contract became their pressing concern.

I would never have known what actually transpired had not Frank Machon, the Glaswegian haulage contractor for Allivane somehow got hold of a letter and memo, which subsequently I discovered had been filed secretly with the Supergun papers in the House of Lords record room. On 2 May 1990, in the welter of activity at BMARC to sweep clean in the official light of inquiry, McNaught delivered a letter to Bob Primrose, Director of Marketing at the MoD, describing the contract:

to produce booster pellets for artillery fuses for Jordan. Astra's customer is Ordnance Technologies Ltd (ORDTEC) of Twyford, Reading. The contract is for the supply of 300,000 M739 booster pellets between March and July of this year.

These pellets are to be matched with their associated fuse components delivered from a US company called Rexon
Technology Corporation of Wayne, New Jersey, and then delivered to a UK port for onward shipment to Jordan . . . My
suspicions have been aroused because I have found a letter on
our file indicating that the main contractor for this project is
SRC Engineering of Geneva . . . I should also add that from the
documentation you will see that the consignee address is the Al
Fao Organisation c/o The Jordanian Armed Forces.

McNaught's 'sudden realisation' about its Iraqi destination, absurd
in the light of the length of time he had been working on it, was
copied to Kock with a covering memo, which was copied to Isles.
I was told that the clean-up operation nearly gave McNaught a
breakdown.

The Ordtec contract and the LISI contract were more or less
visible aspects of the covert trade with which BMARC was
involved with the MoD. The problem of the BMARC production
figures had begun to suggest another tier of covert activity altogether, which did not even make the contract lists. But although
Frank Percival kept digging around and unearthing inconsistencies
and producing figures that continued to make little sense, there
was no real breakthrough up until his sudden death in the
summer of 1989.

This was a shock to us at the holding company, for Frank was
a fit and healthy man with no record of heart problems; we had
no inkling of any health problems of any kind. Of course these
things happen, but I remember being more than a little curious.
Frank was an experienced man and had been digging deep. His
death removed an important light on the dark areas in BMARC.

Frank's passing followed another curious incident – the departure, occasioned by Major-General Isles, of John Green, a man we
had proposed as site manager for Faldingworth and who had also
been contributing to my investigation files. The summer of 1989
was a crucial period in more ways than one, as I will show.

Meanwhile, one of the points I had asked Roy Kelly to look out for was the weight of traffic at Faldingworth, what was coming in and going out. With Kelly's help, I began to establish a dossier of movements of lorries which were unaccounted for. He told me of trucks coming in from ICI and going out the very next day. I couldn't place anything from the company in BMARC's schedule. Kelly said that he had assumed I must know what they were doing there.

The reason I put Kelly on to this was not anything I had seen at the site. As my investigations began to suggest reasons beyond company politics for the factious behaviour at BMARC, I was reminded of a rumour which had been spread around our Richborough plant in Kent in the early days of Astra.

In 1984–5 Gumbley had been asked by Allivane's chief executive, Terry Byrne, to undertake a contract to fill charge bags for them. (For the story of the covert MoD/Allivane trade, see p. 97.)

Charge bags drive shells through the air. In the case of a field gun they are encased in a large brass cartridge case. In order to alter a charge you take off the leather cup and remove one or more of them. In the case of medium and heavier guns, particularly naval guns, the charge bags are loaded into the breech without any casing. We were asked to fill some of these bags for 155mm ammunition for Allivane.

As a result of this contract we built up an on-going relationship, and two MoD/Allivane personnel were assigned to us down at Richborough. One, a man called Taylor, had worked under Gordon Foxley, head of ammunition purchasing at the MoD, who would be convicted in strange circumstances in 1993 for receiving £1.5m kickbacks from the fuse or munitions manufacturers Fratelli Borletti of Milan, Junghans of Schramberg, Germany, and Raufoss of Gjovik, Norway. I will return to Foxley later; the relevant point now is that Foxley worked under a certain Major-General Isles at the MoD.

The other man sent down to us was called Robertson. Under the direction of Taylor, who was also charged in connection with the Foxley case, and Robertson, the charge bag-filling commission extended to other things. I actually became interested in what was going on after I received a report that there was a fiddle concerning our fireworks, that stock was disappearing. I went down to see for myself what was going on. I found no evidence of any fireworks fiddle, but something our site manager, John Green, said to me switched my interest to the activities of Taylor and Robertson. What was rumoured was a regular passage of containers stopping overnight on our site before being trucked out again the following day.

When I asked questions, I never got satisfactory answers, and the matter was complicated by the fact that we were expanding our own production at the time and, in need of extra storage, had bought in a load of containers rather than put more buildings up. So we had containers for our own legitimate purpose on site, and without a full-scale search it would have been difficult to ascertain which were being used for legitimate business and which, if any, were part of the Allivane operation.

I asked questions – I had pursued it to the point of questioning our technical director, Martin Guest, a member of the Astra main board – but didn't make an issue of it because there was no reason to get particularly excited. If I noted a certain uneasiness, I could reassure myself that there was nothing funny going on with the fireworks stock and if we were making a little extra money with Allivane, why should I, Martin Guest, or anyone at Astra be concerned? No one at that stage knew anything of the extent of the arms and propellant cartel business that Allivane and the MoD were running.

As technical director, Martin Guest was the most positively vetted of all from a security point of view. He is an excellent man. If, however, this book shows nothing else, it demonstrates that because of the government's use of companies to further its covert strategy without the consent of managements or shareholders, the burden of official secrecy can sometimes outweigh that of a director's duties to the company and shareholders. Such is the division of loyalties that recently, in a conversation with the journalist David Hellier, Huw Jones of the Prudential (one of Astra's main institutional shareholders) said that he doubted the advisability of quoting arms companies on the Stock Exchange, so much is going on that shareholders will never know.

Interestingly, a year or so later in the latter part of 1986, at the time that Richard Unwin was pressing us to take over his company, which had plant on the Essex marshes so especially well suited to the storage of explosives, Allivane came back to us with a substantial order to assemble M11 charges for use in large-bore (155mm and 203mm) howitzers.

It would be some time, however, before Allivane's haulage contractor Frank Machon provided me with evidence that we were being used by the cartel as a depot in its distribution line through Europe to Iran and Iraq.

In 1991, long after I had parted company with Astra, Richard Norton-Taylor of the *Guardian* received a whole stack of evidence from Frank Machon and asked me to help him to evaluate it. As a result of that I met Machon and one night at about 2 or 3 in the morning he played a tape of a conversation between Gerrard Heneaghan, the managing director of Allivane, and some other party. They talked about a 155mm order worth £100m. 'Is that the one that was sent via BMARC?' the other party asked Heneaghan.

If you need to leave a shipment of explosives overnight you cannot simply stop in a layby or lorry park; you have to find and use a site designed for storing explosives. Our site in Sandwich was an obvious facility, but the BMARC site at Faldingworth was even better equipped, and that was what, in the context of our problems with BMARC, brought this earlier experience to mind.

The site at Faldingworth included an indoor range and engineering shops, a filling plant, old RAF storage facilities, watch towers, electronic detection, dog runs, the lot. I had always wondered why Oerlikon, when they had bought BMARC in 1971 as part of their takeover of the Geneva-based company Hispano Suiza, had deemed it necessary also to buy Faldingworth and then invest in a truly enormous extension of the storage facilities. They bought an airfield big enough to store hundreds of millions of pounds worth of ammunition and put in a whole series of raw material storage magazines, centrally heated bunkers, in addition to the old RAF facilities, most of which were centrally heated, huge in size, and designed to take finished goods. There were also other underground bunkers, great convex shelters with grass growing on the top, where raw materials could also be stored.

It made a lot of sense for a lorry or two to stop there overnight or for other companies' goods to be stored there for longer, awaiting their shuttle to the next stage in the international production line. Machon's shipping documents showed that the scale of operations through BMARC increased substantially from 1987–8, when we took over the company, because they were shutting the Allivane operation down and using BMARC as the prime distribution centre for the arms and propellant cartel. It transpired later that no charges were being levied for much of this storage of goods, confirming the secret nature of the operation.

Fired by my earlier suspicions about Richborough and the information Kelly was turning up, I decided to make the gigantic Faldingworth storage facilities part of my investigative itinerary, while remaining cautious not to upset the delicate situation between BMARC and Astra any further than necessary.

I began by contacting the appropriate staff at BMARC to show me round. On the first occasion I turned up, nothing was amiss. On my second tour of inspection I found myself being taken to the same building once more, and at the end I thanked my guide, but suggested that next time I came down perhaps I could look over one of the other buildings, say right up the other end.

When next time came round they showed me the same magazine again, and when I suggested that my guide go and get the keys to one of the other magazines, he said the man with the keys to those had gone home. So I began to arrive unannounced and the people up there started to get jumpy.

My first 'find' was a whole magazine full of finished ammunition with Argentinian markings. My guide said he didn't know what it was for – (a huge pile of finished ammunition, I thought, and he doesn't know what it's for!) – so I took it up with Isles, who told me that it had been left over from a very large government contract prior to the Falklands War. The story was that it was lying there because they didn't know what to do with it. Well, let me tell you, with a war raging in the Middle East, the government knows exactly what to do with any left-over Falklands ammunition.

Then, looking over an underground bunker one day I found the pot of gold; tons of Muiden Chemie propellant which was quite inexplicable in relation to the order position of the company, historical or current. There was enough raw material to obliterate the Russian army. Isles and his cronies told me, 'Oh, you know, we store things for other people; sometimes we store a bit for RO or GEC; we have to maximise the space.'

But we never saw these items on the order book. I know, I checked. They were not accounted for. I didn't force the issue at this time. I gathered evidence and built up my BMARC file.

Then, in 1988, Muiden Chemie were prosecuted by the Dutch government for supplying propellant to Iraq, and Astra's name was found on documents taken by police in the raid (p. 101). When I heard of the prosecution I began to see what the whole business was about.

As rumours about the government's propellant cartel began to surface, John Reed of *Defence Industry Digest* said to me that he had heard we were involved in the cartel business. I said I didn't know what he was talking about. He told me that it had been repeatedly asserted 'by a source close to *Defence Industry Digest*' that Astra's name was against a contract with Jordan. He referred to it as 'the propellant contract'.

Don't confuse this with the Supergun propellant contract we would find in PRB. Allegedly, the contract Reed was talking about was part of Thatcher's Jordan Package and had Astra's name on it. I protested that Astra didn't have a propellant facility, nor did we until we bought PRB. Reed insisted, and then one day Chris Gumbley came and said that he had caught wind of a secret order book down at BMARC. Pleased that we had come to similar conclusions, I asked him what he meant. He told me that they were running secret orders through the company and it was then that Gumbley began investigations of his own.

I discovered that the 'source close to *Defence Industry Digest*' was Lionel Jones, the executive of Royal Ordnance for whom Graham Willett had worked. Gumbley and I became close to Lionel; at one stage we even offered him a job. In the course of our acquaintance, he furnished me with a great deal of information about RO's dealings with the MoD and the nature of their involvement with the Middle East. He once said that he wished he had taken up our offer of a job, that things might have worked out differently for Astra had I been filled in earlier about what the government wanted of companies like ours.

Specifically on the propellant contract that bore our name, he confirmed that it was one of the ways the missing millions were siphoned off from the government's Jordan Package. Operating the covert trade via a parallel contract in Astra's name was better than manipulating export licences either by declaring false end-users or using an export licence to redefine a contract, as in the 1987 Allivane contract with Saudi. A parallel covert contract in the name of a real company provided the basis for apparently legitimate export paperwork and payment could be made via a parallel bank account set up for the purpose. John Reed corroborated the method, claiming that it was not uncommon for 'defence material salesmen' to act independently of their employers, and that 'in a system characterised by "endless photocopies", it would be possible to forge powers of attorney.'

What Lionel's information amounted to was that we were being involved on a third tier of covert dealing. Besides the illegitimate storage deals and contracts like LISI and Ordtec going via false end-users to Iraq, we were being involved in contracts that we hadn't even touched, that were not part of our official order book, but which bore our name.

How blatant was the abuse was shown in April 1989 when we were one of seventeen companies representing Britain at the Baghdad Arms Fair. Among the others were British Aerospace, Thorn EMI, Rolls-Royce, GEC Avionics, Matrix Churchill and representatives of the defence sales unit of Midland Bank. All of us were sponsored by the British government to the tune of 25 per

cent of our expenses in direct violation of official policy. When I
saw the official Fair Guide, I was absolutely furious. We were
billed on the page opposite British Aerospace, their head office
address (in the Strand in London) appended correctly beneath
their name, while beneath ours was not Astra's address but
'Brooklands Road, Weybridge, Surry (*sic*) KTB OSJ', the address
of BAe in Surrey, the old Vickers factory. The telex number was
brazenly the same as BAe's as well.

At the time I had been furious about the error for other reasons.
New customers use the guide to be in touch after the Fair. It is
singly the most important item in an exhibition presentation and
the purpose of the exhibition guide. Indeed, in spite of great
excitement at the Fair, we had absolutely no follow-up. I took it up
with John Sellens and others, who put the error down to 'those
bloody Arabs', but ours was the only address in the catalogue
that was incorrect. Now it seems possible that the printing was not
an error at all. To certain clients we were a very helpful company
based in Weybridge, Surrey, that sold large quantities of materials
bound eventually for Iraq. Certainly, when I visited Prince
Mishari, half-brother of King Fahd of Saudi Arabia (p. 259), I
would discover that Astra had just such a reputation as a regular
covert supplier to the Middle East, as did the major subsidiaries
we had acquired.

While all my investigations were going on, relations with Kock
became very difficult. He knew what I was up to, and from early
1989 I became aware that he was enticing Gumbley into his circle. My wife, Gisela, claims that she noticed the move from very
early on. Soon after our acquisition of BMARC (early summer
1988), we arranged a dinner with the BMARC management and
their wives at Stapleford Park. When she and I walked in, Gisela
was struck by the fact that Gumbley's wife was kissing General
Isles' wife and being, as she said, very pally. She didn't say anything to me at the time, of course, but immediately went up to
Mrs Gumbley and enquired how it was that she knew Mrs Isles so
well. 'Oh,' replied Mrs Gumbley, 'we all met up in London.'
Apparently Kock had arranged a special dinner to which top

BMARC management and their wives, Chris Gumbley included, had been invited. We specifically had not. As my investigations developed, the wooing of Gumbley by Kock gathered momentum too.

Gumbley and I are essentially different, but we worked very well together, complemented each other. Though at Brocks he had been the production man, he was a very good salesman, a natural. He was also one for all the trimmings, the good car – he later drove a Rolls-Royce – and the generous expense account. I don't think it was bad or good, it was Gumbley, part of whatever it was that made him very valuable to Astra in terms of sales in particular. The trouble was that his extrovert style was accompanied by a tendency not to see the whole picture of what was going on but only what was immediately presented (what my ex-soldier son Christian once called an outlook typical of the military).

All this made him a very attractive vehicle for Kock, a master of flattery and manipulation. Kock made Gumbley feel like one of the hot shots that the old-timer in Syracuse had mistaken us for. Gumbley liked being wheeled around Kock's associates, envisaging possibilities for himself far superior to any he had hitherto imagined. Kock so boosted Chris's self-esteem that when in mid-1989 I courted the idea of opting out of all the shenanegans at Astra and merging with Lord Chalfont's VSEL, a mainstream establishment defence company, Gumbley's understandably inflated personal expectations of Astra actually killed the deal. It was July–August 1989, after our purchase of PRB but before the reporting of the Supergun propellant contract that would put us in such a vulnerable position. We were in a good position financially with a cogent and effective business strategy in America, England and Europe. I was aware, and had perhaps been made more aware by the antics of Kock and the BMARC contingent, that the main Astra board directors were not an especially sophisticated bunch. The last thing I wanted was to have to replace any of them with a bunch of fat cats from the City. The merger with VSEL was a tenable option which would give them and the company security. Chalfont and Frank Noah were in favour of the deal, but Chris Gumbley had insisted on my negotiating a position whereby Astra would dominate VSEL and sell out at a vastly inflated price, all of which was ridiculous. Playing hard to get caused a delay during which Frank Noah disappeared from the VSEL board, and Noel Davis, an establishment defence man keen to establish himself and uninterested in Astra's upstart claims, arrived at the company.

As a result of these factors, we lost the deal. It was my one and only serious effort to put Astra on the establishment gravy train. As events transpired after the Supergun contract emerged, it was probably our last opportunity to survive at all.

Kock's wooing of Gumbley began in 1988 and reached its zenith around December 1989–January 1990, when Gumbley's own investigations finally made it clear that Kock had been playing Fox to his Jemimah Puddleduck. A few months later, the poor man would realise what his true fate was to be.

Meanwhile my profile of Kock was being sharpened by reports of his activities abroad. I learned from Major-General Last, the military head of sales at the MoD, that wherever he went it seemed that Kock would pop up out of the blue. 'I was in Taiwan the other week and your man Kock was there,' he said, 'and would you believe it I was in China later and he was there too!' This was repeated on a later occasion in the East India Club with Tim Laxton in attendance. Kock had told me nothing about these trips. Then I heard from others that Kock had been seen in Africa in different places, and his work with Richard Unwin on Thatcher's Malaysian arms deal began to emerge. Kock clearly enjoyed this process and the charisma it bestowed, but it made him more vulnerable too, my investigations threatening him not only on the company level of Isles and the rest at Grantham, where he had hoisted his flag, but now also on this level of deals he was doing and had done overtly in the government's name.

This began particularly to worry him when, from June 1988, I began to go after PRB. For Kock was all too aware what would be revealed if that acquisition went through.

CHAPTER SEVEN

PULLING
THE PLUG

Poudreries Réunies de Belgique (PRB) was a well-equipped company with a total 'in house' arsenal capability and five or six outstanding plants. It was a compact, commercial enterprise with certain classic developments likely to suit future armament requirements. Finally it offered us a whole new range of customers, contacts and contracts.

It could manufacture extended range ammunition, it had smooth bore technology, and had combustible cartridge case technology. PRB was a main supplier of the latest development of tank gun, 120mm smooth bore, developed by Rheinmetal of Germany (formerly Krupp). Most tank ammunition for the future will be based on that. The trouble with the conventional British tank round is that if you fire it on the highest charge, you wear out the barrel after about thirty rounds. With smooth-bore technology you can fire as many rounds as you like, with much less wear and tear, and at a higher muzzle velocity. When you combine the smooth-bore technology with the concept of the combustible cartridge case – no brass case to carry, just one that disappears like papier mâché – you have a winning formula for the future. PRB was also of course well into shell technology and was a leading ball powder supplier. Ball powder is used as a propellant by most countries other than the UK, in larger ammunition as well as small bore. PRB also had rocket technology through a joint venture with Thomson of France at Fort

Zeebrugge, where PRB had sold the majority interest, and at Kaulille.

Furthermore, PRB's plants and licence agreements could not have been created from scratch for under £500m. The PRB Group had its head office in Brussels, five factory sites in Belgium, at Balen, Clermont, Kaulille, Matagne and Mechelen, two operations in Canada, which included a site at Knoulton, Quebec, and research and development offices in Montreal.

Also important, as we stressed in our shareholders' prospectus, the purchase fitted the concept of defence strategy at the time, which was to take an interest in Europe in preparation for the much touted 'free European market' in 1992. PRB would give Astra the ability to export to the UK from Europe, adding an entirely new dimension to the group.

Finally, and above all, it gave Astra another platform for supply in the heavily politicised arms industry, and would make it difficult for Royal Ordnance to compete adequately, particularly overseas.

PRB was for sale in Belgium by Gechem, its holding company, itself a part of Société Générale de Belgique (SGB), a company so large that it was equal to one-third of the Belgian economy. It had, we were told, come up for sale as a result of an unwelcome takeover bid for the whole of SGB by Carlo Benedetti, the Italian financier. Benedetti's bid had come as a tremendous shock to the Belgian government. It had seemed like a bid for part of Belgium herself by a foreign upstart, and as a result it had been hotly resisted by SGB. By selling off PRB, they alleged they were pleasing their new shareholders – Benedetti (25 per cent) and Indo-Suez Bank of France (51 per cent), who saw the arms trade in the doldrums and wanted higher returns. The fact that we believed that we alone had been approached to buy PRB did not appear at all sinister. On the contrary, we were one of the few companies in the arms field which was expanding and which had a reasonable international concept within which PRB would have a unique opportunity to flourish.

The original price for the whole company was £38m, and I

negotiated it down to £20m with a £2m extra payment, performance related, which we thought was a pretty good deal. But, at first, negotiations did not run smoothly.

In mid-1988, when we had reached a position where we could see clearly all the commercial advantages of buying PRB, we solicited meetings with SGB and Gechem. Initially it was only Gumbley and I who went to see them. They were very slow to react. Nothing much happened.

Kock meanwhile expressed caution over the purchase, stating as his reason that he was concerned about the power of the Belgian trades unions. He was the only one on the Astra board to pronounce reluctance (as opposed to caution) about the purchase, and it must have been pleasing that his old colleague from Midland Bank, Comte Hervé de Carmoy, now chief executive of SGB and managing director of Gechem, the holding company of PRB, was playing hard to get. As I have said, in April 1988 de Carmoy moved from Midland, where he had been director and chief executive of the global banking sector, their most highly paid executive at a salary of around £750,000, and joined SGB/Gechem around August of the same year.

In the light of our increasingly difficult relationship, Kock's caution did not bother me particularly. However, it was also the position taken by Sir John Cuckney at 3i.

Not knowing any of the background to Cuckney's relationship with Kock, this did surprise me. We were in pretty good shape at the time. Our accounts to March 1989 eventually showed a £9.2m pre-tax profit. Moreover the sound proposition of PRB seemed clear, and our three major institutional shareholders – the Pru, 3i, Clerical and Medical – had always been solidly behind us on previous acquisitions. I had looked with confidence to traditional sources of finance for the takeover. When our next meeting with SGB/Gechem in October–November 1988 met with more stonewalling, I began to wonder whether the whole proposition would peter out.

Then suddenly, in February 1989, after further meetings, the Belgians came back to me and piled on the pressure: 'Are you still interested? You've really got to get moving if you want to do this deal.' Immediately I began to cast around for alternative funding for the takeover.

I had met Alan Curtis, who succeeded David Wickens as chairman of Lotus (the company for which Mark Thatcher had gone to work in Dallas), at the 1988 Farnborough Air Show. Like Sir John Cuckney, Curtis was a member of the board of the Society of British Aircraft Constructors, which runs the Air Show. He had taken me to the United Technologies chalet on that occasion and introduced me to all the top people at UTC. Afterwards Richard Unwin, who had made the introduction, urged me to consider Curtis's amenability to helping us out should we ever have any problems raising finance. So now I decided not to wait around for Cuckney or the rest of them. I would go and see Curtis instead.

When I rang him at his Savoy Hotel suite, Curtis said, 'Fine. Come round, let's have a chat . . .', and that was how I found myself in his now legendary suite overlooking the Thames at the Savoy from which he ran his business – the suite that has gained his circle of political and business associates the media soubriquet of the Savoy Mafia.

Curtis is a tall man and very slim, quite a foxy-looking character but very pleasant. He talked quite openly about his relationship with Margaret Thatcher. I believe he was a friend of Sir Denis originally, but he was on very good terms with the prime minister and was a regular visitor to Downing Street at informal evening meetings they called 'slipper time'. There is no doubt that Curtis was well in, although it is likely that he was more minor a member of the group than its particular nickname suggests. It would certainly be wrong to suggest that Curtis was in charge.

There is little doubt that all who were in the Savoy Mafia had contact with people who had access to information from the Joint Intelligence Committee and those closely involved day-to-day with Thatcher's arms policy. I mention in my evidence to the House of Commons Trade and Industry Select Committee Inquiry into Exports to Iraq the occasion when I was with Curtis in his suite and had to leave early when Lord Younger, the Minister of Defence, Peter Levene, Chief of Defence Procurement at the MoD, and Sir Colin Chandler, Chief of Defence Exports at the MoD, and the chairman of Vickers, Sir David Plastow, arrived for dinner. By the time I became involved with Curtis, in February/March 1989, Margaret Thatcher had been in power a long time and all these relationships were well set.

On several occasions when I was with Curtis, Stephen Tipping was also present. Tipping had assumed the position of Mark Thatcher's front man in the business of arms facilitating following Mark's banishment from the scene in 1984.

I never saw Mark himself at the Savoy, but the presence of Stephen Tipping was the first inkling I had of the high position taken by the ex-Monteagle executive in the international arms cabal, and in the light of subsequent revelations about Mark's work for the Savoy Mafia, in particular on his mother's Malaysian arms deal, there is every reason to believe that Mark was somewhere in the wings. On two or three occasions there was someone in the adjoining room of the suite to whom Tipping reported. I always felt that Mark was the one in the next room.

It is a feature of Mark's performance in the USA since his banishment that for security reasons he has operated his company, Grantham, through a front man, Roger Wallace. Both this and some of the methods the company has employed, as revealed recently in TV's Newsnight programme, suggest that he learned a great deal from his Intelligence colleagues during his period as arms facilitator. Grantham, named after Margaret Thatcher's birthplace, is the investment vehicle that deploys the vast sums that accrued to Mark during his period in the international arms business.

That Mark was still part of the arms network while I was meeting Curtis with Tipping we now know from all that has come out in the media. My knowledge of it I owe to the fact that in 1989 he travelled to Kenya with Stephen Tipping, taking Astra brochures with them on our behalf. The main reason for their trip was the pursuit of a big pharmaceutical contract with Nairobi

University, which they won, beating a bid from Fisons.

In the spring of 1989 Curtis introduced me to Sifcorp, Wafiq Said's company in Old Park Lane. I met Said once or twice, but the man who dealt mainly with our business was Dr Zaid Idilby, Said's partner. Idilby sent two men, Hubbard-Ford and Middleton, to Belgium to check out PRB before putting together a deal. The proposal was that Said would invest £30m in Astra which would enable us to buy PRB and would give Said's company a 30 per cent stake in Astra.

When the deal looked like going ahead, I felt bound to go back to our major shareholders to make sure that they would not stand in the way. When they heard the name of Wafiq Said, they dashed off into a huddle, and the next thing I knew was that they said, 'We'll put the money up!' I was amazed.

It was Sir John Cuckney for 3i and Huw Jones for the Pru who did the about-turn and insisted that, after all, they finance the purchase of PRB. I couldn't argue with our major shareholders, of course, as we needed their consent, but it put me in the difficult position of having to cut loose from Said. I told Curtis I'd rather go with him, but I couldn't. He said he quite understood. He wasn't annoyed. In fact I was surprised how readily the situation was understood and accepted. Sifcorp were equally amenable. They did come back to us and ask for a fee for looking at the project, but one was never agreed. Everything seemed suddenly to fall neatly into place.

As soon as Cuckney and Jones decided to go with us, Kock's attitude also changed. Having said initially that he was against the deal, suddenly he couldn't have been more for it. I remember one particular day which illustrated well his change of heart – when the Bank of Nova Scotia was posing one of the main difficulties in the banking syndicate for the PRB deal. (All members of the syndicate had to consent.) Kock rang up the Agent-General of Nova Scotia in the middle of the night from a meeting at our lawyers, and suddenly the problem was brushed aside. It was amazing, and another pointer to the extent of this man's influence. But more significantly in terms of future events, Kock's action demonstrated the completness of his about-turn on the subject of Astra's purchase of PRB. Kock made the crucial call on the eve of the original signing date for the PRB deal, the night of 13 July 1989. It was the first time he had ever sat up at such a meeting, and his call was the crucial final move in settling the acquisition.

Originally we were supposed to sign with PRB on Friday 14 July 1989, but it was delayed until Monday 17 July because the lawyers couldn't get the paperwork together. Completion was scheduled for 11 September, when we would have to pay over £20m.

In the same month there was another Naval Equipment Exhibition at Portsmouth, and Roger Harding, who had been moved six months earlier from Washington to the MoD as Deputy Head of Defence Sales, took Gumbley and me aside and said, 'I am advising you as a friend, if you find any contracts in PRB that are at all suspicious, anything that might be related to Iraq or Iran, report them at once to the MoD.'

It had been a condition imposed during negotiations by SGB/Gechem for reasons, we were told, of security, that while our auditors, Stoy Hayward, should have sight of the PRB order book and be able to verify that the orders were in existence, we at Astra should not be allowed to view the actual contracts until the deal had been signed. We signed a confidentiality agreement to that effect, as did Stoy Hayward. Tim Laxton of Stoy Hayward was later to describe the PRB management as 'absolutely paranoid about any of their customer details getting out to Astra' before the deal went through, but in terms of the highly competitive nature of the international arms market, it seemed fair enough at the time. We were to be told the amounts of the contracts and when they fell due to PRB, which, as the financial aspect of PRB's forward programme, was the key aspect of the deal.

Immediately after the exhibition at Portsmouth we asked the PRB management to give us a list of contracts, and upon completion of the deal when we handed the money over, we were given the list and turned up a number to investigate fully. 'When the acquisition was completed,' Gumbley gave evidence later, 'the

PRB management had resigned from the board and they then began to tell me which were of a sensitive nature.'

It is an interesting side-issue on this that it had been agreed, following advice from their lawyers, that the PRB directors Guy Cardinael and Philippe Glibert should resign from the board and be re-appointed after the takeover. That in the event they refused reappointment struck me as odd, until we began to open the Pandora's box of PRB contracts.

One was a contract for high energy propellant and propellant powder, another for 130mm ammunition, both going ostensibly to Jordan. There were also contracts for 'internal security pyrotechnics' going to Zambia, two more for propellant going to Austria and France, one for 155mm components going to Spain, propellant powder going to America, 155mm propellants going to Singapore and one for demolition charge mines going to Saudi. 'They [the old PRB management] indicated,' continued Gumbley's evidence, 'that the contracts, particularly for propellants, had a capability which was for – and they hinted towards this – nuclear and chemical weapons systems . . . going to Iraq via Jordan.'

What emerged on further investigation was that all the contracts had third-party destinations. The Jordan ammunition contract was bound for Iraq, the Zambian contract was bound for Angola. The Austrian contract was going via Noricum to Saudi, the French contract was going to Morocco via Luchaire, now well-known contraband routes to Iraq used by the arms and propellant cartels. The Spanish contract was in fact destined for Pakistan, the USA contract was bound for Taiwan, the Singapore contract for Taiwan, and the Saudi one for Iraq.

Immediately significant, however, was the propellant contract bound for Jordan, which was found to include 200 tonnes of an unusual solid propellant of a type not used by Jordan and which PRB staff told us was in fact destined for Bull's Project Babylon. It was a contract for making the combustible material used to propel the missiles for Gerald Bull's Supergun.

Now this contract was worth about £38m initially to us, and £50m a year thereafter for about five years, so we had no reason or desire to stop it from a commercial point of view. The Belgian government had already given permission for it to be serviced, and PRB was still a Belgian company. Moreover, it was certain that if the Belgian Intelligence services knew about it, MI6 would also know about it. They were too much in each other's pockets and had been since the Second World War. Nevertheless, for reasons that I will go into, we reported it and took the knowledge of this contract from unofficial to official.

Events went like this. Gumbley delivered our report to Bob Primrose in Defence Sales. I was then met by Roger Holdness, who was sent to me in my office. Pure MI6, Holdness had two phone numbers, one at the Foreign Office, the other at the MoD. After about three hours, and when I had taken him to lunch, I was at a loss to understand why Holdness continued to want to talk about the propellant deal in such detail. In our report we had already told them all that they could possibly want to know. Yet he went over it again and again. It was as though he was desperate to know how far my personal knowledge of Supergun extended. It was nearly six months later that Secretary of State Nicholas Ridley claimed that the government had only 'recently become aware in general terms of an Iraqi project to develop a long-range gun based on the designs by the late Dr Gerald Bull.'

We then had another meeting at the MoD with Primrose, Holdness, myself, Gumbley, and (because he had by then got involved in detailed contract specifications) Bill McNaught.

The interviewing did not stop there. In November Kock asked me to go up to the BMARC plant at Grantham with him. He said he wanted me to meet a delegation from the SAS who were interested in buying some equipment. I couldn't understand why I, the chairman of the company, had to be there, but Kock insisted, said it was absolutely essential. I said, 'For God's sake, we've got all these salesmen and I need to go and see PRB in Belgium . . .' But he wouldn't have it, so I said, 'Do you think we'll get a sale out of it?' And he said, 'Yes, I think they're very serious and as chairman you must be there.' So in the end I went.

We were to travel to Grantham by train from King's Cross.

Kock turned up at the station before me. After I joined him on the platform, two figures arrived, one of which, I was surprised to see was Roger Holdness, with whom we had discussed the Supergun propellant contract. The other was a very tall chap who was introduced to me as Colonel Smith from the SAS, who was supposedly their procurement officer. I was immediately struck by the fact that Kock and Holdness were on Christian-name terms. 'Hello, Roger', 'Hello Stephan', they greeted one another.

When we got on the train, Smith and Kock began waffling away to each other about a lot of SAS wallahs and people they knew, and Holdness started going over the propellant contract again: what I knew, who knew what. This continued through breakfast in the dining car, and not only did he go on about it all the way up on the train, but when we got up to Grantham, when we were supposed to be conducting a tour around the factories to show what we could do, all the time Holdness tagged on to me and kept asking these questions.

In the end I said, 'Look, I've told you all about this; why are you going on about it?' Then, finally, he came out with what was at the root of his concern: had I met Gerald Bull? I said I hadn't, although by then in fact I had. I met him in November 1989 in Brussels, after being shown letters written by him to the sales manager of PRB, Philippe Glibert, expressing concern about Astra and the Foreign Office. Our conversation had focused on the role of Kock, de Carmoy and Cuckney in the purchase of PRB, and the real reasons, which I will explain, why suddenly everyone had turned in favour of our bringing the deal to fruition. To Holdness I played down the Bull connection, said I didn't know anything about him. I gave him purely what I'd got from the paperwork from PRB. I think in hindsight it was very lucky that I did that. A few months later Gerald Bull was murdered.

With the benefit of hindsight we can begin to answer some of the questions that emerge from the chronology of our purchase of PRB, some of the apparently odd coincidences and sudden turn-rounds which occurred, which baffled me at the time but which serve to elucidate the whole policy reversal of the arms cabal in Britain in 1988–89 I described earlier. The first oddity was Kock's declared opposition to it in the face of the obvious attractions of the deal on paper and its logic in the face of EPREP.

IMS, the government-owned arms company, had been involved with PRB for years. Besides the IMS ammunition contracts of 1984, 1985 and 1986, PRB had supplied the kit for a lot of the government's African operations – Kock's 'parish', you will recall. But more to the point, Kock himself was at risk from the very contract, the Supergun propellant contract, that became the focus of attention when the PRB deal was done.

About August 1991, eighteen months or so after I was pushed out of Astra, I learned from the journalist David Hellier that Chris Cowley, the project manager for Bull's Supergun, had met Kock and Hervé de Carmoy in Baghdad in June and November 1988, negotiating the finance for the propellant for the Supergun. Suddenly a whole raft of occurrences fell into place. De Carmoy had been the main board director of Midland Bank in charge of the international division. He had left the bank in April 1988, as MITS was being wound down and put into Midland Montagu (the end of the Iran–Iraq war – 18 July 1988 – was in sight), and he had taken up his position at SGB/Gechem the following August. Kock had been a consultant in the international division under de Carmoy. It makes a lot of sense that since Midland was handling the protocol for Supergun, and SGB (via PRB) was handling these large contracts bound for Iraq, and de Carmoy had an involvement with both, and that Kock had an involvement with Midland and de Carmoy, that they went out together to sort out the finance.

After Hellier rang me up with this news, he set down to writing his article about it. But that evening he was threatened, first on the telephone and then he was nearly knocked over by a car as he was walking along the pavement to his house. He was so petrified that he hid for a week in Wales. He has since listed the car 'accident' among a series of other incidents during the period he was writing in the *Independent* about Kock and Astra:

During this period something happened to unsettle me. I was walking home one night on the pavement of a busy road when a car slid onto the pavement and knocked me to the ground. I was shocked but not badly hurt . . . [Then] on one occasion I spotted a photographer taking pictures of me with one of my contacts [actually two, Tim Laxton and Chris Gumbley] as we sat in a pub during one of his [Gumbley's] days on release from prison. I then discovered that another journalist [Jane Renton], who was working on the same story at the London *Observer* newspaper, had received a warning that something might happen if she continued her investigations. Her paper took this seriously and put her up in a hotel for a few days.

Other things happened to disturb me. One of my contacts died suddenly, days after giving me a lift to the trial of the former chief executive of Astra [Chris Gumbley] who was being charged with corruption. The person in question, Lionel Jones, complained on the way down to the trial about a boil on his neck . . . [1]

Poor Lionel, I will come back to him later. When Hellier fled to Wales after the car 'accident', I was driving up to Cockermouth in Cumbria to my late mother's house, very worried that he had made no contact and that I was unable to get in touch with him. I rang Tim Laxton on the car telephone and told him I had been trying to locate Hellier. Laxton, who had by then left our accountants Stoy Hayward, and himself become involved in trying to unearth the truth about what had happened in Astra, said that he had also been trying to contact Hellier. I said that I had spoken to the journalist's girlfriend, and she had been very distraught.

Eventually Laxton rang up Hellier's editor, who was very cagey. As I continued my journey, I phoned Laxton again and said, 'Why don't you ring Cowley yourself and get the story corroborated.' This he did; Chris Cowley went over it again, Kock in Baghdad, the whole scenario.

Then, at my suggestion, Laxton later joined me in Cockermouth. I picked him up from Carlisle and in the afternoon

of the following day, I told him that I would like first-hand corroboration of the story. 'But,' I said, 'I don't feel able to ring up
Cowley myself because if everyone starts ringing him up he may
get worried and stop talking.' Cowley was having his own problems with spooks, as his book, *Guns, Lies and Spies*, makes clear.
I asked Laxton to ring him up once more while I listened in on the
extension out in the hall. This he did, and Cowley confirmed it all
again.

Clearly, in the light of my investigations into BMARC, the last
thing that Kock would have wanted in mid-1988, if he was off to
Baghdad to negotiate the finance for PRB's Supergun propellant
contract, was for us to buy PRB.

Not only did I have an explanation of why, against all the logic
of the deal and the views of other members of the board, Kock had
been against our purchase of PRB initially, but this news also
gave me an insight into the timing of another extraordinary event
which had occurred in February 1989 at precisely the time that
SGB/Gechem suddenly came onto me and pressed for an early
conclusion to negotiations for PRB.

The moment that SGB/Gechem came to me and said, 'Let's
get going,' Kock rang me and said that Edward Album wanted to
convene a meeting. Album, you will recall, was Astra's other non-
executive director, the one we had inherited from the deal with
Francis Sumner Holdings through which we had obtained a full
listing on the Stock Exchange. I asked him why Album wanted the
meeting. Kock wouldn't say, but pushed for it to be set for as soon
as possible, stressing the urgency and indicating that it was Album
and not himself who was causing the fuss. I told him that the
earliest I could make it was two days hence at 8 o'clock in the
morning, the only time that I had free.

I had been to a meeting at the Gunmakers' Company and
came back early that same evening to the office. As I was about to
leave, I caught sight of the two of them, Kock and Album, coming
through the office door. They pressed me for a meeting there and
then. I agreed and suggested we bring Gumbley in if it was that
important. But they said, no, they didn't want Gumbley along

and suggested we go across the road to the Duke's Hotel. There, over a drink, Kock came out with it: 'Edward thinks that it would be a good idea if you stood down as chairman. We think it would be a good idea to bring in Sir James Blyth . . .' I said something like, 'What on earth for? I know that Blyth has been head of defence sales [he had the position at the MoD from 1981 to 1985], but,' I said, 'not unlike you, he has had nothing to do with building up this company.'

I was of course shattered by the suggestion, but we were a public company and here were the company's two non-executive directors suggesting that I be replaced as chairman. It wasn't something that I could ignore or dismiss. I rejected the idea, but called a board meeting with Gumbley, Miller and the rest for 8 am two days later. It was time to declare our position, I told them. It was clear to me that Kock was using Album as a stalking-horse, and that it was a move connected to my investigations into BMARC and Walters. With me out, effective control would pass to Kock through one of his stooges.

I said, 'I think Kock is using Album to do his dirty work and as far as I am concerned I want to sack Album, so he'll be going anyway on Thursday [the day we fixed for the showdown], but I have been thinking about it overnight and I want Kock to go, too. After I have done that, I want to get on the train to Grantham and sack at least three people up there.'

They went along with getting rid of Album, but caution was expressed over Kock's sacking, the reason given, yet again, that his Midland Bank connection was crucial to the company. There was also a general feeling that we couldn't afford to axe two non-executives on the same day, as it might precipitate a Stock Exchange crisis or some other problem. The fatal mistake I made was that I didn't stick to my guns and press the point.

I said, 'If we want to keep control of this company, we have got to get rid of all the people who are causing trouble. I quite accept that when we retained Major-General Isles after the acquisition of BMARC, I was to blame. But you are making the mistake I made then, worried about what other people will think – the MoD in that case, now the Stock Exchange. We have got to make the right decision for the company. I'd like to bring in Bob Tennant [former managing director of Eley Kynoch] as a director because he has engineering knowledge, and possibly another outsider, either a lawyer or a financial man.'

Chris Gumbley, who agreed to sack Album but not Kock, suggested bringing in Laurence Kingswood from our lawyers Baileys, Shaw & Gillett. I said I wasn't sure whether that was a good idea. I was not keen on appointing the company solicitor, as I could see a conflict of interest, which later the DTI inspectors did indeed seize on in their investigation into Astra which began in August 1990. If he had been a very strong robust person, as opposed to a technical expert, I might have been more amenable. Even so, I didn't feel as strongly about Kingswood as about wanting Kock to go, and that, I regret, I didn't press.

When Kock came into the Thursday meeting (8 February 1989) I had the impression that he must have heard about my plans, for his usual swaggering demeanour had completely disappeared; he looked physically drained. Again I found that odd, as I couldn't quite put so strong a change all down to fear that he might be about to be sacked from Astra.

We sat down. My proposed agenda was to sack Album, get him out the room, give him three months' money and tell him we were absolutely disgusted at the way he had behaved. That is basically what we did, and not only did Kock fail to back up Album and march out of the door after him, he actually voted for me and went out of the office like a lamb. I remember my secretary, Mrs Franks, noticed how shaken Kock was. She asked me, 'What have you done to him?'

Later he would tell the DTI inspectors that he stayed on to 'serve the small shareholders', but in truth Kock stayed on because he didn't dare leave. He wanted me out, but he couldn't leave me to rake over the dirt in PRB, our acquisition of which he now knew from de Carmoy had been given the go-ahead. At the time he must have been terrified that this was the first step towards an exposure of enormous proportions involving a whole raft of covert corrupt contracts involving MI5, MI6 and assorted Intelligence agencies within PRB.

I would learn later from the minutes of a board meeting held by Astra's new management in September 1990 that it was from this time in 1989, following his abortive boardroom coup, that Kock, without the agreement or knowledge of other Astra board members, hired the services of Trowers & Hamlins (Conservative Party lawyers) to develop a more sophisticated strategy to be shot of us all.

How very worried Kock became at this time is demonstrated by an unseemly incident at the Angel and Royal Hotel, Grantham, that followed immediately afterwards. As happens, Kock turned to drink at times of greatest stress. On this occasion he had spent the evening with Isles. Late in the evening Isles delivered Kock back in a chauffeur-driven company car to the Angel and Royal, where he was staying. Karl Bowers, an assistant manager, was in attendance at the hotel, and he wrote the following account of what happened soon after the episode, at 2.30 am.

Approximately 11.30 pm I was in the Angel bar taking a till reading when Marcus and myself heard a voice outside. I went to investigate. There were two people outside trying to get in. I said, 'Good evening. Sorry to keep you waiting.' Then I was subjected to foul language and abuse. Discovering I did not have the front door key I went round over the tap door to start to open the door. By that time he, Mr Kock, had gone into the Angel bar and had words with Marcus. I apologised and asked him to come in while he continued to swear at me. He made bodily suggestions that he was going to hit me. I tried to calm him down but due to his inability to hold his alcohol he continued to be rude and abusive. He then demanded that I call him Sir and said that he would see me out of a job because he was the director of the biggest company in the town that employed the most people – I then warned him of his bad language but he told me to f——k off. He then said he was Major Kock of the ——, which I didn't quite get, then he demanded that I rang Sir

Charles Forte. I said I couldn't do that, and again he threatened me with violence by saying he would put me down. I then said to him if he didn't stop his behaviour I would call the police. He then turned the tables by saying he would call the police. I gave him a line on 300, but he tried or couldn't manage it, then shouted and swore some more and went to bed.

I then called Mr Dain [the manager] at home to let him know what had happened. Then I talked to Marcus, who could not believe what he had just heard. Twenty minutes later Mr Kock rang down asking for bacon and eggs. I told him we did not serve cooked food to rooms, but would he like sandwiches. After much deliberation, he chose cheese and tomato sandwiches, which I did. When I took them to the room, he swore again and said he would have the sandwiches checked by the hygiene people in the morning. I said they would probably be off by then, said thank you, then left.

I have probably left some things out of this, but I don't want to write a story. 2.30 am.

There is of course a comic element in a drunken scene such as this long after the event, but one phrase stays with me because it has a chilling ring of truth. Bowers says, 'He threatened me with violence by saying he would have me put down.' Almost exactly one year later, as I will relate, Kock would use the very same expression to me in a private dining suite at the Berkeley Hotel in London: 'I'll have you put down.' I wonder how many people he said that to when he had the power to effect the threat.

The following day Mr Dain communicated the details of Bowers' account to Isles at BMARC, who tried to bury the incident. But the Astra chauffeur who had driven Kock and Isles to the hotel told John Anderson about it. Anderson looked after transport, among his other duties at this time. Anderson told John Sellens to determine the facts, and Sellens sent an Astra employee, B. J. Watts, down to interview Bowers. His statement, also signed, accords with Bowers'.

With the failure of the boardroom coup, Kock, aided by advice

from Trowers & Hamlins, pinned his hopes on a more sober strategy designed to be implemented a few months later. It
commenced surprisingly by giving me what I wanted.

When I informed Cuckney's 3i and our other two institutional
shareholders that I was about to sell the Saudi, Wafiq Said, a 30
per cent interest in Astra to enable me to complete the PRB deal,
they jumped into action and came up with the finance themselves. This certainly surprised me. Why the change of heart?

The answer is that the period of to-ing and fro-ing over the
PRB sale (mid -1988 to spring 1989) coincided almost to the
month with the complete turn-round in Western arms policy over
a period of nearly twelve months. When the Intelligence-con-
nected finance company, Paine Webber, started me off with great
enthusiasm in mid-1988 to acquire a company riddled with contracts destined for Iraq, government policy was still pro-Iraq.
From this time through the Iran–Iraq ceasefire in July 1988 to
April 1989 when Pakistan got the atomic bomb, there was a
development that culminated in a complete U-turn, if not panic.
Suddenly it looked as if cabal policy to help ISC and Matrix
Churchill and indeed Gerald Bull's SRC, with its potential to arm
Iraq with nuclear capability, was in danger of bringing the estab-
lishment machine down.

When the Americans made the surprise discovery that Pakistan
had developed the atomic bomb, they worried seriously for the
first time about Iraq, and what might be revealed about how far
covert US/UK policy had already taken Iraq's capability. Fear
overcame greed. Commerce, they say, is driven by striking a balance between greed and fear. Fear bred the damage limitation
strategy which would engulf all the relatively small independents
that they had used, Astra included.

Any conspiracy, which is what would be necessary between
SGB and the cabal in Britain in order to wrap up PRB's government-inspired covert operations, requires a close working
relationship between all parties.

The long history of collaboration between the British government and SGB in arms cartel activities (through the IMS and

PRB deals) provided a sound enough basis for conspiracy, perhaps, but the historical liaison went further.

TANKS – Tanganyika Concessions, a major mineral company taken over by SGB, owned 20 per cent of Union Minière in the Congo, the great source of strategic minerals for the British and American defence industry. It had been a British company, but was purchased by SGB, who already owned 80 per cent of Union Minière, to acquire the minority interest. It was and remains a very important shared interest between SGB and the British government, an interest nurtured by having people closely connected with the MoD and the British government establishment appointed as directors. Sir Kenneth Corfield, Midland and chairman of STC (formerly Standard Telephones and Cables) was chairman of TANKS during this period. Comte Hervé de Carmoy, also ex-Midland, became chairman of Union Minière in 1989 at the same time as he was chief executive of SGB.

So there is no doubt that there was a strong line of communication and strategic empathy between the British government establishment and SGB, a company which, as I have said, accounts for around one-third of the Belgian economy, an empathy that was tied, through the de Carmoy – Cuckney – Kock connection, specifically to our case.

There is no question in my mind that SGB consulted with the British government all the time that we were negotiating with the company. When de Carmoy and Cuckney dictated the new policy to secure PRB for Astra, Kock had no option but to fall in line and become an active participant. Later, during the DTI Inquiry into Astra, it was confirmed that the strategy was being steered from within the company. Our finance director Jim Miller and I actually caught sight of a memo from Warburgs, who were handling the deal on SGB/Gechem's behalf, reassuring SGB that there was no danger of the deal not going through because 'we have a man in the Astra camp'.

Kock went to extraordinary lengths at the DTI Inquiry into Astra's purchase of PRB to establish that he had not changed his initial position, which was against the acquisition. He did this partly to distance himself from the event under scrutiny, but mainly because his change of heart was a clue to the conspiracy to saddle Astra with the explosive material at the core of PRB, which would be used so effectively against us. The DTI inspectors heard evidence from myself, Gumbley, Miller, Guest and Anderson that Kock's attitude changed so that he became positively in favour of doing the deal for PRB. 'Mr Miller pointed to the fact that Mr Kock told him he was being pressured by the vendors as to why Astra was delaying the acquisition, and that he in turn encouraged the board to accelerate it,' the inspectors' report had to admit. 'Mr James and Mr Gumbley told us of further specific incidents which they said illustrated Mr Kock's positive support for the acquisition.' But incredibly the inspectors concluded: 'We do not consider it necessary to detail these.'

The whole point is that Kock's change of heart was a necessary tactic in the government's effective saddling of Astra with PRB. With Kock's co-operation it could turn the story of government covert dealing, which was locked into PRB, into a tract against us. For this reason it was not just necessary but the very essence of justice that the inspectors should have detailed our evidence. I have shown Kock's change of heart on PRB in my reference to his sorting out the problem with the Bank of Nova Scotia (p. 223), but it was his day-to-day position. Chris Gumbley gave his evidence as follows, before the House of Commons Trade and Industry Select Committee Inquiry:

> Mr Kock advised at the beginning of the difficulties of Belgium [trades union power, etc.] and he was not 100 per cent for the move forward. His position changed and he became very much in favour of the acquisition . . . I must also add that Mr Kock did ring me early in the morning, once before the PRB purchase and demanded that we get a move on with the purchase. He told me that he had been talking to Mr de Carmoy of SGB. Mr Kock asked for my assurance that we were proceeding with the PRB purchase with all speed.

So what lay behind this sudden change of heart by Cuckney, de Carmoy and Kock? What did they hope to achieve by saddling Astra with PRB?

When in early November 1989 I received copies of two letters written by Bull to the PRB manager Philippe Glibert, I learned more than that Bull had been 'advised of an imminent "accident"' by the Foreign Office following the Lear Fan deal. The second letter, also still in my possession, concerned Bull's own negotiations to buy PRB during the early part of our negotiations with SGB/Gechem in 1988 when they were playing hard to get. This was news to me. (I would also learn that the Bank of Nova Scotia, which had posed one of the main difficulties in the banking syndicate supporting our acquisition of PRB, difficulties which Kock had miraculously solved, had been connected with Bull.)

My visit to Bull in the same month confirmed that he had offered, for a 50 per cent interest in PRB, roughly double what we had eventually paid for the company. Why, I wondered, had SGB/Gechem gone for our lesser offer in preference to Bull's? PRB was a joint owner of Bull's SRC in the early- to mid-1980s, and provided all the development finance for Bull's projects. Bull had been plying his trade with a company close to the Belgian government, and much of the work involved US technology transferred through PRB's Canadian subsidiary, Belcan. It is also clear that Bull and SRC employees such as Glynn Kay and Chris Cowley were reporting regularly to MI6 and British government agencies. Finally, Bull's play for the company involved Noricum and Trebelan to maximise work feed for PRB and the development of new technology. It was a very attractive proposition. Indeed I discovered there had been four or five offers altogether from different sources, but SGB/Gechem had allowed Astra to knock down the price from £38m to £20m. Why?

Why didn't the government or SGB want Bull to have it? The answer must be that Bull was trading with Iraqi money. They couldn't sell PRB to Bull because the political ramifications at this sensitive time were too dire. PRB lay at the centre of the arms and propellant cartel and, as Gumbley and I would discover, much more besides, enough to blackmail the British government into submission. They could not afford to let the Iraqis or Bull have the power over them that PRB would confer. They could not sanction the sale of such a Pandora's box of covert arms secrets. They wanted PRB brought home under the Astra umbrella, where Cuckney and Kock could keep things safe and under wraps.

As we have seen, a similar 'sanctuary' policy worked in the cases of Muiden Chemie and Heckler and Koch, when they were brought into the safe haven of Royal Ordnance, and indeed it worked later in BMARC's sensitive Faldingworth site, when it too was sold to RO and became part of the government's secure system.

In line with that policy, they could not let Wafiq Said have PRB either, whether or not he was utilising Iraqi money (which he probably was). They couldn't let Said have PRB because he was a Saudi and the government 'golden boy' over Al Yamamah. If they found, for any reason, that they had to pull the plug on PRB (and I would give them that reason) the last person they wanted with egg on his face was Wafiq Said.

If, as Kock feared, I spiked their efforts to find shelter for PRB by revealing what I found there, then they would activate the same strategy of damage limitation that was in the mixing bowl for Ordtec, Matrix Churchill, Walter Somers, Sheffield Forgemasters and SRC. They would wash their hands of the embarrassment in the blood of a few main board directors.

As I have stated, my decision to reveal the contracts was taken with our own safety in mind. I have every reason to believe that Roger Harding's exhortation to report any covert contracts in PRB was a friendly piece of advice to get any dubious contracts on record so that the MoD could not use them against us. There seems little doubt that had we not reported the contracts, we would have been the stars of the show trials and arrests to follow.

Unfortunately our decision to report the contracts would trigger the very event that it was designed to avoid – the destruction of Astra – and a process to discredit the founding directors which continues to this day.

Looking back now, it seems to me that whichever option we had taken we wouldn't have won, unless we had gone with Wafiq Said. Said's support would have locked into us an element which would have made us virtually indestructible, and they knew that. This was why Cuckney began pressing us – he rang me three times, once through Sandy Walker at 3i's Glasgow office – to complete the deal with institutional backing.

There is a side-issue which casts 3i's institutional support in an interesting light. Our major institutional shareholder, 3i, which had finally pushed for the deal with PRB, sold three million shares in Astra between our signing of the PRB contract in July and its completion in September. The question arises as to whether, if 3i were warehousing shares for others, these were the three million shares that 3i owned themselves. Although 3i reported to our broker, the company secretary was not directly informed about the sale. Were they perhaps sold to the Iraqis to placate them for losing the deal, or were they, as was suggested to me by Gerald Bull, sold to Israeli Military Industries?

It is worth noting, in regard to this, that at the time of the PRB negotiations the stockbrokers UBS Philips and Drew built up a huge position in various Phildrew Nominee Accounts. Attempts to identify these were time-consuming and abortive. It has been suggested to me both that these holdings were Israeli and that they were Iraqi, and indeed John Reed of *Defence Industry Digest* referred in a memorandum to Iraqi money being used to buy PRB.

What is more closely relevant is that at a time when we were finalising a deal which 3i had encouraged, they were apparently acting to minimise their exposure.

As far as the cabal was concerned, as soon as we reported the Supergun propellant contract, the battle lines were drawn and the strategy of damage limitation proceeded apace. The first step, wholly unpredictable, was an instruction from the MoD to continue production of the propellant for Iraq and to deliver the first shipment.

It was but a sign, however, that we were no longer in control of the company's destiny, for on 5 December, the PRB propellant press at Kaulille was blown up and the Supergun propellant production facilities wiped out. It does not take too conspiratorial an imagination to assign responsibility for this act, as Gumbley indicated to Menzies Campbell MP, with perhaps too much of an eye to the legal implications, at the Trade and Industry Select Committee Inquiry into arms exports to Iraq in 1991–2:

> **Mr Doug Hoyle:** We have heard it [Kaulille] was sabotaged, do you agree with that?
> **Gumbley:** It was very convenient.
> **Mr Menzies Campbell:** For whom?
> **Gumbley:** Well, it was very convenient because we could not now deliver the propellant.
> **Hoyle:** Who would have benefited?'
> **Gumbley:** It would not have benefited the Iraqis.
> **Hoyle:** I think you are right on that, we would agree on that.

During our interrogation by the Select Committee, the chairman Ken Warren tried to promote the idea of 'extraordinary coincidence' by making out that the propellant was volatile material and could have gone up at any time. In fact, although the propellant was subjected to tremendous pressure in the press, it was dangerous only if there was an initiation charge capable of creating sufficient heat to set the material off.

Harris and Partners launched an investigation and privately agreed with me that it smacked of sabotage. The explosion had occurred during a break in production, a tea-break when there were no personnel in the area. Chris Cowley, who has given courses to the SAS in industrial sabotage, is also of the opinion that the explosion bore all the hallmarks of industrial sabotage. He has suggested that it was effected by an army unit from Germany.

I was in no position to lay the explosion at any third party's door, for we were interested not only in a material damage claim but in a claim for consequential loss. What the explosion implied immediately was a serious shortfall in Astra's turnover, some £38m to March 1990.

As I have said, we had of course weighed this up in reaching our decision to report the contract, and I did not regard it as fatal. However, in the meantime, another extraordinary and damaging fact emerged. On 12 September 1989, at a meeting with PRB's comité de direction soon after the acquisition of PRB, John Anderson and Dr Pike were informed that there would be a shortfall in PRB's projected results for 1989 of around £15m.

It then became apparent that the firm order position had been deliberately withheld from us by SGB/Gechem during the purchase of PRB. On 26 June (weeks before the signing of the contract in July and nearly three months before its completion in September) Guy Cardinael, general manager of PRB, wrote a memorandum to Jean Duronsoy, managing director of Gechem and principal negotiator for the sale of PRB, in which he said, 'For various reasons (including "politics" in particular) this scenario [of PRB's results for 1989] will not be kept, it has been reviewed downwards since March 1989. Astra's management has not been informed . . .' In short, it appeared that the sale of PRB to Astra had been built deliberately on a lie.

Later I would discover that when PRB had been separated from Gechem and re-formed as a limited company in preparation for the sale, at least one very major contract, and probably many more, had been taken out of the company for political reasons not solely concerned with the desirability of hammering Astra. How far the deliberate fabrication of PRB's order position and the so-called confidentiality agreement was designed to this end in collusion with those who would see Astra put down is impossible for me to say, but Cardinael's memo made plain that 'politics' were behind it.

There had been ample opportunity for SGB/Gechem to bring the true position to our attention prior to the sale. Our accountants, Stoy Hayward, had examined the orders, and on the basis of the timings (when these orders would fall due), a list of which had been given to them by SGB/Gechem, they had concluded that we should proceed.

But I hadn't left it at that. As I pointed out at the DTI Inquiry, I discussed the 1989 figures not only before we signed the contract but on the telephone in the interim before completion with both Duronsoy and René Grégoire, assistant to Duronsoy on the sale and finance director of Gechem:

> Anything which affected the profit was banged home very hard. They continually gave us assurances that the company would make its minimum profit projection [£2m] for the year [1989] . . . Mr Duronsoy told us that they would make the minimum profit . . . We discussed any reservations which were expressed by Stoy Hayward. We discussed them exhaustively and extensively with Duronsoy, Jous [Philippe Jous, Gechem's corporate affairs vice president, legal and administration], Grégoire . . . We had a long period when we were closeted with these Belgians before we signed the agreement, when they were on hand for several days . . . Our main concern was their ability to make the profit that they had predicted for the year.

Adrian Haxby, assistant director of Warburgs, who acted for Gechem in relation to the sale, also assured us that they were on line for maximum profit.

What this revelation meant immediately was that I had to look around for short-term support. In the long term I remained confident that we would weather the storm. Once we had integrated PRB into our international strategy of inter-company technology transfer (US–UK–Europe), I was confident that our strong forward position would make us unassailable. This was not over-confidence on my part, neither was it solely my opinion. Our accounts to March 1990 detail that with PRB, Astra had an order book approaching £300m – £100m in PRB, some £200m in the rest of the group. Also, PRB meeting minutes of 12 April 1990 (note this was after my removal), record a 'positive' sales forecast for PRB and the view of government ministers and senior military staff within the MoD that PRB remained an important European defence asset and that its future should he assured. Moreover, we were working on a deal with Taiwan worth in total, $1.5bn, which had been quite a coup for Chris Gumbley. Astra was to be the main contractor (like BAe in Al Yamamah) in a deal which involved a huge amount of Oerlikon equipment, a project for the 105mm light gun, for which RO was manufacturer, and other assorted ammunition and weapons. By the spring of 1990 we had progressed beyond competitive bids and agreed terms. Around the time I was removed in April 1990, the Taiwanese agents were over, and it was all ready to be signed.

In the event, however, the shortfall in PRB's 1989 results was used by the government/Intelligence/SGB alliance as a 'plausible explanation' for why PRB failed to meet targets after we had reported the propellant contract and deprived Astra of over £30m of business, and I believe the revelation of the 1989 shortfall in PRB was contrived to their purpose, which was to close the lid on its secrets by bringing Astra down. Otherwise, why did SGB refuse to settle with Astra for the shortfall (compensation was required by Belgian law)? It would have cost SGB a mere £12m rather than, as happened, all the adverse publicity and a £40m loss on the banking side alone? I shall return to this.

Once we began to broadcast the corrupt contracts in PRB, the disposal of the company became the priority and would proceed with inordinate haste. In the same month as I resigned as chairman, while I was still on the board, the new management, with Kock in the saddle, arranged the sale of key parts of PRB to the French company Giat, and the rest was closed down. This was done with no Board minute showing approval of the sale, a fact which was not commented on by the DTI inspectors in the ensuing inquiry. Commercially it made no sense at all. Recently there was a BBC television documentary by Jane Renton, which concluded that Britain might well end up buying all its ammunition from France, from PRB and Giat. That it was politically motivated is beyond doubt.

At the same time, the $1.5bn Taiwan deal was let go, and the disposal of BMARC within the government secure system more than two years later, during which time it was starved of new

orders under the new Astra management, would be further confirmation of the political motivations for the break-up of the
company. BMARC was sold to British Aerospace/Royal Ordnance
for £8m despite the fact, reported in March 1994 by David
Hellier, that an Anglo-Austrian consortium offered £12.7m.
Graham Rushworth for the consortium said with regard to the
Receivers, Coopers & Lybrand, 'My own view is that your firm,
for whatever reason, chose to favour Royal Ordnance. We are
considering, therefore, what remedies are open to us.' Again, Ed
Walters told me that an American consortium would have paid
£20m for BMARC, but the Receivers would not hand over the
prospectus.

They sold Faldingworth and certain assets and the name of
BMARC to RO. Grantham they retained and put it into a company called Springfield Road Ltd (named after the location of
BMARC's Grantham site), a company of which Kock is shown in
documents I have from Companies House, as director, receiver
and manager. A receiver and manager winds up a company, takes
the power away from the shareholders and tries to get the maximum return for the banks, who have first call. He is also named
as receiver for Astra. This means that Kock was working for the
banks and for the company and was in control of the funds at
Springfield Road Ltd. He was in control of everything that
happened, in particular where the money ended up.

Who bought Astra's American companies? One of those principally involved was John Lehman Associates (the Intelligence-
connected John Lehman, boss of Brian Havill of Paine Webber)
with Charter Industries Singapore (false end-user on BMARC's
Iran-bound LISI contract and Cyprus contract, among others
destined for the war zone in the 1980s).

We were well stitched up, there is no doubt about it. The DTI
Inquiry would persist in saying that PRB's 1989 profit shortfall
was the reason for the break-up of Astra and that our failure during negotiations to spot it was our fault. There was no mention of
the role in our financial difficulties played by the loss in revenue
due to our reporting of the Supergun propellant contract (clearly

greater than that played by the PRB profit shortfall), nor at any point were we given any credit for having reported the existence of the contract.

It is my belief, and I have stated my reasons, that even taken together, these two incidents need not have led to Astra's break-up, and the contention that it was our fault, the fault of the Astra directors, cannot, in my opinion, be backed up on the evidence available.

Besides my own enquiries of SGB/Gechem, which I have listed, and reports on PRB commissioned by Astra over a period of fifteen months, we had a battery of advisers who had been similarly duped.

We were advised by the accountants who were auditors for SGB (Touche Ross), we were advised by our own accountants, Stoy Hayward (with no axe to grind), we were advised by Baileys, Shaw & Gillett, our lawyers, we were given assurances by Warburgs and Slaughter and May acting for SGB/Gechem, we had Paine Webber, a major US investment bank with specific knowledge of the defence industry, and our stockbrokers Hichens Harrison, who also looked at the cash position. It is difficult to see how much more rigorous we could have been in our pursuit of a true financial picture of PRB. Not one of these advisers, who had access to all the information made available by SGB/Gechem, at any time, on any occasion, advised us not to go ahead with the purchase.

Most telling of all, Générale de Banque, an SGB subsidiary which provided the bank facilities to PRB, did its own study of the cash position prior to our acquisition. With its own historical knowledge as banker for PRB, and with a close knowledge of the defence industry, it gave PRB a clean bill of health and it gave us a positive report and it granted us the facilities. So did Indo-Suez, SGB's new controlling shareholder. Yet SGB's Générale de Banque was the main loser (up to £40m) at the end of the day. It was the price paid to wrap up the British government's embarrassment and to exonerate SGB, and it was dismissed as irrelevant by the DTI inspectors.

*

Back in September 1989, being primarily concerned to sort out our short-term financial problems caused by the Supergun contract and order book shortfall, I began to realise that the fact that we had signed for PRB under Belgian law was a significant bonus. I was advised that our case for compensation in the event of fraud was better under Belgian law than under English law. If the PRB sale was built on a lie, according to Belgian law the vendor was liable to make full reparation on those terms alone.

Before bringing this to bear on what was going on, I went to Duronsoy at Gechem and informed him that we had had to report the Supergun propellant contract; also that I was very concerned to hear from PRB that they had not made full disclosure about the timing of orders, and resulting cash flow downturn, which threatened to translate into a loss for PRB in 1989 of around £8m, and that consequently I was looking to them to help out.

I went to him with a workable scenario to rectify the situation. I suggested that SGB take a 30 per cent stake in Astra that would push our share price up and get us over the difficulties. If, subsequently, they didn't want to keep these shares they could unload them over a period.

One reason why I believed that this would make sound sense to SGB was, as stated above, that Générale de Banque, part of the SGB Group and banker to PRB for many years, had itself, on my insistence, produced a report on PRB, on the strength of which the bank had agreed to grant a working capital facility of £18m to PRB, its sister company. This had given me great confidence during negotiations and now, surely, SGB would be amenable to finding a way to protect its own bank's interests. At first Duronsoy said they might be interested. But of course, in the event, it didn't fit in with overall SGB/British government strategy.

When finally he turned my proposition down, I put in a claim for compensation. I was prepared to negotiate down from £23m to around £12m. Sir Kenneth Corfield, chairman of TANKS and SGB's man in the UK, agreed that this was the best solution. Even the people in PRB itself said: Hang out for the £12m; you'll get it.

Again, as an alternative to legal proceedings, the compensation offer made obvious sense to SGB. But the wrangling went on and on so that it remained unresolved by the time I was pushed out of the Astra chair. The new management with Kock finally settled with SGB for £3.5m cash on 5 April 1990, which was absurd. The fact that they did not sue SGB/Gechem for the false information they gave us might make more of an interesting investigation on behalf of Astra shareholders than was entered into purportedly on their behalf by the DTI four months later.

I was told later that SGB's refusal to deal with me cost them in the region of £40m. They lost some £16m of the £18m put up by Générale de Banque as a working capital facility for PRB and the bank also had to stump up guarantees on contracts lost in the process of the new management's disposal of PRB. No company chooses to lose £40m if they can bail out with a share deal that would cost them nothing in the medium term (because they could have sold their shares), or £12m cash in compensation, unless, of course, there is a sound political reason and someone is prepared to make up the shortfall. The only conceivable reason for their refusal to deal with me is that it was a political decision.

No investigation into SGB/Gechem's misrepresentation of the 1989 order position was ever made by the inspectors in the DTI Inquiry which ensued in mid-1990 because, they declared, 'the principal Belgian personnel involved in the matter did not consent to be interviewed by us.' Cardinael and Glibert, who were among those who might have shed some light at the Inquiry, had opted out of their commitment to be part of the new PRB board. 'We have therefore not had the opportunity,' the inspectors concluded, 'to put the critical factual matters to them in person and this has greatly inhibited our capacity to make any findings in fact.' It was quite an admission.

An investigation had been promised by the Belgian police, which never materialised, although later the Belgians set up an investigation under the former deputy prime minister André Cools into the circumstances surrounding the sale of PRB, among other matters related to the arms trade. On 18 July 1991, as he was opening his car door, Cools was shot by five bullets through his throat and left ear.

I learned of this from the *Independent* while on my way by train to Bristol to visit Chris Cowley about his claim to have seen Kock in Baghdad arranging the finance for the Supergun contract. It emerged that Cowley had had contact with the *Independent* about the Cools murder. A day or so earlier he had read about the shooting on his way by plane to meet Monique Sauder, a Swiss magistrate who had all the information about commissions paid to secure the first PRB shipment of Supergun propellant to Iraq.

Those who had an interest in keeping Cools quiet also had an interest in this most explosive aspect of the PRB Supergun deal. For the record, when, as directed by the British government, we shipped the first and only (trial) consignment of Supergun pro-pellant to Iraq, it travelled in a Belgian Air Force aircraft, in containers marked as if they contained chocolate. Two commis-sions were paid, totalling £240,000. One went to Bilder Trading, a UK-registered company with links to King Hussein, the other to a Panamanian company, whose directors and shareholders remain a mystery. I would very much like to know where (and to whom) these companies lead.

In the autumn of 1989, as I attempted to deal with our short-term financial problems in negotiation with Duronsoy, I came under immense pressure by Kock, first through our major share-holders.

Huw Jones of the Prudential rang me one day in October, just a month after I had reported the Supergun contract and a month after we learned of SGB/Gechem's withholding of information about the downturn in 1989 profits. We met for lunch and he asked me how it was going with PRB. I told him there were one or two problems because we had had to report a number of dubi-ous contracts, which obviously had deprived us of a lot of turnover. I said I was pretty confident in the long term, but in the interim, results would not be seen to do us any favours.

We also discussed the Wafiq Said deal, and I put it to him that it would have been better for everyone if that deal had been allowed to go through, especially as Said was so close to other potential deals in the Middle East. Financially the company would have been in a far stronger position with a really powerful player as the major shareholder. I asked him why they had rushed in.

I also asked him why he thought that Sir John Cuckney, who had previously taken no interest whatever in the deal, had come on to me on three occasions, pressing me to complete the acquisition? Finally, I asked Jones why, at the eleventh hour and without any warning, 3i had sold three million shares in Astra.

I told him that these matters concerned me, as there seemed to be a hidden agenda about which I was not being informed. I said that I was concerned in particular about Kock as the fulcrum around which these suspect or damaging activities turned. I told him that I had been considering bringing in someone like Campbell Dunford (ex-MITS), who, besides anything else, would get on with the re-organisation of the company's banking arrangements that Kock had said he would arrange but never had.

I had had misgivings from the start about the banking arrangements made through Paine Webber to cover the inter-company loan aspect of the deal with Oerlikon for the BMARC acquisition. You will recall that Paine Webber had organised the banking at the last moment through Bank of Boston when Midland Montagu had withdrawn.

One Chuck Ball at the Bank of Boston, a friend of Brian Havill, had organised the facility via a multi-currency loan syndicate. As feared, there had been problems. Boston hadn't syndicated the loan fast enough, also the covenants were very tight and unnecessarily complicated. With the time restriction within which we had had to acquire BMARC in 1988, we had had to go along with it. In the situation we were in now, with Kock snapping at my heels, I wanted to ensure that it would not prove the last straw in our increasing financial burdens.

I had met Campbell Dunford back in 1987 when he was a member of MITS. Kock had suggested we invite him to our box at the Royal Tournament, which we sponsored. At MITS, Dunford had just the kind of banking and defence industry experience the Bank of Boston problem needed, and I had considered employing him then as a consultant. However, he had subsequently taken up a position in London with the Moscow Narodny Bank. I learned later that Kock had arranged the job for him.

I had then lined up a deal with one of the Touche Remnant investment trusts, whereby I intended to do Maxwell/Hill Samuel Investment Trust type of deal, merging with a redundant investment trust, Astra issuing shares to take over their funds, which would have paid off the Boston loan. Unfortunately I gave the details of the package to Paine Webber to sort out, and they lost the deal to someone else. They had taken so long that it had seemed almost as though Paine Webber hadn't wanted us to escape the clutches of the Boston Bank deal they had arranged (certainly Boston was making a lot of money out of it). It should go down as the first of many occasions that I felt trapped in the arrangement.

Thereafter great play had been made by Kock that Midland would take the loan over. There was, however, still the problem of the disputed Midland Montagu fee on the BMARC deal. I had a meeting with the top man from Midland Montagu in London, where it was agreed that if we paid them they would take over the Boston loan. Kock then arranged a meeting in New York with Ray Giess, our manager, now at a main City branch, Ian Mullen, deputy head Midland Montagu Corporate Banking, and Paul Bartley, vice-president corporates, Midland Bank Plc, New York.

It was suggested that Gumbley, Miller and I fly over there and sort out the details. For some reason Kock was never able to get a visa to America, and did not come. So off we three went on a trip that nearly turned out as costly to us personally as it would to the company. Due to time pressures we flew by Concorde and found ourselves on the same flight as a large corporate team from the Tiphook company (who were involved in an acquisition in the US) – lawyers, Queen's Counsel, the lot. The aircraft nearly crashed. Suddenly it began to shake uncontrollably, luggage flew out of lockers, trolleys veered up the aisle. Computers controlling air intake on the engines had failed, we were told, though it was 30 minutes before we had the explanation. By then the aircraft had gone subsonic and lost altitude to 20,000 feet or so, and there was considerable doubt, owing to the extra fuel used up, that we would make Bermuda, let alone New York. The incident occurred at the point of no return, a portent perhaps for both Astra and Tiphook. Had the aircraft gone down, it might have been simpler for everyone, including the spooks.

When finally we met with Midland we found them, as expected, happy to take over the loan but only on condition that we paid them the disputed Midland Montagu fee. We paid them, and they never came up with the deal. The whole charade cost the company more than £400,000, and we were no further forward. I was very annoyed. There followed a series of board meetings in autumn 1989 at which I insisted that Kock sort out the loan and, if he did not, that there was no room for him at Astra.

Now – at the end of 1989 – I had heard that Campbell Dunford had left the Moscow Narodny Bank, and I thought about contacting him again. I had wanted to ask Huw Jones what he thought of the idea of having Dunford on the board to take over Kock's brief on the loan package as a test. As one of our major shareholders, he would surely back an attempt to sort out the company's banking problems. But if, as I suspected, Kock was already getting through to him, he would be less likely to back any attempt to reduce Kock's control over such an important area.

Well, I am afraid that Jones was pretty non-committal and as loath to disrupt Kock's position as he would be later when Kock was arrested for shooting up an unfortunate motorist who had broken down outside his Scottish home (see p . 266), and I sought Jones's assistance in removing Kock from the board. I have no doubt that our conversation accelerated the decision to deal with me in the way that they did. I guessed Kock had already spoken to him, but Jones wasn't frank enough to say, neither did he deny or explain any of what had been going on at 3i over the PRB acquisition.

OK, I had put him in a difficult position, but I was fed up with the subterfuge and felt it was time to flush out the opposition. The only suggestion Jones made was that he might know a useful non-executive director. The name he came up with was Roy Barber, whom we will meet shortly.

After this meeting I saw Sandy Walker of 3i in London. He was in fact in charge of the 3i Glasgow office, with which we had been involved from the start. Back in 1980–81 their man Colin Ironside had handled negotiations for a possible management buy-out of Brocks before we made our bid for Astra. Ironside had made a favourable impression at that stage and helped cement a good relationship with 3i in Glasgow that bore fruit when it came to the Astra bid. Later, when Astra grew, I elected to stay with the Glasgow office. There had been pressure for us to move to their London or southern branches, but I felt that we had got to know them in Glasgow and the Scottish office was more down-to-earth. Then Ironside left, and about 1986 in came Sandy Walker, a nice enough chap, perhaps a little more ambitious or thrusting than Ironside, whom I found first class. He came in first as deputy manager and then manager.

When I met Walker in London after my meeting with Huw Jones of the Pru, however, I was very uneasy about his demeanour. Also, from our conversation, it was clear to me that he had been speaking with Gumbley and Miller as well as Cuckney. Nothing wrong with that, one might think, but it was not protocol, and Kock's wooing of Gumbley had made me aware of the dangers of the board being split at this crucial time. So I wasn't at all happy. I was more direct about what I had surmised was going on beneath the surface over the PRB fiasco even than I had been with Jones, and when I asked him whether he had indeed been talking to Gumbley and Miller, Walker went very red.

When the whole balloon finally went up a few months later, I rang Walker and was told he was unavailable because he was leaving. Later he rang and apologised for not being able to speak to me but he was preparing to go to Australia where he had been posted by the company to set up an office. He said, 'I'm sorry about all the chairman thing, I am sure you'll land on your feet.'

I feel that he might have been a useful instrument at the DTI Inquiry in bringing to the surface a vestige of truth at the 3i end. From his sudden and timely departure I can only deduce that I wasn't the only one to think so.

It was in November–December 1989 that I discovered Campbell Dunford was available. It had been understood that when he returned from Moscow Narodny he would be employed again in MITS. However, in the meantime, due to the end of the war and the political furore, Midland had reduced MITS, de Carmoy had gone off to PRB, and what was left had been sub-sumed under Midland Montagu. Consequently they didn't have a job for Dunford.

I told Miller, our finance director, what I had in mind – to bring Dunford in to do Kock's job. Miller didn't disagree. Although he was finance director, he was more of an operational accountant, battering people to get the profit projections and budgets in, rather than a City man. This isn't a criticism. I found him very direct and honest and a very decent person, but when it came to the City, he probably deferred to me.

While all this was going on, I began to be pressured from another quarter. Our brokers Hichens Harrison suddenly advised that we should produce the half-year figures in December, in spite of the fact that they were normally produced the following January–February. I would spend the whole of that Christmas (1989) in the office working on the final drafts, which I knew would be disappointing.

Now the first half-year in the short-run ammunition and usable commodities end of the defence industry is always worse than the second half, certainly on a year end of 31 March. Defence budgets both in America and England are April to April and it is in the last half in our sector when the bulk of sales are invoiced. With the problems we were experiencing with PRB however, these figures were bound to be especially disappointing, and I was very concerned at this sensitive time not to create, as I felt I was being pushed into creating, a false crisis of confidence.

In fact, although the mid-term figures were poor, when the new management produced the full year's figures to March 1990 – which did not emerge until the summer, long after the decks had been cleared of original pro-Astra directors – turnover was only £6m down on the previous year at £90.2m, even after £40m had been shifted into the March 1991 year end to bolster the abysmal (in fact non-existent) sales performance of the new management. In that year (1991), in spite of a nil sales performance, turnover was £86.6m on the basis of orders won by the original Astra team.

But back at the end of 1989 I was dealing with the first-half picture to September 1989 for the year ending 31 March 1990, which would result in a £3.8m pre-tax loss, and I was more than ever concerned to straighten out the mess with the Bank of Boston.

When I suggested Dunford's appointment at a board meeting, Kock immediately said, 'Ah, Dunford, good idea. I'll have a word with him.' I told him there was no need for that, I would get him in myself. Kock did however approach him. Dunford agreed to join us as an outside consultant, immediately starting work on re-financing the loan package, making several impressive presentations in the City.

Before long he raised the question of permanent employment with Astra and a position on the main Astra board. I was for it, but Kock at once objected, saying that there would be a problem. Dunford, Kock claimed, wouldn't get security clearance to be a director on the main board of a British defence company because he had been working for the Russians. In fact, as Kock well knew, and I would discover, Dunford, far from being a security risk, had already been checked out by MI6 and the CIA. Kock's duplicity would be exposed when I personally got Dunford a top-rate security clearance with no trouble at all through our security officer in BMARC.

Kock was concerned about Dunford's wish to have a place on the board in the first place because the Bank of Boston would be the means by which Kock and the new management controlled the company in the end.

Great play was made at the DTI Inquiry that Astra was in

default of Boston banking covenants. Although this was not a problem at the time of the 1989 interim report, Kock had identified its potential value in his strategy and interpreted as a threat my desire to have Dunford on board to deal with the problem.

Furthermore, Dunford's presence as a director would pose a complication in Kock's strategy to clear the Astra board of all present directors except for himself and replace them with his own and Cuckney's men. Dunford's background may have been MITS, but he took his work for Astra seriously and he would be unlikely to conspire in the destruction of the company that he was working so hard to further in the City.

The solution to our banking problem that Dunford proposed was Manufacturers Hanover Bank. Together with this bank, we re-negotiated our Bank of Boston loan facility, a move which if ratified would have greatly lightened our financial commitments. Kock was clearly put out when he heard about it.

Dunford knew Kock from his MITS days, of course, and was aware how dangerous he could be. So when he received a particularly nasty threatening call from Kock one night in which he made it clear that he did not want Dunford on the board, Dunford arranged to get hold of a telephone-taping machine and wired up his phone so that he could have evidence of precisely what was said. I have that tape, and this is a telling extract of what was said the next afternoon. It was a Saturday.

Stephan Kock: I tried phoning you this morning . . . Campbell, I didn't want any misunderstanding between you and I. We've had a reasonable relationship for some time.
Campbell Dunford: I've always thought so, Stephan. Yes, absolutely.
SK: But there are a number of matters which you wouldn't understand because you are not directly involved, and what I am saying to you is, don't be impatient.
CD: Right.
SK: Also what I am saying is that as adviser and consultant on the banking matters, whether you are on the board or

not makes really no difference to your income? OK?

CD: OK, fine.

SK: And I will see to that. I mean, there's no question about that.

CD: I hear you very clearly, but obviously you understand my life's been on hold and I've done my best for Astra as requested by you, by Gerald, and I really need to get on with things. I wasn't aware there was any sort of on-going internal problem.

SK: There is no on-going internal . . . I am in command.

CD: Right. OK.

SK: There is no question about that.

CD: Right.

SK: I am in command because of all the various people that have taken a great interest in Astra.

CD: Yep.

SK: I am not going to move the chairman. I'm not going to move the chief executive . . .

CD: I have no axe to grind except that I didn't realise that I was stepping into what potentially looks like a minefield. I didn't have any information on that.

SK: They all speak to me now.

CD: And the other thing is that I have got to have enough income to survive, because I have in fact . . .

SK: I will arrange that as soon as I get back to London.

CD: When are you going to be down?

SK: Well, I'm trying to not go next week because I have to be in Belgium the week after, but I will certainly be down within a week. But as far as you're concerned, your particular situation will be done formally and I hope in a most satisfactory way.

CD: OK, fine, well, er . . .

SK: And I'm sure that once that has happened, I am sure that your immediate concern about whether you do this or that will be removed immediately. What you have already produced banking-wise has been appreciated, whatever our sort of individual beliefs.

CD: Well, I hope I haven't upset anybody.

SK: No, you have not.

CD: I . . .

SK: No, you have not.

CD: And I . . .

SK: No, no, no, no, you haven't.

CD: And I have delivered the goods as requested.

SK: What I am saying to you is that we will see to that forthwith on an on-going basis.

CD: Right.

SK: You know, in about three or four years. The question of directorships is a very delicate one.

CD: Clearly. I didn't know I was walking into this sort of delicate sit . . .

SK: I am really in command of that because no one other than . . . Well, I'm not going to go any further, but I had to tell you last night that that particular aspect has to be . . . not cancelled but only postponed.

CD: Not rushed, in other words. I understand. It's purely that the first thing I heard was that . . . to be told by a third party that I wasn't acceptable for security reasons, all of a sudden, I must say, I took umbrage.

SK: You must not be surprised at that.

CD: No, but equally you know that I've been checked out by our side, the CIA, etc., and you know bloody fine I'm straight as a die.

SK: I do, heh, heh, heh.

CD: It was because of . . .

SK: I would leave that one alone.

CD: Right . . .

SK: So, my dear Campbell, please relax.

CD: OK.

SK: Do apologise to your wife about me bothering her on Saturday.

CD: Look, good heavens, no. I got back to you as soon as I could. I left a message on your machine, which I hope you got.

SK: We have another line, which is a secure line, which I'll give you the number of when I next see you.

CD: All right, fine.

SK: Bless you, Campbell, and how nice to have talked to you . . .

I was away in Belgium when representatives of Manufacturers Hanover Bank arrived at our Grantham offices to organise the details of Dunford's big new package. Kock got to hear about it, came down from Scotland and kicked them out of the company.

So desperate was he that we should not alleviate the Boston situation that he was instrumental, through Boston, in bringing in Cooper Brothers to do a useless report that cost us £140,000 and caused further delays. I became pretty stroppy when I heard about it and went down for a meeting with Coopers with Miller and Gumbley.

Coopers sent two partners to that meeting. One was the chap who was going to do the report, but the other was from the Receiver's department, a serious breach of accounting ethics as there was no question of receivership then, but a clear sign, too, that they were already anticipating receivership as our ultimate fate.

The financial shenanigans go only so far to re-create the underlying tension that existed in Astra during this period following the report of the Supergun propellant contract when the strategy for our eventual demise was unfurling.

Among the more crucial elements in the drama was a sales trip I made to Jeddah, Saudi Arabia, with John Sellens. We were to see Prince Mishari, half-brother of King Fahd. Mishari had been anxious to meet Gumbley and myself since July 1989, but the trip had been repeatedly postponed partly because of Gumbley's other sales trips and also because Kock and Jonathan Aitken, who was on the BMARC board, clearly did not wish me to go. Aitken had gone to the lengths of getting a letter from the Foreign Office saying that Mishari was an 'undesirable', who had shot dead the British consul in Saudi in 1953.

I subsequently discovered through Admiral Robin Hogg (nephew of Lord Hailsham) of Midland's arms department MITS that Saudi in the 1950s was a bum posting where sundry Foreign Office no-hopers were sent. The consul in 1953 had been a drunkard and womaniser, who had molested Mishari's sister and apparently deserved to be shot.

We flew to Jeddah and received VIP treatment from the start. We were waved through Customs, a car was there to meet us at the airport, and we were put up in a very fine hotel, where we had dinner with various people in the prince's entourage. Later I discovered from Mishari and his advisers that he wanted to get involved in the huge trade which was apparently being conducted through Astra and in Astra's name. This was no particular surprise to me as I had already been given this impression by Mishari's UK agent, a man called Henderson.

Mishari was particularly interested in the weaponising deal for Blackhawk helicopters, which he had heard Astra was doing with Westland, and a large 155mm artillery project, which Mishari told us was a PRB deal. Both were part of Thatcher's celebrated Al Yamamah contract with Saudi. The manufacturing part of the 155mm contract, I discovered, had indeed been one of PRB's which had been taken off PRB's order book prior to the company's sale to Astra by SGB/Gechem.

Mishari's interest was in the capacity of agent for spares and follow-up contracts to these deals, but mine increasingly was to know the reason why we had been deprived of such a large 155mm contract. Had it been deemed too sensitive for us to handle or too profitable?

That 155mm order would have been very useful to us then, but both these British government contracts were certainly sensitive. Mishari confirmed that they were destined for Iraq.

We were away in Saudi for a week, and on my return I had to dash off to Germany for a regimental function with the 1st Grenadier Guards, my son's regiment, which used the Warrior armoured vehicle which was armed with the RARDEN cannon that we manufactured at BMARC.

When I returned, on Monday 16 December, I learned that Kock had been in a state of consternation over my visit. I also learned that he had taken the opportunity to have 'quiet words' with Chris Gumbley, drinks at the Special Forces Club, and so on. When Gumbley appeared in my office, he said he had something very serious to talk to me about. 'We want you to stand down as chairman,' he said.

I asked him who exactly wanted me to stand down.

'It's the institutions,' he said, 'Kock has been in touch with 3i and the Pru. Cuckney in particular is concerned.'

I was sad to hear it come from Gumbley. I said, 'Cuckney is also the person who wanted to push through this deal with PRB a few months ago, so why do you suppose they are all pretending to be so alarmed about it now?' Then I told him that PRB was involved with this 155mm contract and asked him why he thought it had been kept back from Astra. He said he didn't know anything about it.

Chris Gumbley's reluctance to trust his suspicions about Kock, BMARC and PRB was understandable. We were so close to events, and Kock's influence was palpable. Survival is a strong instinctive urge which can blind one to the best strategy to effect it. I tried to show him a little of what was coming down, and then said that there was a lot still to be discovered about PRB.

I had noticed that my file on Kock had begun to fill with notes of conversations overheard between Kock and others concerning Thailand; faxes and telexes had been sent to Thailand by Kock on our office machines. One of Kock's contacts in Thailand in December 1989 was someone called Bernard, whom I believe to have been Bernard Wheeler, Kock's connection, you will recall, with Tory Party funds.

The documents, while not in any way incriminating in themselves, were none the less important enough to have been taken from my files by MoD police in the cover-up which ensued. I put it to Gumbley that he should make a trip to the Far East and investigate some of PRB's other contracts. I thought it about time for Gumbley to see a few things for himself on the spot. The trip was arranged for early January. Gumbley would go out with Harry Krantz, an agent and friend of Gerald Bull who worked for Astra, and a man called Binek, who had worked for both PRB and Bull.

At a board meeting that week to discuss the interim results, badly affected as they were by all that had been going on, I noted that Kock seemed nervy and red-faced. The tension between us was by this time noticeable. In one ludicrous interchange he accused me of spreading a rumour that he had fired shots into the ceiling at a board meeting, an idea soon to be not so very far from the truth.

Over Christmas I dealt with the interim figures, approaching all the directors for input, including Kock, though he would later deny this to the DTI inspectors. Then on 10 January, I heard from John Anderson that a secret meeting had been held by Kock at the White Hart Hotel, Lincoln, at which Major-General Isles, Lt-Col. Avery, McNaught and a Col. Forsyth of the MoD (Isles's nephew), plus at least four assorted spooks had been present. I now know that at this meeting it was revealed that a decision had been taken to break up the group and put the lid on all the covert dealings before I pulled the rug on everyone involved.

We were in a state of pure anarchy at Astra at this time. We were due to have a board meeting in Brussels around the middle of the month and Gumbley suggested that we – Kock, myself, Gumbley and Miller – have a private dinner in a suite at the Berkeley Hotel to try to get everything into perspective. It was an absurd idea, born of Chris Gumbley's good intentions, divided loyalties and fated at the outset. But I agreed to it. We were to meet at 7.30 pm on 11 January.

The Berkeley, which used to be in Mayfair, is now in Wilton Place near Knightsbridge. It is a Savoy Group hotel and although not really very small, it gives the feeling of understated comfort and appears smaller and more intimate than other hotels in the group. It is much favoured by business people, particularly by Americans of the white Anglo-Saxon Protestant variety. Tiny Rowland also dined there regularly at that time.

I arrived before Miller and Gumbley, and asked to be shown to the suite, but then saw Kock sitting drinking in the lounge. Although he drinks Scotch, on this occasion he was drinking dry white wine, presumably to keep his wits about him. I sat down opposite him. The atmosphere you could have cut with a knife. I said something about the quality of the surroundings, and he replied, 'Oh, I don't know. It's not the sort of place I go to very much.' I said, 'No, Stephan, I don't suppose so', and I believe we left it more or less at that, Kock looking, I noticed, even more flushed and bloated than he had been of late; in need of some sleep, I remember thinking.

Then Jim Miller, a svelte, rather better-looking edition of Rocco Forte, and Chris Gumbley, short and stocky with his infectious grin, arrived together and we all went up to the second-floor suite. Gumbley tried to make small talk in the lift to relieve the tension which seemed to be magnified by the confined space. In the dining room, we positioned ourselves round the table and ordered drinks from a waiter who then returned to distribute the menus.

I don't think any of us knew what would be said; Kock was obviously ill at ease. It occurs to me now that he was probably worried that I knew more than I did at that time about what he was getting up to. Gumbley again broke the ice with – 'The purpose of the meeting is to try and secure a better atmosphere for the Brussels board meeting . . .' He looked round, smiling at us all.

I said, 'I have no problem with that,' my eyes settling on Kock.

Kock began, 'Well, I don't know why we are having this. Having dinner with James is rather like supping with the Devil.'

'Well, the reason I came along here,' I said, 'was that Chris felt there might be some problem at the board meeting and it looks like he might have been about right. I may as well push off.'

A few conciliatory remarks from Gumbley and Miller evaporated in the air before either was really heard.

'Perhaps,' I went on, 'you should begin by telling these two just who you are and what you've been up to with Astra.'

'I don't need to account to you or anyone else,' Kock said.

At this point the waiter returned, and we all ordered soup. I decided I would shake Kock up with a few bits of detailed knowledge concerning his movements. An old friend of mine from my Barings days called Gordon Davison, a lawyer, an ex-SAS man and a member of the Special Forces Club, had been doing some sleuth work at my behest since I came back from Saudi. I mentioned dates and times of various meetings – at 3i, the Foreign Office and the MoD.

'I have a pretty good idea what you have been up to,' I said to Kock. 'But I'm going to hold my fire. It will be very useful at the right time.'

The results of this were immediately more satisfying than ever I had hoped. The features on the face across the table creased into a tattoo of reds and blues.

A comment or two more from Gumbley and Miller (introduced to be helpful, but banal in the circumstances) seemed to come from another room before I plundered my advantage: 'The trouble with you, Stephan, is that however hard you try you'll never really belong to the club.'

'What's that?' he snapped back at me.

'It's Englishmen only,' I said. 'No one belongs where you come from.'

That seemed to do it. Kock was looking through me now and appeared to be having trouble breathing. 'I'll have you put down,' he hissed. 'I will have you put down, eliminated, I'll have you killed!'

Gumbley and Miller, who had been sitting with their jaws open as if watching the ball bounce to and fro in tennis match, began to protest.

But I said, 'Why don't you start now? I'll wrap this bloody chair round your neck,' and stood up, grabbing the back of the chair I had been sitting on. 'Come on,' I said, 'Do something on your own for once. I'd like nothing better than to give you a lesson for the damage you've done our company.'

On cue, the waiter came in again and asked if we were ready

to choose our main course. We two froze in our respective frames while Gumbley told the poor man to get out and come back in ten minutes. What, I wondered, was I suppose to do for the next ten minutes? It could surely only go downhill from here.

Miller looked very concerned and suggested we should both simmer down, and Gumbley said he had hoped the dinner would improve the atmosphere but it had only made matters worse. I said that there could be no compromise with Kock, 'as he has to get rid of me to prevent the roof falling in, despite his high-level protection. And once I have gone,' I added, 'you wait, you'll all follow afterwards.'

I told them that the chairman of British Aerospace had been advised not to worry about Astra putting Royal Ordnance out of business, because 'Astra will wither on the vine by April'.

It may sound like a scene out of a Greek tragedy, but it was real at the time. The oracle was right to the very month – none of it predestined, all skilfully worked, and the puppeteer was sitting there among us.

We all of us, by 11 January, had a date and a time.

Chris Gumbley suggested we break up, and I said I was going anyway. The waiter returned and was told to forget about dinner. As I walked to the door, Kock rose to his feet and said, 'We will get you anyway.' It was a phrase that would be repeated a few months later by the new chairman as he saw me off the premises, watched by Kock and Tony McCann, who would by then have replaced Chris Gumbley.

Gumbley walked with me to the lift, hitching his trousers at the waistband two or three times, a sure sign he was nervous. As I got into the lift, he said, 'We have all got our skeletons and problems. Perhaps we shouldn't expect Kock to be any different.' I told him, 'You just don't know what has been going on. Kock will finish it all. It's up to us to do something, but it is probably too late already.'

The lift took me back down. I walked to the cloakroom, collected my coat and asked the doorman to find me a taxi. It was 9.30pm.

The following morning in the office I told Campbell Dunford

what had happened. He said, 'You must go to the police.' I told him not to be silly. 'You don't understand,' he said, 'you'll have it on record.' He was right. It was why he taped all his phone calls with Kock. It is always a good idea to have something on file.

The pressure Kock felt that his cover might be blown was measured a few days after the Berkeley Hotel incident on a lonely moorland road in Argyll.

A car with two men in it pulled over to the side of the road, one got out and started to change a wheel. As they were doing this, another car approached from a side road. A figure emerged from this car, beckoned the van driver over, then suddenly pulled out an automatic pistol shouted, 'I'm a soldier, you know!', firing two shots over the man's head.

The driver's misfortune was to have broken down near Kock's Scottish hideaway at the point when the pressure of my investigations had reached its peak. A few months later when the matter came to court, Kock's solicitor pleaded in mitigation that his career had been 'delicate in both nature and locations' and he had 'a security problem and was acutely aware of his own safety'. He was fined £650.

Upon further investigation, the *Independent* reported, 'Police admit privately that their investigations [into Kock] were stymied by protestations on Mr Kock's behalf by the intelligence services.' On talking to colleagues, possibly Dunford or Cowley, both of whom have expressed these sentiments, the newspaper described 'former business colleagues' as 'genuinely frightened of him'.

A few days later Gumbley went to Thailand with Krantz and Binek, which would turn out to be a very significant trip in Gumbley's life. After Thailand, Gumbley never again sat on the fence. As I suspected it might, Thailand opened his eyes to what was going on in PRB, but because the ramifications of what he revealed concerned not just PRB, but Kock and the covert arms policy of the Thatcher government, and turned in particular on the personal financial interests of those who were involved in it, both in Britain and Belgium, this Thailand trip would seal Gumbley's fate.

Kock's connection with Thailand came through Malaysia, his old SAS stamping-ground. But now, in the late 1980s, the stakes were no longer anything to do with the suppression of communist insurgents. What Gumbley touched on in Thailand was the operation of the arms cartel, but more particularly the disbursement of kickbacks to officials in the highest echelons of power.

As 'architect' of Thatcher's Malaysian arms deal, the appellation accorded Kock by former Midland Bank colleagues and reported by Chris Blackhurst in the *Independent*, Kock became involved in a project to build a huge special forces complex in Thailand just across the border from Malaysia. The project complemented the special forces base project in Malaysia, a part of Thatcher's Malaysian arms deal.

Specifically, as far as we were concerned, the Thailand project was the subject of a £16m contract drawn with PRB for 155mm equipment with a company called Lopberi, which we discovered involved commissions for £5m and which Gumbley went to investigate.

'What Mr Gumbley threatened to uncover during his few days in Thailand was an arms ring which reputedly spreads from Whitehall to Washington via Belgium and other loosely regulated countries to some of the world's most pernicious regimes, including Saddam Hussein's Iraq,' was how the *Independent* would cover the trip long afterwards.

Gumbley in fact unearthed a number of PRB contracts going to Iraq via Thailand. But the one for 155mm shells worth £16m, was extraordinary because of the level of commissions and kickbacks involved – nearly 30 per cent. Five million pounds is a heavyweight commission for a contract worth £16m, and he discovered that the pay-offs were going to senior placed officials and politicians in Belgium and England.

When he returned, Kock noticed the change in Gumbley and really began to sweat. Pergau, the Malaysian arms deal, was Kock's crowning glory but what troubled him was that he knew how much we might discover about the commission flow from the entire £1.3bn deal. I have shown you the nature of the covert

economics of Margaret Thatcher's big arms deals, but in early
1990 Gumbley and I really had no idea what we were digging
over, or had yet grasped how much bigger than us or PRB was the
scam we had tapped into. We are talking here about the personal
financial interests of some of the most powerful politicians and fixers in the cabal. People were about to die over what Gumbley had
locked into. Gumbley's trip following so hot on the heels of my
escapade in Saudi was the final straw, really.

The following month, February 1990, I was staying at the Hotel
Stephanie in Brussels for PRB meetings. Gumbley and Krantz were
also there. It was the hotel we had used to address PRB staff and
employees shortly after the takeover in September 1989. I had had
a late meeting and supper with two colleagues and was about to
have a drink in the bar with John Anderson before turning in,
when Gumbley came in with Harry Krantz and said, 'Come up to
my room, Harry and I have something you should see.'

I went up to Gumbley's room on the fifth floor and was offered
a beer. Sandwiches were ordered and Gumbley handed me a
three-page official-looking document described at the top as telephone calls received and made by Philippe Glibert, then sales
director of PRB. The phone calls had been monitored over a two-
day period. I wasn't at all sure what I had in my hands, but I
realised at once that it was the kind of professional information-
gathering that only Intelligence services undertook. I looked at the
information it contained. There were calls overseas which carried
addresses as well as numbers. I noted a number of calls made to
our Belgian bankers, to Mr Klibanski at Générale de Banque, with
whom Glibert had no obvious reason to be in touch in the course
of his duties for Astra. Two calls, I noticed, had been made to Alan
George, a freelance journalist whom I knew worked for the
Engineer and the *Observer* and had written an article, in which
McNaught had been named, about BMARC trading with Iraq.
The article could not have been written without access to
Intelligence information.

The document had come via Bull to Krantz, his friend. Bull was
walking a dangerous tightrope if his business depended on playing

games of 'who had what on whom' to keep going. There were no company boundaries any more in the arms business. Covert deals undertaken by the cabal had seen to that. Now that policy had changed, power was defined by what you knew. It was a dangerous situation built on the threat of exposure. My fight to keep Astra going by threatening to expose Kock and the rest of them, and how we had been used by the cabal, was doomed to failure because, as in the case of Gerald Bull (who would pay with his life), the interests of the cabal ultimately would take precedence over everything.

This document, which Gumbley had delivered to me with a smile and saw only in the context of Astra and PRB and the proof it seemed to contain of covert activities in the company, worried me because it linked us with the man who probably had more knowledge than anyone about the cabal's covert activities since the war had begun.

What Bull had at his fingertips and which was his insurance, we needed to know in order to win our particular battles over Astra's future. But such knowledge was a very dangerous commodity.

Some two days later my secretary called to say, 'Mr Kock wants to have a meeting in the St James's Place office with some Ministry of Defence people at 9 or 10 o'clock in the evening.' I told Kock that as a non-executive director he could have access to the office only in normal business hours, and no strangers could be admitted without regular staff being present. This provoked a furious argument that culminated in my telling him that I would have him thrown out of the office altogether if he caused my secretary any more trouble. With all else that was happening, the idea of having Kock in the office with a couple of MoD cronies and the company files did not appeal to me.

That it was an indication that matters had reached a terminal point became apparent when I returned to London. It was swift when it happened.

The financial problems had been exacerbated by SGB's firm refusal to negotiate the compensation claim. I had enlisted the

assistance of Sir Kenneth Corfield (chairman of TANKS) as a
quasi-arbitrator following a derisory counter-offer by SGB, which
involved a £5.5m interest-free loan to be 'repayable on return to
better fortune; Gechem shall eventually abandon the debt if
PRB's financial position has not improved by December 31,
1990.'

In mid-February Tim Laxton and I attended a meeting with
Sir Kenneth. He reiterated that we would get the £12m compensation we had demanded, and said also that Cuckney had fallen
out with de Carmoy.

At a board meeting held on 21 February, it was agreed that I
should write to Duronsoy and reject his counter-offer. I told him
that PRB needed financing to the tune of £20m plus. Générale de
Banque had recommended a cash injection of £16m into PRB and
further money for restructuring costs. I suggested a further meeting with Gechem, SGB and Général de Banque. Corfield then
spoke to Duronsoy and Jous, but the result of our representations
was that on 27 February Duronsoy formally withdrew his offer of
£5.5m.

I was told on the Thursday morning that they wanted to bring
Roy Barber in as chairman under the auspices of the Pru and 3i,
and there wasn't any point in making a fight of it because they
had all the votes. At this stage I retained my position as a director
on the board.

I then went round to the Pru with Anderson, and Gumbley
came along to hear what was said. I told the Pru I was very disappointed about what had happened; I thought I had been very
badly let down and that they hadn't behaved honourably, but that
I was sufficiently responsible to do what was in the interests of the
company provided there wasn't anything going on which I didn't
know about. I said I wouldn't obstruct the appointment of Barber
provided he could give me these assurances. Jones was so nervous
at my arrival (his handshake was damp and clammy) that he had
another person with him to make sure he didn't say anything
wrong. I knew something was seriously amiss, but the personal
pressure was enormous and had been for three months.

I went back and they agreed a package of £300,000, a car, the value of the pension, BUPA, etc. Theoretically it added up to about half a million. In the event I got nothing.

Laurence Kingswood, our other non-executive director and representative of Astra's lawyers, Baileys, Shaw & Gillett, suggested I see Boodle Hatfield, who were the lawyers to the Duke of Westminster. I asked him why on earth would I need such a high-flying lawyer.

'Well,' he said, 'I used to be with them before I joined Baileys. They've got a very good partner who deals with contracts. We can't act for you because we are acting for the company.'

Baileys had been my personal solicitors; I brought them into the company. Since then they had come a long way, acting for the Iraqis in the purchase from TI Group of Matrix Churchill, for Bull and the Iraqis on the Lear Fan carbon fibre project, and latterly for Matrix's managing director Paul Henderson. I agreed to contact Boodle Hatfield.

In the course of that day John Anderson, who had been my associate when we first purchased Astra, came in to see me and said he wanted to go. 'If you are going, I don't want to stay and I can see that you're right about Gumbley.' I had warned him that Gumbley would be next to go.

This created a complication from my point of view because immediately there was another couple of hundred thousand to be put on the table and he was not being forced out like me. Still, I couldn't stop Anderson, and we went together to the solicitors, Boodle Hatfield, the following day and went over the situation in great detail. The partner we saw, the employment expert, a Mr Drake, took notes, and I told him there was to be a board meeting the following day, when I wanted it all tied up without any fuss.

Next morning I got a phone call from Boodle Hatfield saying the partner we had briefed couldn't attend, but he had delegated the job to another partner, Robin Peile. I was quite angry, and said, 'This is very important from my point of view. How can you delegate this complicated affair to someone who hasn't been properly briefed?' I was told not to worry, that the new chap had been briefed correctly.

Then Peile came on the phone. We had a long conversation and at about 10 o'clock I said, 'Well, this board meeting is at half-past one.'

He replied, 'I'm very sorry but I cannot possibly make it at half one. I've got a luncheon meeting which I simply can't cancel.'

I couldn't believe it. I said, 'If you can't come and your other partner has called off, I want another partner here.'

This man said, 'I will get there as soon as I can after lunch.' Anderson and I went absolutely berserk about this. We asked them to postpone the board meeting and they said they wouldn't postpone it. There were further complications when correspondence regarding the package was faxed to us. At the end of the day the board meeting went ahead and it was agreed in principle that compensation would follow but we got no actual signed letter on the grounds that our lawyers were not present.

I received bills from Boodle Hatfield for around £10,000 for some two weeks of writing letters and failing to turn up. I paid the first, about half of the total, and refused to pay the second half. They issued a writ against me and I counter-claimed against them for all my compensation, some £500,000. It eventually came to a Registrar, a taxing master, in Chambers. I represented myself. They were represented by another firm, Reynolds, Porter and Chamberlain. They expected to be able to settle the substance of their writ, in other words to have me ordered to pay their second bill, before my counter-claim had been settled. The Registrar held the opinion that my claim went to the root of the matter and that that should be heard and settled first, only then would it fall clear whether there was any justification for their call on me.

Then, quite suddenly, during their Uriah Heap presentation to the Registrar, Boodle's lawyers said, 'Oh, there is one matter which we seem to have overlooked. Mr James has actually overpaid us £900 on his first bill.'

The upshot of this – a piece of pure farce that brought the hearing to an end – was a stalemate. Both claims are still held in abeyance. From my point of view, I see no point in pursuing my claim until I have shown the full extent of the damage done to me and the illicit way in which I was forced out of Astra and the company was put into receivership and dismantled. From Boodle Hatfield's point of view, after their farcical performance at the hearing, they have not shown themselves eager to pursue me.

I went next to David Kleeman, a former senior partner of a firm of lawyers I had worked with in the past and who was then a commercial consultant. He advised me to go and see D.J. Freeman.

Meanwhile Roy Barber had got rid of Baileys and on 20 March 1990 brought in a new and very tricky firm called S. J. Berwin. It is interesting to note that the same firm and partner, Robert Burrow, were brought into Asil Nadir's Polly Peck just before the rug was pulled there. Freeman's got absolutely nowhere with them. Berwin's were spinning the affair out so incredibly success-fully and Freeman's were charging me about £240 an hour, that finally I went back to Kleeman and said, 'Look, I am prepared to settle for a sum, however reduced from the offer first made, because at this rate it is going to cost me the whole amount of compensation in legal fees.'

So the idea was that I should settle for a quick £50K or £60K, which would about pay for the legal advice I had had so far. Barber strung Kleeman out even beyond the point where I told Kleeman to give up, and the whole thing went on until Kleeman's bill had reached £4K or £5K, at which stage I felt totally exploited, even though, in comparison with the extortionate demands of the others, Kleeman's fees were reasonable.

There seemed no way out of the web that Kock and Barber were spinning. It began to seem as though they were not to be sat-isfied with my resignation, that they were out to break me, and the legal system which was there supposedly to defend my rights was, in the feet-dragging way that it operates when given rein by the opposite side, acting in their interests.

I made a silly mistake at this point. I was so fed up with being led on by one lawyer and another that I told Kleeman he should take his money out of the tens of thousands that I had paid his

friends, D. J. Freeman. Understandably, Kleeman issued a writ
against me for his fees. I defended it by saying that Kleeman's
advice had been poor, first by sending me to Freeman's who failed
to produce a result and then persisting in flogging a dead horse
after I had told him to cease. But of course he won his case. My
only satisfaction was that the judge did say that he had every
sympathy for my position.

At the time that actually meant something, though goodness
knows it cost me enough. Finally, of course, two years after my
departure the company went into receivership and they got me all
right, as Kock had promised they would .

As predicted, Gumbley went too. He had written to Alan Clark
putting the problems at Astra into the perspective of the EPREP
agreement, the secret monopoly agreement between the MoD
and Royal Ordnance. Had it not been for EPREP, we would not
have needed to buy PRB when we did. PRB had been conceived
in part as a solution to the problems created by EPREP. Our
strategy had been to buy PRB to put Astra in a position where
the company could compensate (by its immediate ability to compete) for the loss of revenue in BMARC which resulted directly
from the secret agreement.

So Gumbley had written to Alan Clark pointing out that our
problems had been seeded in EPREP, and we were looking for
arms contracts to replace the shortfall in PRB. Casting aside all
political motivations in the demise of Astra, it was a reasonable
enough request. Why should the MoD, when we had always done
their bidding, refuse us the opportunity to sustain PRB and operate a company which, as it turned out, would have been
invaluable in the approaching Gulf War? We know the answer to
that, and by this stage Gumbley, too, knew the answer. But
EPREP's secrecy was important to the government, so there was
something of a lever on the government in Gumbley's request to
Alan Clark, though naturally Gumbley did not spell that out.

Just how sensitive an issue EPREP was to the government
was shown a few days after Gumbley wrote to Alan Clark, when
he was arrested by the MoD police. The MoD police inspector in

charge of the case told Gumbley, 'there are two groups of people in this country whom you can't afford to upset, and you've upset both of them.'

Kock wanted Gumbley out, and he wanted (and got) all the rest of the original Astra directors out too. The arrest filled the bill perfectly in Gumbley's case and was perfectly in tune with what else was going on. At the time, the government, Intelligence and Customs were deeply involved in another frame-up, his arrest more or less coinciding with the seizure by Customs of the Euromac 'nuclear' capacitors.

It was revealed at Gumbley's trial that the order to arrest him emanated from 'very senior levels of the Ministry of Defence procurement executive' and that a 'government minister' was involved in the decision.

You will hear that Gumbley was eventually put in prison for corruption, a distinctly dubious charge in itself, as I will describe, but the point is that, at the start, corruption was nothing to do with it. It was a political matter. At the Trade and Industry Select Committee Inquiry into Exports to Iraq, Gumbley explained what happened.

The MoD police (a political police force, the very organisation posted to guard our supposedly independent competitor, RO – no regular force participated in this charade) turned up at his house one evening, unannounced. 'By the time they searched the house and office and had got me to the police station I think it might have been 10 o'clock [pm]. My interview with the police finished at 2.22 in the morning.'

Mr James Cran asked, 'What were the range of questions you were asked by the MoD police which might give us an idea, and indeed you an idea, as to why you were arrested in the first place?'

Gumbley replied, 'All the questions were around this agreement [their concern was whether he had a copy of the EPREP agreement which he had mentioned in his letter to Alan Clark]: what I knew of it, what I considered the implications were from a political situation, what I thought the security classification of documents was . . . They subsequently found out the agreement had nothing to do with me whatsoever and moved on to other matters. I got the impression that if they could not get me on the agreement, they would get me on something else.'

As in my case for compensation, legal representation became a critical factor in Gumbley's disposal. I have already mentioned Trowers & Hamlins. They are the firm of lawyers that 'process' donations to Tory Party funds. Anthony Gosselin Trower is a director of the 'river companies' and now a consultant to the Trowers & Hamlins practice. He is a former Intelligence and SAS officer.

Appropriately enough, Trowers & Hamlins are also the firm which Kock recruited in the spring of 1989 to help him map out his strategy in the boardroom battles that culminated, successfully for him, in the ousting of the Astra directors and their investigation by the DTI. He did this without the permission or indeed the knowledge of any other member of the main board of Astra.

In December 1990, long after we had all been thrown out, he sought at a board meeting to approve payment to Trowers & Hamlins out of company funds. In effect, Astra was to pay for its own scuttling. T&H is minuted as having been enlisted 'to provide independent advice during the period of board room battles . . . to catalogue events and evidence to be handed over to S. J. Berwin relative to the DTI Inquiry.'

Now, in Gumbley's hour of need, who should Kock recommend to represent him?

'Messrs Trowers & Hamlins were recommended to me by a director of Astra Holdings PLC, one Stephanus Adolphus Kock,' recalled Gumbley under oath after T&H had served Gumbley with a Statutory Demand in the sum of £15,909.40 on 28 June 1993 in the bankruptcy court.

'Astra,' Gumbley continued, 'had been set up by the government as a cover-up for unofficial sales of certain arms to Iraq. It is my belief that I was set up by the authorities in order to discredit Astra over these sales . . .[Kock] was involved with the Security Services and acting on behalf of the government. I have also discovered . . . that Trowers & Hamlins were not only acting for Mr

Kock but also were responsible for the handling of certain funds held by the Conservative Party who were and remain part of the government. I therefore believe that there was a considerable conflict of interest.'

Kock put T&H on to Gumbley before any charges had been made. Police interest had however already switched from the EPREP agreement, which clearly, Gumbley had never had, to possession of an MoD telephone directory, to a gift of a second-hand car he had made to a friend in the Ministry of Defence some while earlier. This charge had been dumped on Gumbley by someone at BMARC.

It was reported in the press that Gumbley, 'believes that his letter to Clark prompted the Master General of Ordnance, General Sir John Stibbon, to contact his old colleague Major-General Donald Isles [of BMARC] and acquaint him with a concern that Gumbley was digging too deep. Certainly the former managing director Bill McNaught has confirmed that the "Grantham faction" laid information with the MoD police that led to Gumbley's arrest.'

It is worth mentioning that Stibbon was on the MoD panel with Trefgarne at the Press Conference at the British Army Equipment Exhibition in 1988 when Trefgarne promised a reply (which was never forthcoming) to a question about competition between RO and Astra on ammunition supply. This occurred just a week or so before the EPREP/RO monopoly became known.

Chris Gumbley's neck was in the noose, and people were lining up to help pull it tight.

In a handwritten letter dated 9 March 1990, after Chris had been questioned but before his arrest, his solicitor at T&H attempts at one and the same time to relieve Gumbley of £5,000 for his defence, to influence and temper his 'approach' to my replacement in the Astra chair (Roy Barber), and to conjure a friendly, even family, atmosphere in which T&H is to 'represent' Gumbley and at the same time to advise Kock on company strategy, a crucial plank of which is Gumbley's resignation, not to say prosecution!

Barstow, the writer, seems to be enjoying every moment of the charade, giving his client (Gumbley) the idea that he is more important even than a Saturday night with his friends.

Dear Chris,

This is for your private eye and is privileged as between solicitor and client. Colin and I can't be sure we're right, but this is how it looks to us at the minute.

My telephone on Saturday night with friends is 0296-75-238. We are expensive animals who charge by the hour and you can imagine how much time and midnight oil this sort of thing involves. I will send you a formal engagement letter next week but ought to warn you we shall need to be put in funds at the outset now. It will all drag on, I fear, and it would be realistic of me to suggest you let me have £5,000 now which I shall put in client a/c, rendering bills to you monthly, or more frequently if the amount of work done seems to justify it. I hope very much that the Company will judge it right to enable its servants to defend themselves in such circumstances as these (which are a long way from 'hand in the till'); and I think you should seek to establish that as quickly as possible. It makes your approach to Roy Barber that much more crucial from your point of view. Good wishes from,

Gerry

I've just called your daughter & have heard you are all coming to London tomorrow morning. I've asked her to ask you to call me at my flat en route.

Gerry Barstow was subsequently sent out to run Trowers & Hamlins' office in Abu Dhabi, which was set up in June 1993.

Having been saddled with solicitors creatively involved in advising his prosecutors, Gumbley is next advised by Barstow to resign from Astra even before charges have been made against him by the police. Resignation from Astra is presented to him as behaviour likely to result in avoiding conviction, which is hard to credit.

Another March letter from T&H suggests – 'I think that on how you behave now depends, to a large extent, your chances of avoiding a criminal conviction . . . It may be appropriate for you to offer him [Barber] your immediate resignation on whatever terms will seem fair in the circumstances . . . I feel it would be bad from your point of view vis à vis the company if you were to delay approaching Roy Barber [with your resignation] until after the MoD police seek to interview you.'

The priority is to get Gumbley out, then to drive a wedge between Gumbley and any support available to him: 'Assuming, as you must (for sheer safety's sake) that Gerald James or some colleague of his is the source of the tip-off,' the letter warns, 'all those who knew about the matter . . . will now wish to distance themselves from it to protect themselves . . . I do not think that you should attempt to draw James out on who tipped off the MoD. It could be James or it could be others on his orders . . . I should avoid frightening any of them more than you have to.'

Does it not make your skin crawl? Dutifully, Gumbley met Barber on 11 March and offered his resignation. Barber – whether or not he knew that Gumbley was to be arrested two days later – urged him to think about his position and to offer his resignation at a board meeting scheduled for 15 March, by which time, following his official arrest on the 13th, there was no possibility for the other directors to object.

Following his resignation, on 22 March Gumbley travelled to Brussels and met Harry Krantz, Gerald Bull and a lawyer. In evidence to the Trade and Industry Select Committee Inquiry into Exports to Iraq, he said:

I had a phone call from a colleague of mine who suggested he would like to see me and suggested he could help me. I went, it was a perfectly natural thing to do . . . [Bull] suggested to me that the sale of PRB by Gechem and SGB was incorrect and he felt he would like to help in assisting me as a private shareholder in suing SGB for the sale of PRB to ourselves. He also informed me my demise at the particular time had been

engineered to remove me from Astra and he was willing to
provide evidence and proof of that so I could help fight that
particular case as well . . . I had been arrested by the MoD
police . . . He did say that my arrest by the MoD police was an
engineered manoeuvre . . . He said [my removal from the
Board of Astra] was carried out to discredit me and to cause me
to have to resign from Astra.

Mr Doug Hoyle: Did he suggest who might be doing that?
Gumbley: He did suggest it, yes.
Hoyle: Who was it?
Gumbley: He suggested it was the British government with
SGB . . . What happened was we were due to meet the following week, on the Monday . . .
Hoyle: Who is we?
Gumbley: Dr Bull and a solicitor or lawyer he had appointed
to try to help fight the case and we agreed to bring as much
evidence together as we had. We agreed to meet on the Monday
to discuss this and see the best way forward. After I left him
and I flew back to the UK in the morning, at 5 o'clock I had a
phone call to say he had been murdered.

On his return to Gatwick from seeing Bull, Gumbley telephoned
me at home on his car telephone, asking me to go back with him
to Brussels the following week and bring any files on PRB. He told
me he had seen a friend who would be helpful. Immediately I said,
'Ah, the good doctor.' He seemed surprised that I knew.

Bull was in fact murdered little more than an hour after
Gumbley had left him, shot from behind with a silenced 7.65mm
pistol as he fumbled for his keys to the front door of his apartment,
which was on the sixth floor of a modern apartment block in
Avenue François Folie in Uccle, Brussels.

'I must confess,' Gumbley added to the committee, 'from that
point onwards I have maintained the lowest possible profile I
could adopt. I have not spoken to anybody, I have not got involved
in anything, I have not discussed it with anybody until this day.'

Following Bull's murder, Gumbley wrote a letter to the Prime Minister, Mrs Thatcher, about his case, only to be re-arrested on the eve of the seizure of Supergun barrels at Teeside docks, and held overnight in police cells. The police said that 'who I had seen when I was there [Brussels] had caused a lot of trouble,' recalled Gumbley later. He made his court appearance on the morning that Supergun became front page news. Shortly afterwards he received a letter from the Prime Minister's office which told him, 'I hope that now you understand the government's view.'

Gumbley was sentenced to nine months in prison.

A man called Tony McCann had been brought in by Barber to take Gumbley's place on the board on 13 March. He spent his time reading newspapers with his feet on the desk while Kock and Barber got on with the dismemberment of the company and the disposal of the remaining directors. Anderson meanwhile had employed the Queen's solicitors, Farrer, and settled for £50,000 compensation. He resigned formally on 9 April. Miller and Guest, accused by Kock of having known about Gumbley's gift of the car, were compelled to resign on 22 March, the day of Gerald Bull's death. Kingswood was forced into resigning on 21 May, after the new management contested Baileys, Shaw & Gillett's fees over the PRB acquisition, and it was said that Kingswood found himself faced with a conflict of interest in the matter. I resigned formally as a director of the board on 12 April 1990.

Kock alone was left of the board that had acquired PRB.

Some time later Anderson was harassed in his home in Scotland by MoD police, who arrived without an official warrant, arrested him and took him down by car to Glasgow and then by air to Gatwick. He was treated like a common criminal, and a MoD police car met the aircraft and took him to Ramsgate. En route, driving like madmen, the police became involved in an accident near Canterbury which caused Anderson a neck injury which has left him unable to drive more than twenty or thirty miles without stopping. Later Anderson said, 'The arrest came completely out of the blue. It has affected my health, my family relationships and the ability to get a new job.'

Following the accident, Anderson was turfed out to find a friend
to stay with near Canterbury. The next day he was told to report
to Empress Building, the MoD building near Earls Court in
London. After a few brief questions, he was given an air ticket to
go home.

The MoD police have no jurisdiction beyond a certain distance
from an MoD base, and they cannot act except through the ordinary police. Moreover, there was no right of arrest in Scotland on
an English warrant and the Prosecutor Fiscal would not issue a
Scottish warrant. In spite of complaining for several years to the
Police Complaints Authority, no action has been taken. A letter
from Charles Kennedy, Anderson's MP, to the Ministry of Defence
was answered by the Junior Defence Minister Viscount Cranborne
to the effect that 'Mr Anderson was only wanted as a witness'.
This prompted a reply from Kennedy, 'If that is how you treat a
witness, God knows how you treat a suspect.'

The sales director John Sellens, though never a member of the
main board, having accompanied me to Saudi, also had to be dis-
credited. The risk of what he might have found out was too great.
When the boom went up, he was run off the road by a lorry and
nearly killed. It happened near Bristol on the M4. He was run into
the central barrier and was in hospital for a fortnight. This was
May or June 1990. Subsequently he was arrested on yet another
trumped-up charge about a motor car.

In Gumbley's case, the MoD man, Dennis Stowe, to whom he
had given a car was an old friend from the earliest days but not in
a position to influence contracts. There was no question of bribery.
Stowe was, in addition, reportedly in trouble on his own account
with the MoD and the charge followed on that. With Sellens, it was
even more ludicrous. We had employed a chap, Major Larry
Hollingsworth from Abu Dhabi, who had been in the Royal
Ordnance Corps. Sellens had known him from previous operations. Hollingsworth had been at Longtown – the central
ammunition depot where half the Falklands stuff was sent from
and where Allivane stored its ammunition – before going out to
Abu Dhabi, and Sellens used to go up there and see him. Sellens

was questioned about supplying a Volvo car to him, which was true, but what happened was this.

Hollingsworth had been going to join us in January 1989; he was due to leave the army in December 1988, but at the last minute the MoD told him that the ruler wished him to stay on, and if he did they'd not only make up his pay but would raise him from the rank of major to lieutenant-colonel. He had been open about it, but his wife had fancied the idea of him becoming lieutenant-colonel and possibly improving his pension and so on, so that is what he did, staying on for another year in Abu Dhabi.

Sellens, in the full expectation that he was going to join us in January 1989, had already provided him with the normal perks which we seemed to provide to executives, including a Volvo. To confirm our intention to keep the position open to Hollingsworth and show goodwill, Sellens had let his wife have the car before he arrived. When Sellens told us, we said to Hollingsworth, 'Well, hang on to the car until you come.' He offered to pay so much towards the car, and I believe the fee that was agreed was £2,400 or £4,000.

That was the sum of it, but they seized on it and said again that we had provided a servant of the Crown with a car, which was of course quite true but demonstrably not in any sense corruption. That was the basis of the alleged case against him, which of course was dropped. But it was used by the MoD police to intimidate him, to shut Sellens up.

Hollingsworth, who has since distinguished himself on relief work in Bosnia, dealt with the MoD police in a traditional military manner. When asked any questions he refused to answer other than with name, rank and number – that's training for you!

Another man whom I believe suffered as a result of his connection with Gumbley and me was Lionel Jones, the man who told us we were being used to siphon off the missing millions from the Jordan Defence Package.

The first time I met Lionel was at an army equipment exhibition when he was working for Royal Ordnance. In fact two of the people who came to us from RO had worked directly under him –

Graham Willett, who knew all about the Cyprus contract during all that rumpus with Isles, and a man called Trigger, who rashly had been sacked when his knowledge of the relationship between the RO and the government would have been invaluable.

Later Chris Gumbley and I did in fact ask Lionel himself to come and work for us, and he told me that he wished he had because his knowledge could have saved us much heartache. Lionel latched on to Gumbley and me, and became something of a shadow to Gordon Foxley as well.

At the time of the privatisation of RO (1987), Lionel Jones had been sales supremo at the company. Afterwards he became personal assistant to Peter Kenyon, RO's then chief executive. It may be that Lionel first began keeping in contact with us with something of an official interest in how much we knew about the covert activities – you work for RO, you work for the government.

We certainly made an odd trio, Foxley, Gumbley and I. Foxley, you will recall, was a former head of ammunition purchasing at MoD convicted in October 1993 for receiving £1.5m kickbacks from Fratelli Borletti of Milan, Junghans of Schramberg, Germany, and Raufoss of Gjovik, Norway – fuse or munitions manufacturers. His alleged corruption had not come to light until some five years after it was supposed to have been committed. Perhaps more to the point, Foxley left the MoD in 1982, staying on at their request for one more year. The contract he was blamed for occurred long after his departure. I have very serious doubts that he was put in prison for the reasons for which he was charged. I believe he may have been involved in something sinister because of his specialist knowledge and that he is afraid to defend himself properly. When his appeal came up recently, it received very little publicity.

Among Foxley's expertise at the MoD, where he had worked under General Isles, had been in the nuclear arena, as an expert in the fusing of WE 177 (the free-fall bomb) and Redbeard. The history of BMARC's Faldingworth site is that it was a Lancaster bomber base for a Polish squadron in the Second World War and was then developed as a nuclear weapons storage facility for 'V' bombers stationed at nearby Scampton. Its 800-acre area had runways, security towers, double security fencing and a huge investment by the RAF on bomb, weapons storage, and other buildings. Like Foxley, the site had thus been involved in nuclear arms technology – the most sensitive of issues.

The official reason for giving up the site as a nuclear storage facility was said to be its betrayal to the Russians by a Swedish colonel, which struck me as remarkably thin when the Russians would know such potential targets as a matter of routine.

Its official removal from the UK nuclear map did not, however, remove its capability. After Astra acquired BMARC, the Faldingworth site, which fell almost exclusively under the control of Major-General Isles, was still equipped for nuclear storage, and remained so at the time we became aware that it was being used covertly by the government-approved arms and propellant cartel.

If the reader is inclined to question the logic in any desire by the West to arm Iraq with nuclear weapons, it is a fact, corroborated in Congressman Henry Gonzalez's Inquiry into the Trade with Iraq, that Iraqi scientists were present at an advanced thermonuclear detonation seminar in Portland, Oregon, in September 1989. Listed among the registrants are M. Ahadd, S. Ibrhim and H. Mahd, all of the Al Qaqaa State Establishment, P.O. Box 5134, Baghdad, Iraq. Al Qaqaa was the 'sensitive establishment' where the *Observer* journalist Farzad Bazoft was arrested, later to be executed in March 1990.

On one level, when Lionel Jones came on the scene, the only connecting link between Foxley, Gumbley and myself would appear to be that in our own ways we had thwarted the status quo and had to be squashed at all costs. There was very real concern, for example, about the extent of our knowledge about the government's EPREP agreement with RO. But that is to ignore the odd focus of Lionel's brief on Foxley, who was approached in 1988 by Isles and Avery to participate in a 'fusing' programme at BMARC.

I believe that an investigation into the connection between the MoD, BMARC, and RO (to which Mr C. J. Barlow of Coopers &

Lybrand, the receivers, safe-sold Faldingworth after we had
resigned), particularly in the context of the facilities which
BMARC had to offer as a covert staging post at Faldingworth,
would cast a more illuminating light on what it is they fear we do
know.

What is for sure is that when Lionel Jones came over to our
side, he laid himself open to risk.

Lionel gave the journalist David Hellier a lift down to
Gumbley's trial, which was in March 1991, and a real manipu-
lated farce. Lionel complained to Hellier that he had a boil on his
neck and was feeling run down. He went home afterwards and I
spoke to him that evening, apologising for not being there the
day he had attended. He sounded terrible on the phone, his
speech slurred. He said he didn't feel very well. I asked him what
was wrong, and he said he didn't really know.

The next day I rang, and he was in a coma. He never came out
of it. I spoke to his wife when he was developing additional problems such as pneumonia, and said, 'For goodness' sake, he is an
employee of Royal Ordnance; they must have some sort of health
scheme. Don't bother about your local doctor, get the best specialist.' I asked her, 'What the hell is Peter Kenyon doing for him?
British Aerospace has access to aviation medicine, which involves
breathing and lungs and what have you. You can get the best
advice possible. What is going on?'

There followed some mix-up with his doctor – he didn't go into
hospital quickly enough, he didn't get the right specialist. I rang
Kenyon up about it, and he said he couldn't believe it, no one had
told him. I said, 'I can't believe this. This man is terribly ill, he's
now developed pneumonia, and here you are, supposedly his boss,
and you tell me you don't even know about it. Get down there and
do something.'

Lionel's poor wife was running around in circles. I gather RO
then did get involved and were apparently advised that such-
and-such a specialist was going to look at it.

They said he had been careless over his insulin prescription
(either taken the wrong insulin or forgotten an injection), but I was

very uneasy about it. I knew that he had been a diabetic practically all of his life, and diabetics who have a lifetime's experience of the disease and travelled the world tend not to make mistakes like that.

I told John Reed of *Defence Industry Digest* what I suspected because Lionel had been one of his best sources of information on the propellant story. No one apart from his family seemed to do anything about him. He seemed to go down so quickly, and no one did anything. Then, after all that, he was cremated, so there was no possibility of an autopsy.

Reed expressed no surprise; Lionel's demise fitted a clear pattern in what was happening – the arrests, the threats, the comment on Gumbley's arrest by the Prime Minister's office, the murders of Moyle and Bull, the extraordinary activities of the MoD police, and the assassination shortly afterwards of André Cools, the man investigating the circumstances surrounding the sale of PRB.

Lionel's funeral was in April 1991, just a week or so after Gumbley was sentenced to nine months in prison. I didn't like many of the people from RO, but Lionel was a human being, a very decent man. It worries me still, and always will, that he died because he was trying to help us. I attended his funeral, as did Gordon Foxley. Poor Chris Gumbley was by that time framed up in jail. When I visited him in May 1991 and told him of Lionel's death, the first words he uttered were, 'Was he murdered?'

In June 1990, Kock and Barber took the unprecedented step of inviting a Department of Trade and Industry inquiry into the activities of the company for which they worked. Simultaneously a press campaign began which served to undermine the position of the old Astra directors. This was mounted by a firm called Shandwick which became Astra's PR company as soon as we were kicked out. Shandwick, a firm run by Selwyn Gummer's brother, Peter, would become the PR company for the MoD during the Gulf War. No company had ever previoulsy asked for a DTI Inquiry into itself. Anyone with the least knowledge and

experience of such charades would question how it was supposed
to help the shareholders.

This move to discredit us proceeded from December 1990 to
April 1992. The DTI report, dated April 1993 and published the
following July, which followed the inquiry was 545 pages long
without appendices (200 pages longer than the British and
Commonwealth Atlantic Computer Report, where £1.5bn was
lost), took a year to write up and cost the taxpayer £2.2m plus.

It was submitted by the Inspectors, Colin Percy Farqharson
Rimer QC and John White FCA to the Serious Fraud Office, and
was thrown out. I am told the SFO said that they didn't want to
be used for purposes of political victimisation.

There is a great deal that I could say about the report from the
pro-Astra directors' point of view, which could be of interest to our
shareholders, but in a book of this nature, the purpose of which is
to raise the lid on a box of tricks generally kept hidden from the
public and raise issues appertaining to the interests of the public
as a whole, I shall restrict myself to a few major points about the
defence industry and the nature of public inquiries in general.

If this book has shown anything it is that the government,
through the civil service and its Intelligence agents in the City
and elsewhere, is wholly involved in every aspect of the defence
industry.

In arms, unlike in other manufacturing industries, the government plays a key role. It is a participant. There is nothing that
goes on in which government is not principally involved.

This means ultimately that the government shares in a defence
industry public company's responsibility to its shareholders. It is
not enough for the government to do its dirty work, step aside, say
enough is enough and slam the company directors on the head.

In the case of Astra, let me give you one example of intervention
in our business by the government, which materially affected the
validity of Astra's representations to its shareholders. The example
concerns Astra's prospectus for the rights issue to purchase
BMARC, and the decision by the government secretly to sign the
EPREP agreement two months earlier.

EPREP was motivated by the government's need for secrecy after they had sold Royal Ordnance to British Aerospace as an expression of their avowed policy to introduce competition to MoD arms and ammunition

We prepared a prospectus for the purchase of BMARC on that basis. The section 'Reasons and benefits of the Acquisition' recommends to shareholders the purchase of BMARC on the basis that it would establish Astra as a competitor with Royal Ordnance for MoD business. The prospectus was published in May 1988.

However, in March, the government had already signed EPREP, a monopolist agreement to give RO 80 per cent of its business behind our backs, and felt so guilty about it that they didn't even announce it. News of EPREP seeped out in July 1988, four months after it had been signed, two months after Astra's prospectus had been submitted to the DTI and gone unquestioned by them.

What this means, and we should be quite clear about this, is that the government knew that what we were promising our shareholders was false and did nothing to put matters right. We did not know. Neither did we have any reason to.

The decision by the DTI inspectors to ignore completely the government's responsibility to Astra shareholders lies at the very root of what was wrong in Thatcher's Britain. Despite all the puff about free markets and competition, it was a Tory government committed to self-interest and we are reaping its stale yield to this day.

What's more, this failure by the inspectors to identify government culpability was inevitable, and arises out of an essential incongruity.

The inspectors were employed by the government through the DTI, up to its neck in illegal exports of arms, and it had a vested interest in the outcome of the inquiry. Would the inspectors turn on the hand that feeds? There was never any danger of their investigating the government's role in Astra, and they swept aside the very idea of it on the third page of their report.

DTI inquiries, as presently constituted, are an adjunct of the establishment's abuse of power. It is more than coincidence that no major City scandal has featured a DTI inquiry, be it Lloyds, BCCI, Prudential Assurance (losses of £1bn on estate agency investments), Royal Insurance (losses of £4–500m for four or five years) or Guardian Royal Exchange (losses on an Italian sting of some £500m). There are many other examples, the most notable recent one being that of my former employers, Barings.

In Astra's case, had the inspectors been independent of government, they would have been free to examine those aspects of the business in which government was involved. But they were not independent.

Colin Rimer and KPMG Peat Marwick's John White were tied to government by the same strings that work every contract between a buyer (in this case the government) and a seller (in this case Rimer and White) a sub-text that speaks, at the success level, of the mutual satisfaction of both parties' needs.

There is a lesson for the future in this, which I believe is very much in the public interest, and it is a pretty obvious one.

Inspectors on public inquiries should be independent of (and never appointed by) parties involved with the subject under investigation.

Unfortunately, in our case, there were strings attaching our prosecutors to interested parties in all kinds of ways, which in a court of law could have excluded Rimer and White from any participation.

Colin Rimer and John White were appointed as inspectors by Peter Lilley at the DTI. I became aware after they were appointed that Peter Lilley was a school friend of Colin Rimer. He was a direct contemporary at the Dulwich Junior School, the Dulwich College Senior School, and indeed at Cambridge University. Chris Cowley obtained information from within the DTI that they had been at school together, were great friends and had actually been seen driving off together in a chauffeur-driven car together while the inquiry was on.

The position of John White is even more interesting. He is a senior partner in KPMG Peat Marwick. He was the Middle East partner in KPMG and was apparently personal adviser to the rulers of Abu Dhabi and Dubai. His firm were also auditors to British Aerospace and Royal Ordnance, who were our main competitors.

On those grounds alone his appointment was surprising, but there is more. Peats were also advisers to ISC Ferranti on their merger and became joint auditors of ISC Ferranti afterwards. Peats were also auditors to BNL, who were the main source of funds for Iraqi armaments in the 1980s when $5bn worth of US funds were channelled through banks like BCCI, Chemical Bank, Irving Trust and Morgan's to Iraq by various routes, exclusively to buy arms. Peats were the auditors to BNL in the US, giving clean audits for the five years before the alleged scandal broke. In their Brussels office, Peats were advisers to Gerald Bull, SRC (Bull's company) and the Iraqis on the purchase of the Lear Fan carbon fibre plant in Northern Ireland. That purchase was actually finalised but had to be unscrambled following objections by the Israelis and the Americans, who, it has since been claimed, were objecting only because they wanted to sell them an American carbon fibre plant.

What makes Peats' involvement stranger still is that the former manager of their Milan office, Tony Natelli, became involved in the Avenel project in the United States which was funded through BCCI and its American banking offshoot. Nobody knew where the funds came from; there was supposed to be a $12.5m transfer from Basel in Switzerland, but nobody knew the original source.

Natelli was the developer of the property that miraculously went to senior figures in the Bush administration who were involved in the Iran–Iraq supply, and leading figures in the banking industry. It is a very prestigious development. There was an inquiry into it, but no one got anywhere. But again Peats was involved.

The other main aspect is that KPMG Peat Marwick, with the other five leading firms of accountants, but particularly Peats and Price Waterhouse, are the main beneficiaries of £millions of funds to assist in the privatisation operations conducted by the

Conservative Party. So, as a company, Peats is a terrific beneficiary
of government largesse and obviously our interests were of no
significance to them in relation to government interests.

The DTI have written letters to me about the independence of
inspectors, when in my opinion they are about as independent as
the balls on a bull.

Perhaps the last word should go to Sir John Nott, whose
thoughts on using DTI inspectors to investigate alleged fraud
and corporate wrongdoing were published in the *Sunday Times*
on 10 October 1994: The system, he said, 'is in disrepute. DTI
inspectors increasingly make no sense . . . You tend to get a
couple of pompous, publicity-seeking inspectors who set themselves up to be a legal court. It is all too much like a star
chamber. As a result a terrorist who murders 30 people in Oxford
Street has many more rights than a person suspected of City
fraud.'

From the DTI Inquiry into Astra Holdings PLC, let us move to the
House of Commons Trade and Industry Select Committee Inquiry
into Exports to Iraq, undertaken of course by members of
Parliament, which started late in 1990 and got back into full
swing after the Gulf War in July 1991. Naturally Astra figured
prominently, but as with the DTI Inquiry by Rimer and White,
Kock figured hardly at all.

In the DTI Inquiry, evidence I gave about Kock was actually
omitted from the report altogether, specifically my description of
his death threat to me in the Berkeley Hotel. Gumbley had the
same story. When I objected to the omission, I was told that my
evidence had been delivered off the record, when the inquiry was
not in proper session. But is any evidence submitted to a public
inquiry off the record?

On this point of what is permitted as evidence, the Trade and
Industry Select Committee (TISC) fared no better. I must mention
in particular the successful attempt by the MoD and ministers to
prevent the summonsing of Roger Harding and Bob Primrose, the
two MoD officials to whom Gumbley and I reported the Supergun

propellant contract, on the basis that it 'would be inappropriate and unproductive'.

In regard to this, Sir Richard Scott pointed out to Sir Robin Butler that paragraph 10 of the Osmotherly rules suggests that the Select Committee has the power and right to call a witness other than the nominees of the minister.

Sir Robin agreed that 'both sides have a certain power', but added that the minister also 'has a power to instruct the person called, whether they were mute or co-operative'.

Are we to understand from this that there was no point in the committee exercising its right to summon Primrose and Harding, as, in any event, the two persons in question would have been told how to respond by their civil service masters, and nothing or nothing significant would have been forthcoming from them? If that extraordinary admission by the Cabinet Secretary were true, and in the case of Harding, whom I like and trust, I somehow doubt that he would have avoided the truth, then what was there to prevent their appearing?

What actually happened was made clear in a letter dated 14 February 1992 from Nicholas Bevan (MoD) to the Cabinet Office. The Cabinet Secretary and the PUS at MoD advised ministers that 'following inter-departmental consultation, which has included Sir Michael Quinlan and Sir Robin Butler, Ministers have been advised to respond that since Messrs Primrose and Harding are retired . . .'

Now let us look at the importance of Primrose and Harding to the deliberations of the TISC over Astra. Roger Harding had been involved with Astra from 1983, when we had met him as Defence Counsellor in the British Embassy in Washington, at the Las Vegas Defense Exhibition.

Harding had guided, and then with the assistance of Dick White, helped implement our American (and Canadian) policy. With Harding we had always felt that there were possibilities, there was optimism and above all trust. I have absolutely no doubt, too, that he was instrumental in our introduction to Accudyne and the Walters Group, probably our most successful acquisition. By that, I mean that he was responsible for involving us in the MoD fuse deal that led us to Walters, as well as generally in the US for the implementation of the Thatcher/Reagan special relationship, so far as it affected defence sales.

When Harding returned to England to become Deputy Head of Defence Sales at the MoD, he worked under Chandler, one of the inner coterie, but he nevertheless took it upon himself to tip us off about the Supergun contract at PRB.

There were good reasons for the MoD not to want Harding to testify, but I must say that it was low even by MoD standards for Mr Bevan, having advised his absence, then to blame Harding at the TISC hearing on 27 February 1992 for taking the decision not to inform ministers of the said propellant contract.

Primrose was a rather different kettle of fish, very much more in the background, although he had been among the first on the scene to look round the plant and storage facilities of BMARC on behalf of the MoD after we acquired the company from Oerlikon.

Kingswood had spoken to Primrose as he went round the plant and learned from him that he had been in Intelligence and hoped to return to it shortly. By the time Primrose met Chris Cowley over the Supergun, he was being referred to, in classic spook style, simply as 'the Colonel'. It seems likely, all-in-all, that Primrose, to whom Gumbley passed our information on the Supergun propellant contract, was Intelligence liaison for defence sales.

Between them, Harding and Primrose might have been pressed to shed light on the peculiar and developing relationship of the MoD with Astra, Walters/Accudyne, BMARC and PRB.

The Select Committee might have asked Primrose, for example, about the part played by the EPREP agreement in the saga, its highly questionable legality in the context of monopoly, and what lay behind the MoD's seductive assurances that led to our purchase of BMARC, when the ammunition business had already been contracted secretly to RO.

The presence of Primrose and Harding at the inquiry might have cast a more interesting light on Kock, too. Gumbley, Miller and I looked across at each other in absolute astonishment when, at the committee hearing in which Kock gave his evidence, he tried to steal our thunder by claiming that it was *HE* who had reported the PRB Supergun propellant contract!

> **Kock:** Initially I did it by telephone, a very brief discussion on, I think, the Monday following 20 September. Then the first time I could get down was 11th October when I had a meeting. I did speak of course later to the MoD people and I know quite a lot of them quite well . . .
>
> **Dr Keith Hampson:** Did you actually report this directly to the Intelligence services without consulting or informing the chairman of the company or the chief executive of the company?
>
> **Kock:** Yes, I did, sir.
>
> **Hampson:** You did?
>
> **Kock:** Yes.
>
> **Hampson:** You actually went straight to Dr Pike and Major-General Donald Isles?
>
> **Kock:** Yes.
>
> **Hampson:** You did not first go to the chairman of the company?
>
> **Kock:** No, I did not.
>
> **Hampson:** Is this the normal approach of a non-executive director; would you not normally consult with the chairman?
>
> **Kock:** It depends whether he needs to be consulted.
>
> **Hampson:** Quite an interesting thought.

Kock was not in fact allowed to get away with it. Nicholas Bevan confirmed that no one had heard anything about the contract until we reported it.

What was more unsatisfactory was that the chairman of the committee, Sir Ken Warren, was, like Kock and Viscount Monckton, part of the Maidstone Mafia, with Middle Eastern and South African connections, hardly an appropriate choice for chairman in the circumstances.

Ricks, with manifest Intelligence connections, of course moved in this circle too; his company, MFA, was based there. Before

Kock moved up to Scotland he had an estate in the Maidstone area next to Viscount Monckton's property and had known Monckton's late father since the 1960s in his Rhodesian days. Warren lives in Kent and knows Kock well, and is a member of the Special Forces Club, like Kock. Moreover, Warren and Monckton were chairman and deputy chairman of Gulf (now Ashley) Guarantee Trust owned by two Iraqis, the Khan brothers.

I have papers on one of the Khan brothers – Kamal Mustafa Khan – from French Intelligence sources, which indicate that he was used as a 'conduit for negotiations between various Western governments and the Hizbollah over the hostage issue', and has connections of a business nature with an Iranian called Farhad Azima, at some time under the protection of the CIA and owner of an airline, Global International Airways, now in receivership, that acted as a front for the CIA 'to ship arms to Egypt between 1981 and 1983 . . . [and] was instrumental in transporting arms to the Afghan Moudjahidin rebels.'

Of the Ashley Group, my Intelligence report says that it 'is still very active in foreign currency dealing . . . [and] it is obvious from the results of our research to date that [it] has been marketing its services quite heavily in the Middle East.'

Warren did not declare his friendship with Kock or his Middle East connections during the committee hearing.

There were one or two rather obvious incidents that reflected a neighbourly attitude to the cabal. Following evidence that Sir John Bourn had visited our BMARC plant by helicopter as a guest of Kock after Bourn had left the MoD and taken up his current position as Comptroller and Auditor-General (p. 139), Warren suddenly intervened when evidence was being heard in an entirely different context, and insisted on correcting the record that Bourn was in fact still part of the MoD when the visit occurred. The interruption was both laughable and wholly wrong.

But we had some fun with him. One and a half hours into my evidence, Warren, the chairman, had to leave, and Crowther took over. Signalling his exit, he waved a newspaper cutting at me and asked, 'What do you know about this?' He was referring to an

Independent on Sunday article about the Savoy Mafia. He said, 'Do you know who they are?' And I said, 'Well, I know who some of them are.' 'Right,' he said, 'we will want a list of the ones you know.'

Then he left, and Crowther assumed the chair.

I didn't produce a list, and later the Committee insisted I did. I said I didn't particularly want to, but they said that I would be in contempt of Parliament if I did not. (I don't know why they don't use these arguments with ministers.) So I produced this letter. Copies were ceremoniously handed out to members of the committee, and Warren found, to his horror, that his name was on it.

One of the least appealing aspects of the inquiry, however, was the nobbling of witnesses. Prior to giving his evidence to the Select Committee, Chris Cowley promised us that he was going to spill the beans about Mark Thatcher and commissions and about Kock's role, etc. But the night before he was due to appear, he was nobbled by the chair. Warren quite improperly rang Cowley at his hotel and took him out. Warren says that they had dinner; Cowley that they went to a committee room. But it doesn't matter; they spent some hours together.

Tim Laxton wrote that when he spoke to Warren nine days after he had taken Cowley out, 'he said he had met Chris Cowley on January 14, 1992, because he was worried about the state of Chris Cowley's mind and because Chris Cowley was a reluctant witness. Sir Kenneth said to me, "He might have been going to jump off the Clifton suspension bridge for all I knew." Sir Kenneth's story is now somewhat different.'

Warren was quoted in the *Observer* by the journalists David Hellier and Rosie Waterhouse as saying, 'I certainly wasn't trying to coach him or something like that. I just did not want him to feel there was any pressure to say things that he was not sure of. I was very interested in the Committee getting the facts.'

Cowley thought that the purpose of Warren's contacting him was to derive intelligent questions for the next day from what was a very complicated issue, but he said that he was very angry when Warren ran it like a kindergarten idiot's exercise.

But I know that Cowley was asked the right questions by Jim Cousins MP, who gave him several opportunities to name and identify Kock, and he didn't. What pressures were used on him, I don't know. Cousins told Tim Laxton that when afterwards he asked Cowley why he hadn't named Kock, Cowley said that there was only one person that he had been afraid of in his life, and that was Kock.

The night before my evidence I received a phone call from the Tory MP Gerald Howarth. He told me that he was now representing Margaret Thatcher's interests in the Commons as her parliamentary private secretary, and he advised me 'not to go over the top' in my evidence.

Howarth later said, 'I rang James as an old friend and told him it was very important that he was armed with some detailed facts. I told him not to be too wild because it wouldn't be helpful to him.'

I had indeed known Howarth for some years, which was precisely why I was immediately suspicious as to his intention in telephoning me. He was around way back when he leapt on the bandwagon of the Tory groups led by George Kennedy Young and Airey Neave. In 1971 he set up an Immigration Committee at the Monday Club. He was also a director in Kock's friend Richard Unwin's company and came to public notice when, in the 1980s, it was reported in *Private Eye* that private detectives had been hired to investigate a man called Gerry Gable, editor of an anti-fascist magazine called *Searchlight*. Gable was allegedly the subject of an assassination plot to clear the air of such socialist radicals.

Howarth was always tagging on to someone. He came into Astra on Unwin's coat-tails and teamed up with Jonathan Aitken. Then, while a consultant to Astra, and with the government agreement, EPREP, pointing the way for the future of our arch-competitor, Royal Ordnance, he saw no conflict of interest in accepting sponsorship from RO's owners, British Aerospace. Although I had not known of his connections to BAe/RO when I was at Astra, at the time of the Select Committee Inquiry there was little likelihood that I would take him seriously.

*

Unlike Gumbley, who has understandably made a deliberate effort to steer clear of the whole business since his prison sentence, I have, to the consternation of some of those around me, made it a main purpose in life to find out the truth of what was happening in Astra and elsewhere in the defence industry in the 1980s, and to research and open the public's eyes to where real and permanent power lies in the government of Britain today. I have been hampered in this by a number of difficulties, not least by a failure of investigators to see where the goalposts are really set, in particular the DTI inspectors on the Astra case, Rimer and White, who started their report, paragraph 1.11, page 3, by declaring what I have sought to show in this book is central to the issue, as irrelevant:

> The views volunteered by Mr James covered a wide range of subjects, certain of which apparently had little or no direct connection with Astra and included allegations involving senior UK politicians and civil servants and allegations of illegal arms deals involving foreign governments and government agencies and the security services of the UK and of other countries. Whilst Mr James impressed upon us his own view that we ought to investigate and report on these allegations, we concluded that to do so would have involved inquiries which went beyond what we regarded as the boundaries of our role as inspectors appointed under the Companies Act 1985 to investigate the affairs of Astra. We accordingly concluded that it was inappropriate for us to embark upon an investigation of these allegations.

It was tantamount to saying that they had decided to ignore the context in which Astra had conducted its business. There was of course always a fear about what I might release about the covert dealings in Astra, which was presumably why the new board of Astra insisted on an unprecedented seven-year silence in return for any compensation payment to me (which was never forthcoming anyway).

In one way or another, as I have shown, the story of Astra touches on almost every aspect of the government's covert strategy in the 1980s. Because they realised this, the government could not afford to let me be heard, and to inhibit me, they refused for years to return sensitive material and personal documents, including tax files, taken away by the MoD police and Customs at the time.

Some of my belongings were eventually returned to me in an absurd 'cloak and dagger' way by a Customs officer, J. W. Cassey of the Special Investigation Unit, who masqueraded as Astra chairman Roy Barber's assistant. Cassey has figured since then in the Atlantic Commercial (or Dunk) case (p. 70) with three Foreign Office officials who were criticised by Lord Justice Scott and are currently being investigated by the police for perverting the course of justice. In that case, the Foreign Office and Customs facilitated a conviction by preventing witnesses from the Jordanian and Iraqi embassies, who would have shown the defendants' innocence, from attending the trial.

But there are still many documents missing, including for example some concerning the Ordtec contract with SRC, which I have been told were 'destroyed'.

I have been endeavouring to retrieve documents essential to my own case for more than five years, first in correspondence with the DTI and latterly with the MoD police, DTI inspectors, and court officials appointed by the DTI, namely the administrators of Astra, the receivers Cork Gully/Coopers & Lybrand. In January this year, Barlow of Coopers actually demanded 'confirmation that you will meet any reasonable costs of locating and copying these documents', which it was my right to see, and which were my own property!

Meanwhile I have had to undergo the DTI Inquiry and Trade and Industry Select Committee Inquiry without any of my personal copies of board minutes, papers, diaries and other documents, which, as Kevin Cahill, Bureau Chief of Global and Western, wrote to the Executive Council of the Joint Disciplinary Scheme, 'is a cut and dried breach of natural justice . . . The

[DTI] Inspectors were aware of the existence of the documents and were at all times capable of calling for them and supplying them to Mr James. Not only did they fail to do so, knowing, as they surely must have, that this would eventually call into question the whole basis of their Inquiry, with the very real possibility that £2.4m in public money would then be wasted, but they may have done this deliberately.'

When in 1994 they sought to disqualify us as company directors (the ultimate move to discredit us, see p. 305) they still refused to let me have the documentation essential to my defence. Then, when persuasive efforts were made by other people such as Kevin Cahill, and I began to copy my correspondence to Lord Justice Scott, when questions were raised in Parliament, and threats made about court orders, the situation at last began to change and newly-released BMARC board meeting minutes caused the furore in the press about Jonathan Aitken's involvement as a director with a company (BMARC) known to have been dealing with Iran and Iraq.

Stephen Byers MP tabled a motion in Parliament alleging that Aitken, as minister for defence procurement, had signed a PIIC order preventing the disclosure of 'reports relating to the supply of arms to Iraq by BMARC, a company of which he was a director at the relevant time' (*Sunday Times*, 11 June 1995). The suggestion that there may have been a conflict of interest here seems to me to be but a surface cut into a matter about which there has been wholesale obfuscation, and deliberate confusion by the government of public with private interest.

The LISI contract going to Iran via Charter Industries of Singapore caught the media's attention. It didn't emanate from me (although I could have told them that Aitken was in Singapore at Charter Industries in November 1989). The point is not the degree to which Aitken was aware that we were dealing with Iraq or Iran, but why should that surprise? He was hired as a non-executive director to BMARC precisely because of his Middle East contacts. Presumably he was made Minister for Defence Procurement for similar reasons.

All of this media attention is really missing the point, which has not been driven home, namely that the whole bias of Thatcher's economic and foreign policy was to make hay out of a war between two of the richest nations in the world, that the government did this in a covert way, that it deliberately misled Parliament and, when the truth began to emerge, that it cast around for scapegoats to take the rap.

As significant in economic terms, because they failed to get the money from Iraq in particular, their strategy led to an economic boom which was a phantasm because it was paid for by the tax-payer (you and me) through ECGD, which is why we are in such desperate straits today.

The DTI knew this, and did everything in its power to dampen speculation. Michael Heseltine admitted to the House of Commons on 13 June this year that the DTI knew about the LISI contract four years ago, as early as March 1991, and yet they still did not regard my allegations of what had been going on as justi-fying 'initiating a full inquiry'. How could they? It would be an inquiry into themselves. They would rather see a few directors done away with, they would even (so it now seems) rather serve up a few junior ministers, than have the whole rotten can of worms subjected to public scrutiny, because the Conservative Party would be finished if they did.

It is at this point, with unbelievable arrogance, that they equate their own survival with the public interest.

Who leaked material from the Scott Inquiry which so damaged Waldegrave, Clark and Trefgarne? And why? It wasn't under-cover work by Fleet Street. The leaks came from inside Whitehall. Why? Perhaps the answer should be looked for in the effect that the leaks had on the press, which was, in a case of such enormous complexity, fortuitously to focus the spotlight on these three junior ministers and make believe that that was the whole story.

Is not this precisely the same tactic as that used against the directors of Euromac, Matrix Churchill, Atlantic Commercial, Ordtec, Forgemasters, Somers and Astra? Find a scapegoat, and

satisfy the appetite of the idiot public with a few sacrificial lambs?
Arrogance is not the word for it.

Even when the pressure was on them to release the documents, they didn't give up easily. In April this year Coopers &
Lybrand were forced by Scott into delivering documents to the
inquiry, but wrote to me that if I wanted them I should see them
only if 'Sir Richard Scott can be persuaded that you can assist
them with any inspection of documents'.

For some time I was told by the DTI that all the documents
were with the receivers. When I discovered from the Treasury
solicitors in the Law Courts that the DTI and DTI inspectors did
indeed have them, both provided copies and lists inconsistent
with those from the receivers. For example, the Treasury Secretary
provided me with twenty-nine sets of BMARC minutes, Coopers
with only five.

There is still a great deal that I have not received – personal
files on Kock and BMARC, my diaries and records and address
systems – and there is material that no one could admit to having
without incriminating themselves, namely diaries and papers
stolen from my house.

The major burglary occurred in London in December 1990
when I went up to Cockermouth for Christmas. It was reported at
the time in the *European* newspaper. I didn't leave London until
Christmas Eve, and almost immediately someone broke into my
house in London and pinched a number of files, the same technique – a pane of glass cleanly cut and removed – as that used in
a later break-in to my late mother's house in Cumbria.

Oddly, on that occasion, entry was faked. The alarm did not go
off, but a towel supposedly used to deaden the noise of breaking
glass was lying on the lawn, and had come from upstairs. They
must have broken the window after entry.

There have been other instances when I was quite sure that
people had been in the London house, things moved around and
so on. On several occasions up in Cockermouth, there have been
definite signs that someone has been in – the flap over the lock left
up, doors left open that were kept shut, objects moved round, and

so on. Once there were even signs that someone had had a tin of something and marked the carpet when they made a cup of tea.

On one particular occasion Miss Davison, who spent two or three nights a week at the house looking after the place, and came up every day to make sure everything was all right, noticed that the door of the front bedroom appeared to be locked. All the bedroom locks are painted up and cannot be secured by a key, yet Miss Davison could not open the door, try as she might. Concluding that it must be being held from the other side, she left the house as quickly as she could. Indeed, she was so frightened that she didn't go to the police straight away but rang me after about half an hour. When the door was tried again, it opened easily.

Then another large-scale burglary occurred in Cockermouth on 18 January 1993. The family had been in Cumbria for Christmas, and left me alone when they returned to London. On the 17th I had decided to go and see Chris Cowley. I went down to London on the evening of the 17th and then caught the train to Bristol on the 18th, which was a Thursday. On the evening of the 18th, the Friday, there were very stormy gales in Cumbria, and Miss Davison went to the house. As soon as she entered the sitting room she felt a draught when she opened the door, and when she walked through, she found that the french window had been smashed. She looked round, and the best ornaments were missing. They had rummaged through documents and taken quite valuable pictures from upstairs and a revolving 365-day clock. I couldn't understand why the alarm hadn't gone off – the police had claimed it was supersensitive and we have had a number of false alarms. The alarm firm came and tested the system, and it worked perfectly.

And then I found the burglars' calling card. Lying out near the garage was a place-mat-sized advertisement for elderflower wine, the sort of item you might find in a pub. What was notable about it was that it came from Burford in Oxfordshire. The 'burglars' had taken the backs off all the pictures and photographs, which were all off the walls with their backs loosened or removed. They had gone in looking for documents and then moved on to the antiques. If they had come in for antiques alone, they would have taken a lot more. It looked as if the stolen antiques were merely a bonus or smokescreen for what they had really been after. But it was odds on that whoever left the calling-card knew how to pass on antiques.

Then of course there have been phone calls, some threatening, some where people simply don't talk, or the phone cuts out in mid-conversation and a voice says the caller is engaged on another call, or, again, you hear a tape re-wind, sometimes only one caller hears it, the other end going blank . . .

But in spite of all these unnerving incidents I feel that my policy of openness has been my best defence, though I am a good deal more solicitous now than I used to be about what I say and to whom. In the late spring to early summer of 1994, I decided to write this book and submitted a 30,000 word synopsis to half a dozen publishers. It proved something of a turning point.

In some cases the synopsis remained, as requested, confidential. But in one case, after a flurry of interest and entertainment, the publisher became suddenly immune to contact and has remained so to this day, never returning the text. In another, the synopsis was sent by the publisher, after reassurances of confidentiality, for legal advice. I was not so naive as to suppose that what I had to say was without legal risk, but that the legal opinion consulted should have been a firm retained by the Prime Minister himself was surely (at the very least) a mark of the publisher's own naivety in what he was dealing with and also more than premature.

Once the book project was known to the establishment, a move by the DTI to disqualify me and five of the original directors of Astra under the Company Directors' Disqualification Act, 1986, followed forthwith.

The decision announced by the Joint Disciplinary Scheme (JDS), a committee attached to the Institute of Chartered Accountants, to let the courts decide whether the DTI inspectors were right in their report to censor the Astra directors for their purchase of PRB, was taken all of two years after the case had been thrown out by the Serious Fraud Office.

The timing of the announcement, hard on the heels of my submission to book publishers, could hardly have been coincidence. The government had decided it could not simply sit back and wait for what I had to say.

There followed an outcry in some quarters of the press, suggesting that there would be a very large number of directors quaking in their shoes if so heavy a hammer could be wielded by the establishment against Astra for an acquisition (PRB) that left the company weakened but surviving, and weakened only because we had uncovered and reported a contract that the government should have been pleased to cancel. Indeed the government should have been pleased to encourage others to report similarly illicit contracts by supporting Astra in its subsequent financial difficulty. You will recall what happened to Gumbley when he asked Alan Clark and then the Prime Minister for such support. They responded by slapping him in jail.

Michael Meacher MP wrote to the Trade and Industry Secretary Michael Heseltine, describing the move to disqualify us as a 'shabby and sordid affair', the aim clearly to intimidate us 'because of what [the Astra directors] revealed about the illicit arms trade with Iraq and the government's connivance in it.'

There also ensued other pressures to keep me too busy to write the book, most notably the Inland Revenue. There was nothing new about the Revenue's interest in me, which had been going on for six years, but it had lapsed. There was a sudden swell of activity that coincided precisely with the announcement of the legal proceedings against us. It is a tactic that Paul Henderson, managing director of Matrix Churchill, told me was used to tie him up in the build-up to his trial, as well as some of my Astra colleagues and Michael Cruddas, whose company was used to launder offshore funds from arms sales mainly to Iran and Iraq.

On 30 November 1994, I wrote for the third time to Sir Anthony Battishill, chairman of the Board of the Inland Revenue, asking for assurances that its apparent campaign of harassment was independent of the government's campaign against me. For the third time I received only a fudging response from a minion.

It is this self-interested, self-obsessed and cowardly attitude of the establishment, which amounts to an abuse of power, that deprives this Tory government of respect and will lose it the next election. The very notion of political service to the nation has been so warped by them that when junior disciples, who have been brought up on it, reach high office they show themselves to have progressed no further than the level of playground bully.

Some time – some five or six weeks – before the announcement of disqualification proceedings was made, I received a letter from Jeremy Hanley, then the new Tory Party chairman. It was dated 8 June 1994.

Hanley was cross with me for asking him about a series of Army Board dinners he had hosted during his period of office at the MoD, at the Royal Hospital, Chelsea, in December 1993, and at the Tower of London in February 1994, to which key members of the cabal had been invited, including Lord Weinstock and Sir Denis Thatcher, the Sultan of Brunei and assorted spooks (at the second, Sir Colin McColl, head of MI6, and Stella Rimington, head of MI5).

His last sentence, and the parting shot of his riposte, was, 'I await the Institute of Chartered Accountants' deliberations with interest.'

At that time, neither I nor any other member of the public knew that there was a move afoot to take disciplinary action against us.

The story is actually more than a bad joke at my expense, for it demonstrates the moral and intellectual bankruptcy of a leading politician capable of reducing a matter, purportedly of such national importance that more than £2m of public money had been spent investigating it, to the level of spite.

It demonstrates too that confidentiality means one thing to the Tory establishment and another to the individual on the outside, for it has emerged that Hanley actually went to the trouble of writing to the JDS specifically to discover whether I was one of the directors involved in their confidential deliberations, and the information had been freely given.

The timing of this disqualification move against the Astra board is but one anxiety. Collusion that spells frame-up is another. But the most transparent victimisation is the sole and glaring omission from the list of directors to be clobbered – Stephan Adolph Kock.

NOTES

Chapter One: Hot Shots in America

1. *Arms and the Man: Dr Gerald Bull, Iraq and the Supergun* by William Lowther (Macmillan, London, 1991).
2. *Spider's Webb* by Alan Friedman (Faber & Faber, London, (1993).
3. *Guardian*, 6.2.95.
4. *The Silent Conspiracy* by Stephen Dorril (William Heinemann, London, 1993).

Chapter Two: Roots in Britain

1. *Smear!: Wilson and the Secret State* by Stephen Dorril and Robin Ramsay (Fourth Estate, London, 1991).
2. Ibid.
3. *Lobster*, issue 19.

Chapter Three: Thatcher's Militarised Economy

1. *Independent*, 25.1.95.
2. *Independent on Sunday*, 30.8.92.
3. *Guns, Lies & Spies*, Christopher Cowley (Hamish Hamilton, London, 1992).
4. *Spider's Webb* by Alan Friedman (Faber & Faber, London, 1993).
5. *The Silent Conspiracy* by Stephen Dorril (William Heinemann, London, 1993).
6. *Sunday Times*, 9.10.94. *Enemies of the State* by Gary Murray (Simon & Schuster, London, 1993).
7. Richard Norton-Taylor in the *Guardian*.
8. *The Silent Conspiracy* by Stephen Dorril (William Heinemann, London, 1993).
9. Ibid.

10. *Independent*, 23.11.93.

11. *Guardian*, 2.11.93; *Guardian*, 14.12.93; *Independent*, 26.11.92.

12. *Guardian*, 29.7.94.

13. *Economist*, 7.5.94.

14. *New Statesman & Society*, 17.5.94.

15. *Guardian*, 16.6.93.

16. *Economist*, 7.5.94.

17. *New Statesman & Society*, May 1994.

18. *Independent*, 8.9.93.

19. *Sunday Telegraph*, 29.5.94.

20. *Arms and the Man: Dr Gerald Bull, Iraq and the Supergun* by William Lowther (Macmillan, London, 1991).

21. *Guns, Lies & Spies* by Christopher Cowley (Hamish Hamilton, London, 1992).

22. Ibid.

23. *Guardian*, 16.1.92.

24. *Unholy Babylon* by Adel Darwish and Gregory Alexander (Gollancz, 1991).

25. *Independent*, 13.11.92.

26. *Today*, 2.6.94.

27. *Independent*, 12.11.92.

28. *Guardian*, 3.11.93.

29. *The Silent Conspiracy* by Stephen Dorril (William Heinemann, London, 1993).

30. *Economist*, 7.5.94.

31. *Guardian*, 11.12.93

32. *New Statesman & Society*, 17.6.94. *Economist*, 7.5.94.

33. *Economist*, May 1994.

34. *Business Age*, July 1993.

35. *Independent*, 4.1.94.

36. *Economist*, 7.5.94.

37. *Guardian*, 30.12.93.

38. *Spider's Webb* by Alan Friedman (Faber & Faber, London, 1993).

39. *The Silent Conspiracy* by Stephen Dorril (William Heinemann, London, 1993).

40. *Independent*, 26.11.92.

41. *The Silent Conspiracy* by Stephen Dorril (William Heinemann, London, 1993).

42. *Guardian*, 23.11.91.

43. *Sunday Times*, 6.3.94.
44. *Sunday Times*, 9.10.94. *Thatcher's Gold* by Paul Halloran and Mark Hollingsworth (Simon & Schuster, London, 1995).
45. *Guardian*, 25.5.92. *BusinessAge*, November 1994.
46. *Profits of War* by Ari Ben-Menashe (Sheridan Square, New York, 1992).
47. *Business Age*, November 1994.
48. *Daily Telegraph*, 8.2.94.
49. *Sunday Times*, 20.2.94.
50. *Sunday Times*, 13.3.94.
51. *Observer*, 30.1.94.

Chapter Four: The Cabal

1. *Guardian*, 17.6.94.
2. *Spider's Webb* by Alan Friedman (Faber & Faber, London, 1993).
3. *The Silent Conspiracy* by Stephen Dorril (William Heinemann, London, 1993).
4. Ibid.
5. *Smear!: Wilson and the Secret State* by Stephen Dorril and Robin Ramsay (Fourth Estate, London, 1991).
6. *Independent*, 14.3.92.
7. *The Silent Conspiracy* by Stephen Dorril (William Heinemann, London, 1993); *Smear!: Wilson and the Secret State* by Stephen Dorril and Robin Ramsay (Fourth Estate, London, 1991).
8. Ibid.
9. *The Silent Conspiracy* by Stephen Dorril (William Heinemann, London, 1993).
10. *The Silent Conspiracy* by Stephen Dorril (William Heinemann, London, 1993). *Smear!: Wilson and the Secret State* by Stephen Dorril and Robin Ramsay (Fourth Estate, London, 1991).
11. *The Silent Conspiracy* by Stephen Dorril (William Heinemann, London, 1993).
12. *Observer*, 17.10.93.
13. *Guardian*, 10.2.94.
14. *Guardian*, 14.12.93.
15. *Economist*, 10.9.94.

Chapter Five: Astra UK, 1986–87: Infiltration by the Cabal

1. *Private Eye*, 27.1.95.
2. *The Silent Conspiracy* by Stephen Dorril (William Heinemann, London, 1993), and *Enemies of the State* by Gary Murray (Simon & Schuster, London, 1993).
3. *The Silent Conspiracy* by Stephen Dorril (William Heinemann, London, 1993).
4. Ibid.

Chapter Six: The Entrepreneurial Fallacy of Thatcher's Britain

1. *Dispatches*, Channel 4 Television.

Chapter Seven: Pulling the Plug

1. *New Internationalist*, November 1994.

COMMISSIONS ON MARGARET THATCHER'S DEFENCE CONTRACTS

A. The Rooker Memorandum

The following memo (see pages 104–7) was sent anonymously to Jeffrey Rooker MP, who was involved in a Public Accounts Committee inquiry into government use of public money in the financing of Margaret Thatcher's big defence packages. It is explicit in its allegations about how huge commissions were incorporated, that they were going to the Tory Party, and about the role played by Mark Thatcher. Mr Rooker sent it to Mrs Thatcher for information, who wrote back that she had put it in the hands of 'the appropriate authorities'. Some extracts are shown here.

To: Chairman ▓▓▓▓▓   From: ▓▓▓▓ Copy No.: ▓▓▓▓

Classification: Restricted   2nd May, 1989

Newspaper articles on BAe and HMG bribes to obtain
           Tornado etc. business
----

1. Jordan.

The inflated contract/ITP was cancelled,not "suspended". The
price BAe hoped to obtain was in fact 112% above the
comparative price charged to the RAF according to an insider
report(active executive).

· · ·

T! Jordanian middlemen resident in London, Ghazi Shakr and
Munir Attalah, are extremely upset and tried to personally
intervene with Mrs. T. to rescue the deal.

· · ·

2. Saudi Arabia.

Ballast Nedam and their work on the intended huge airbases
(clearly meant for use by the USA in case of tension) has
come to a complete stop and their team has left Saudi Arabia
and been told that the project is "suspended". The company's
resident Dutch manager has left for an extended leave for
Holland.

There are constant phone calls between Mrs. T. and King
.ahd and Sir Peter Levene and Prince Sultan. Levene was in
fact the person that made the crude oil arrangement which was
invented to enable HMG/BAe to pay the huge commissions to the
Saudis and their middlemen

· · ·

The same source also states that there is a sizable payment
to the Conservative Party ("a huge sum") which is being
administered by Wafiq Said in conjunction with Mark T.

B. Trip Report to K.S.A.

This is an extract from an internal company memo, an exhibit in the case of Thomas Dooley (see pages 119–20), which concerns the second part of Margaret Thatcher's Al Yamamah arms contract with Saudi (AYII, see page 62 and *passim*). Mark Thatcher is again implicated, but more devastating is the size of the payment – $4bn – required to secure the deal. No UK company is big enough to put up this sort of cash; only the government could have made it available. The $4bn must have been taxpayers' money, and receiving it even worried the Saudis. ('Bandar' refers to Prince Bandar, actually nephew of the Saudi King Fahd, see page 106.)

```
                    PARTIAL TRIP REPORT - COMPANY PRIVATE

SUBJECT:  Trip report to K.S.A. 18-27 April 1989

.  Meetings with U.S. Embassy staffer in Riyadh brought to light the following
   concerns:

   .  MG Farrington Chief USMTM, to be replaced by Col. (?) Kaufuan in June-July
      89.  Kaufuan will be "frocked" to BG.  He has served with USMTM before as
      a Section Chief.   Present position is with USAF staff Pentagon in
      International Programs.

   .  Significant message traffic from U.K. and Wash DC vis-a-vis the commissions
      involved in AYII.

   .  Armitage involved.  Very concerned.  Read message from him.

   .  Rolls-Royce and Bae have moved approx. 4 bil. U.S. to a Saudi to delay the
      engine decision.

   .  RSAF/SALFAAC want G.E. engine definitely.

.  Note:  This 4 bil U.S. was mentioned in connection with M. Thather's son.
         7.
.  "A son of the king" is also concerned about the credibility factor for the
   kingdom and the alleged payoffs.  This reference was clearly made to Bandar. No
```

APPENDIX II

JONATHAN AITKEN, BMARC, AND IRAQ

Following the arrests of Chris Cowley and Peter Mitchell (25 April 1990) and those of other executives involved with Gerald Bull's Supergun (1–2 May), BMARC managing director Bill McNaught anxiously puts on record to Bob Primrose of the MoD two of the company's visible liabilities re: arms exports to Iraq and Jordan, well-recognised as a conduit for Iraq. See pages 70–1, 84 and 206 etc. 'Astra Defence Systems' was, for a short time, the name under which BMARC operated.

The BMARC Board minutes implicate non-executive director Jonathan Aitken (later to become HM's Minister for Defence Procurement) in BMARC sales to Middle East conduits for Iraq, in particular his crucial part in the Saudi-bound Vosper contract, part of Al Yamamah. See pages 121–4.

The Rexon pallet label for the Iraq-bound Ordtec contract shows its destination as the Al Fao organisation, a Baghdad arms factory. Orders for the removal of the incriminating label were appended before the shipment left FX, BMARC's Faldingworth plant, where all hands were washed clean.

without incls.

Astra Defence Systems Ltd
Springfield Road · Grantham
Lincolnshire · NG31 7FB · England
Tel: (0476) 68222 · Direct (0476) 68 111
Fax: (0476) 68214 · Telex: 37828 (ASTDEF G)
A subsidiary of Astra Holdings PLC

(36.)

PRIVATE & CONFIDENTIAL

R C Primrose Esq
Director of Marketing Services
Ministry of Defence
Defence Equipment Services Organisation
Stuart House
23-25 Soho Square
LONDON
W1V 5FJ

Your ref :

Our ref : WMN/yk

Date : 2nd May, 1990

Dear Bob

JORDAN

As a result of all the recent activity in the Press relating to the sale of potential weapons to Iraq via Jordan, I am in the process of reviewing all contracts undertaken by Astra over the past few years where the End User is Jordan. For instance, in the past 2 years we have delivered 20mm and 30mm naval guns and ammunition to Jordan, the guns being supplied via Vosper Thornycroft for 3 Hawk class patrol vessels and the associated ammunition direct to Jordan. I have no reason to believe that these are not perfectly legitimate contracts and certainly all the export documentation is correct.

However, I have recently examined in some detail a small contract currently held by Astra Defence Systems to produce booster pellets for artillery fuzes for Jordan. Astra's customer is Ordnance Technologies Ltd (ORDTEC) of Twyford, Reading. The contract is for the supply of 300,000 M739 fuze booster pellets between March and July of this year. These pellets are to be matched with their associated fuze components delivered from a US company called REXON Technology Corporation of Wayne, New Jersey and then delivered to a UK Port for onward shipment to Jordan. ORDTEC are responsible for all of the US and UK import and export documentation: My suspicions have been aroused because I have found a letter on our file indicating that the main contractor for this project is SRC Engineering of Geneva.

. . .

Kind regards

Yours sincerely

R. R. McNaught.

BRITISH MANUFACTURE AND RESEARCH COMPANY LIMITED

Minutes of a Meeting of the Board of Directors
held at Grantham on Wednesday 2 November 1988
commencing at 9.00 a.m.

Present:

    Mr G R James   (Chairman)
    Mr C W Gumbley
    Mr W W McNaught
    General D E Isles
    Mr J R C Miller
    Mr S A Kock
    Mr J W P Aitken   MP   (Part-time)

    Mr R A Smith   (Company Secretary)

. . .

3.8   Direct sales approach to Saudi Arabia

Mr. Aitken proposed that a presentation should be arranged to be made in Saudi Arabia during January 1989, products to be as selected by BMARC. Accepted that no orders could be obtained for delivery by 31 March 1989 but orders for 1990 year important.

Consideration given to question - which countries are financially assisted with their defence budgets by Saudi Arabia? Decided that funding did not necessarily produce any influence over the receiving country's defence orders.

The agent acting for Mr. Aitken pulled off the Vosper contract, is ambitious and is working hard at establishing relationships.

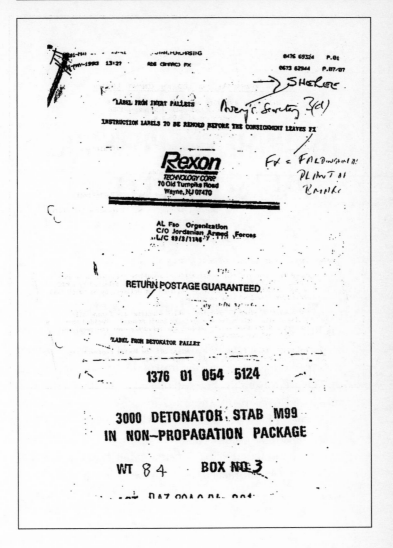

LABEL FROM INERT PALLETS

INSTRUCTION LABELS TO BE REMOVED BEFORE THE CONSIGNMENT LEAVES FI

Rexon
TECHNOLOGY CORP
70 Old Turnpike Road
Wayne, NJ 07470

AL Fao Organization
C/O Jordanian Armed Forces
L/C 89/3/1146

RETURN POSTAGE GUARANTEED

LABEL FROM DETONATOR PALLET

1376 01 054 5124

3000 DETONATOR STAB M99
IN NON-PROPAGATION PACKAGE

WT 84   BOX NO 3

THE COVERT GOVERNMENT-SPONSORED ARMS & PROPELLANT CARTEL

A. Allivane, Astra and Muiden Chemie

Extracts from the official report of the investigation into Joost de Graaff, managing director of Muiden Chemie of Holland. Allivane, at the centre of the cartel supplying Iran and Iraq, and set up with the help of a grant from the Scottish office (see page 96 etc), was first introduced to Astra by the MoD in 1984/5 (see page 109 etc). The contract between Allivane and Muiden Chemie in 1986, which named Astra as a supplier, never appeared on Astra's books (page 213 etc) and was the first indication that Astra's name was being used on illicit contracts to disguise the covert trade.

'ECONOMISCHE CONTROLEDIENST' (ECONOMIC INVESTIGATION DEPARTMENT)
OF THE MINISTRY FOR ECONOMIC AFFAIRS

'Centrale Afdeling Recherche' (Central Investigation Bureau)

Official report no.: 156.857-H

OFFICIAL REPORT

On Thursday 22 September 1988, at about 10.45 a.m., at the head
office of the Economic Investigation Department, we:

Johannes Cornelis Godefridus Hubertus VERMEULEN
and
Aart-Jan BOGERD,

who are investigators with the Economic Investigation Department
in The Hague and the Central Investigation Bureau of that Department, in particular, and who are also unpaid members of the
'Korps Rijkspolitie' (National Police Force), heard the
defendant:

Joost Ubbo Rutger Allard DE GRAAFF,

born in Amsterdam on 10 June 1940 and domiciled at Noorderheide 2
in Laren (Province of North Holland), who had appeared voluntar-
ily at our request.

Having been informed that he had a right to remain silent, he
made the following statement:
"(...)
I will now tell you what I know of the Allivane-Portugal affair.
It must have been around 1984 that I first got into contact with

Allivane in London. At the time, I used to speak with Terry Byrne
Jr. and Sr. and, at a later stage, with Thisthlewaite. I got to
know the company as a young firm with an American background and
agressive sales techniques. They travelled around the globe to
obtain orders in the field of strategic goods. In that period,
they had also begun co-operating with Astra Pyrotechnics, which
is established in England as well. I knew Astra only by name, but
in the course of time I came to understand that the company is
engaged, among other things, in the field of munition deliveries
and also performs certain assembling activities. The contacts
with Allivane resulted in a number of small orders for MC. They
concerned deliveries of base bleeds and smokeless gunpowder.
These products were assembled by Astra for Allivane's benefit,
following which the finished products were delivered to Singapore, among other places.

(cont.)

In the same period, around 1984/1985, there was a worldwide
interest in powder for so-called M11 charges which were used,
and are still used, in large-bore howitzers. Examples are the
155mm and 203mm howitzers of the GHN-45 and GC-45 type and many
others. At a certain point of time, in the third quarter of 1986,
I believe, Allivane was also interested, and decided to contact
MC. During my first meetings with Allivane, it appeared that the
company would have the M11 charges to be delivered by MC further
assembled by the aforementioned company, Astra.

. . .

In regard to Allivane, this company placed a substantial order
with MC in 1986 for M11 charges, which would be further assembled
by Astra. In total, the order involved 2,550 tonnes of powder at
a price of US$9= per kilogram, 150,000 ignition tubes (nitrocel-
loluse tubes or poröse stränge) at a price of US$11= a unit, and
150,000 base bleed grains at a price of US$65 per unit. On 24
February 1987, MC sent Allivane pro forma invoices for these
quantities, nos. 4001-4015. Said invoices all refer to the number
106808/4, which does not ring a bell. MC must have been given
this number by Allivane.

B. Baghdad Arms Exhibition, 1989

Astra's name was being used on illicit contracts which the company had never touched. At the Baghdad Arms Fair in 1989, Astra was among the companies sponsored to exhibit by the British government. But it was given the Surrey address and telex number of British Aerospace, the company close to government which owns Royal Ordnance, a participant in the covert trade (page 92 etc). Great interest was shown in Astra's products, but never converted into orders received by Astra (page 214).

REPUBLIC OF IRAQ
MINISTARY OF INDUSTRY
MILITARY   PRODUCTION
AUTHORITY

BAGHDAD INTERNATIONAL
EXHIBITION FOR MILITARY PRODUCTION
(EXHIBITION GUIDE)
28 April - 2 May 1989

ASTRA HOLDINGS PLC

Brooklands Road
Weybridge
Surrey KTB OSJ ENGLAND
TLX : 27111

ASTRA HOLDINGS is one of Britain's largest companies involved in the manufacture of defence equipment. It is also a major U.S. and North American defence contractor through its three U.S manufacturing companies and its canadian subsidiary.

204- BGD INT. EXB. MIL. PR.

THE COVER-UP

When the truth began to out, the strategy of damage limitation took various forms (page 74–91 and Chapter 7: Pulling the Plug), all 'underhand methods of policy making' which, in the letter below, Sir Nicholas Bonsor MP admits was what did for Astra. But in some cases, as with Gerald Bull (page 81 and 279/280), even that was not enough. Bull's letter of 31 October 1989 to Philippe Glibert, an employee of PRB, one of Astra's companies (see extract below), preceded his assassination by less than five months.

Sir Nicholas Bonsor, Bt., M.P.

HOUSE OF COMMONS
LONDON SW1A 0AA
071- 219 3000
0525- 270644

14th December 1993

G.R. James, Esq.,
2 Laurel Road
London SW13 OEE.

Dear Mr. James,

Thank you for your letter of the 30th November. Whilst I note and understand the
concerns you feel about the likely outcome of the Scott Inquiry, I am afraid that
I do not have the resources available to my Committee to try to second-guess what
the Judge may find. If, as you say, you have letters establishing that Gerald
Ball was being threaten by the Foreign Office and was involved with the M.O.D. in
the Northern Ireland office some six months before his murder, I hope very much
that you will make these available to the Scott Inquiry so that this aspect of
the whole affair can be fully and properly explored.

I am more than grateful to you for your kind remarks in your closing paragraphs;
I can assure you that I and the Defence Committee will do what we can to secure
the future of our national defences and to prevent the re-occurrence of any of the
underhand methods of policy making which clearly led you and your company, together
with many others, to disaster.

With best wishes,

Yours sincerely,

THE S.R.C. GROUP OF COMPANIES ②

SPACE RESEARCH CORPORATION

D· G.V. BI··
PRESIDENT

Mr. Philippe Glibert
PRB
Av. de Tervueren
1150 Bruxelles

October 31, 1989

Ref. : GVB.pf.239

Dear Philippe,

Since our meeting many developments have occurred. Some undoubtedly have been brought to your attention since the English press went berserk.

. . .

19. I addressed a blunt memorandum to the Foreign Office on the whole matter. Through publicity, they were making me a target of terrorist groups. I was advised in a letter of an imminent "accident". The Foreign Office was advised about the curious fact that accidents often happen in series.

After the memo was delivered, the matter was dropped from the press. Also we were assured that the action was by "a few irresponsible juniors and did not reflect the Foreign Office views of myself, our companies, the past etc."

. . .

With best wishes

DR. G.V. BULL

BIBLIOGRAPHY

The Silent Conspiracy, Stephen Dorril. William Heinemann, London, 1993.

Profits of War, Ari Ben-Menashe. Sheridan Square, New York, 1992.

Smear!: Wilson and the Secret State, Stephen Dorril and Robin Ramsay. Fourth Estate, London, 1991.

Arms and the Man: Dr Gerald Bull, Iraq and the Supergun, William Lowther. Macmillan, London, 1991.

Spider's Webb, Alan Friedman. Faber & Faber, London, 1993.

Unholy Babylon, Adel Darwish and Gregory Alexander. Gollancz, 1991.

Guns, Lies & Spies, Christopher Cowley. Hamish Hamilton, London, 1992.

Enemies of the State, Gary Murray. Simon & Schuster, London, 1993.

BCCI, Peter Truell and Larry Gurwin. Bloomsbury, London, 1992.

Thatcher's Gold, Paul Halloran and Mark Hollingsworth. Simon & Schuster, London, 1995.

ACKNOWLEDGEMENTS

While I am indebted to the following for their support and research, which I hope to have interpreted correctly, the views expressed in this book are mine and mine alone, made possible by my own bleak experience at Astra. It would be impossible to thank everyone who has worked with me since the forces I have described in this book began their work on Astra and its directors. But I would like to mention in particular the writer and editor Piers Dudgeon, without whom this book would not have been written or indeed published.

My thanks and appreciation also go to Stephen Dorril for his ordered and thorough research on the intelligence and security services evinced by his books and magazine, *Lobster*, a unique and regular appraisal of the activities of the services. Others who have provided tremendous support are Tim Laxton, Kevin Cahill, Mrs E. Wood, Kenneth de Courcy, Harry Hilton, Kevin Robinson and Dr Mark Phythian. Also, I must particularly thank those journalists who still seek the truth, among them Paul Foot, Graham McLagen, Charles Grant, Peter Koenig, Richard Donkin, Richard Norton-Taylor, Paul Brown, David Pallister, David Hellier, Chris Blackhurst, John Pilger, David Monroe, Mark Lloyd, Mark Watts, Andrew Veitch, David Baxter, Peter Kirwan, Jonathan Foster, John Davison and Adrian Levy.

To the many who have paid a terrible price for doing no more than to work hard on terms set by the government, I hope this book helps in some way. In particular I mention the late Gerald Bull, Christopher Cowley and Stuart Blackledge of SRC; the late

Lionel Jones of Royal Ordnance; my own colleagues in Astra, John Anderson, Chris Gumbley, Martin Guest, Jim Miller, the late Frank Percival, John Green GM, John Park, Dr Roy Kelly, Lt. Col. John Kent, Dave Whysall, Brigadier Charles Smith, Paul Croney and Ken Wingad; Ali Daghir and Mme. Speckman of Euromac; Paul Grecian and his father, Bryan Mason, and Colin Phillips of Ordtec; Paul Henderson, Trevor Abrahams and Peter Allen of Matrix Churchill; Reginald Dunk and Alexander Schlesinger of Atlantic Commercial; James Edmiston of Sterling Armaments; Lorrain Osman; Carl Gibbard and Steve Gilmartin of B & J Industries; Michael Cruddas.

I would like to thank the following Members of Parliament for taking a healthy interest in this affair: Sir Nicholas Bonsor, Michael Meacher, Harry Cohen, Brian Wilson, Tam Dalyell, Doug Hoyle, Jim Cousins, Stan Crowther, Allan Rogers, Dale Campbell Savours, Stephen Byers.

INDEX